THE BACK

GARDENER

THE BACKYARD
GARDENER

SIMPLE, EASY, AND BEAUTIFUL GARDENING WITH VEGETABLES, HERBS, AND FLOWERS

KELLY ORZEL

LYONS PRESS

Guilford Connecticut

An imprint of Globe Pequot

Distributed by NATIONAL BOOK NETWORK

British Library Cataloguing in Publication Information Available

Library of Congress Cataloging-in-Publication Data Available

ISBN 978-1-4930-2657-9
ISBN 978-1-4930-2658-6 (e-book)

The author and Lyons Press assume no liability for accidents happening to, or injuries sustained by, readers who engage in the activities described in this book.

♾™ The paper used in this publication meets the minimum requirements of American National Standard for Information Sciences—Permanence of Paper for Printed Library Materials, ANSI/NISO Z39.48-1992.

Printed in the United States of America.

TO MY FAMILY
WHO'VE GIVEN ME LIFE, LOVE, AND MY WINGS.
AND ESPECIALLY TO CJ, MY BEST FRIEND, WHO
SHARES THIS INCREDIBLE JOURNEY WITH ME.

CONTENTS

INTRODUCTION

All the important things I've learned about growing, I've learned by sinking my hands deep into the dirt. Be adventurous in the kitchen garden, try new varieties, always save room for your staples, and remember that a garden should always evolve.

Gardening isn't all that complicated. Plants are wonderfully resistant. If something's not thriving, dig it up and grow it somewhere else, or try another crop. I'm not ashamed of my gardening mistakes—or as I call them, *experiments*—and you shouldn't be either. Many times these were the moments in which I learned the most.

I laid out this book the same way I garden. The first couple of chapters cover the basics: soils, tools, what plants need to thrive, and how to propagate them. The middle is the heart of the book in which I discuss my favorite organic growing techniques and organize the vegetable, herb, and flower sections based on how they should be planted in the garden. Unlike most gardening books, I divided the plants into groups based on their familial relationships and cultural needs, grown together in a specific sequence. With this book, you'll learn how to enhance your garden by making it work for you—not the other way around. And finally, I've included a monthly garden chore guide to give you a seasonal blueprint. When I started my kitchen garden, I wished I'd had a roadmap tell me what to do and when to do it. Your schedule can always be tweaked and altered, but having a place to start is invaluable.

This is not simply a garden reference book. I've combined facts with personal experiences, anecdotes, and time-honored tradition to be your guide. My hope is that *The Backyard Gardener* inspires you to become a more successful gardener. So go out and get your hands dirty! Happy gardening!

CHAPTER 1

GARDENING FROM THE GROUND UP

Once you've decided to start a garden, it's tempting to grab the biggest shovel you can find and rip up the entire yard. While I experience the same urge every spring, there are a few things you need to consider before you start, such as the type of soil you have, light conditions, how to design your garden, and how to keep it alive. No matter how exciting digging new beds can be (and it is), you don't want to run amok, because if you don't plan in the beginning, you will be less than impressed when it comes time to harvest.

THE NITTY-GRITTY: YOUR SOIL

It's important to have a clean start (sort of). Healthy soil is the most important part of gardening. It costs much less to do it right the first time than if you cheap out and buy bargain brand soil. Not only will you wind up with unremarkable—even poor—produce, you'll only have to spend more money and resources in the long run.

I think of my soil as a living thing—something to be nurtured, fed, and cared for. Lots of microorganisms play various roles in developing your soil's structure, aerating it, and mobilizing nutrients. Therefore, you need to know what's going on under your feet before you can plant.

Not all soils are created equal. Loam is the gardener's best friend: it contains the perfect balance of sand, silt, and clay particles, along with organic matter. This translates into good drainage, as well as nutrient and water retention, which creates the ideal environment for most plants. Other soil types like clay, sand, silt, and chalk are more difficult and often require more attention to keep your garden healthy. Clay soil is the most

It only takes soil, seeds, and time for your kitchen garden to go from nada to knockout in a single season!

THINK OF YOUR SOIL AS A LIVING THING.

fertile since its wet, sticky structure holds nutrients and water tightly. Unfortunately, clay leaves little room for air and water movement, which can lead to root rot. In addition, clay also reacts to temperature extremes: cold, wet soil in cool weather—and hard, dry soil in warm weather. Sand is the opposite of clay. It drains well—a little too well—and readily loses moisture and nutrients. Cacti and succulents thrive in sandy, often acidic, soils, but most other plants will suffer from the lack of water and nutrients. The main benefit to sandy soil is that it warms more quickly in the spring, which is good for germination. Silt falls somewhere between clay and sand, producing light, moist soil that drains well, but also compacts easily. Chalky soil is often shallow, overlays rock, and is more alkaline due to its high lime and calcium carbonate content. The classic ball test will help you figure out what type of soil you're working with. If you grab a handful of soil and it falls apart the minute you release, you have sandy soil. If it stays compact in a ball, you have clay soil, and if it's more crumbly, you have desirable loam.

There are some things you can do to improve your soil structure. Adding leaf mold, decomposed manure, and compost to sandy soils will prevent them from draining too much. Conversely, incorporating ample amounts of bulky organic matter or gravel to clay will improve drainage. Unfortunately, you don't

Loam is the next best thing after compost. It's a perfect blend of sand, silt, and clay with a bit of organic matter.

Correcting your soil pH is easy: incorporate lime (right) to go up and sulfur (left) to bring your pH down.

have a lot of options when it comes to chalky soils. My advice: embrace what you have and grow arid, alkaline-loving plants.

The next step is to run a soil test to find out your soil's pH, its organic matter content, and what its fertility demands are (you can get your soil tested for a small fee through your local cooperative extension office). Think of pH as your soil's temperature; every species has its own optimal temperature and soil is no different. The pH scale runs from acidic to alkaline, 0.0-14.0, with 7.0 being neutral. A soil pH of 6.5 (5.5-7.5) is optimal for most vegetables. Once you know what you're dealing with, it's simple to adjust. Raising pH is a lot easier than lowering it; just add limestone in the fall or winter. Lime is available in multiple forms (fine dust, granular, pelletized, or hydrated) and should cover the area completely— and, if possible, be worked into the soil. It should be spread at least two to three months before you plant since it takes time and moisture to neutralize the acidity. The finer the lime, the more quickly it will work. To lower the pH of highly alkaline soil (most common in arid regions), work aluminum sulfate or sulfur into soil. Aluminum sulfate works faster, but if you have several months before planting time, sulfur will work just as well.

Depending on how you amend and rotate you garden, you may also need to add organic matter to help your soil hold moisture and nutrients better. Your soil test will tell you more about your organic matter and fertility needs, but we'll talk more about that later.

To dig or not to dig? Unless I'm creating a brand-new garden bed or working with severely compacted clay soil, I do not dig or till. There is a method to my madness, and it has to do with soil structure. Healthy soil is full of earthworms and other soil microbes that naturally till and incorporate your compost into the garden. When I top my beds off with compost, I don't bother mixing it in. As counterintuitive as it may seem, undug soil will reward you with good drainage, more air space, higher moisture retention, fewer weeds, and stronger, better anchored vegetables. To sum it up: compost feeds soil; tilling destroys it. The microbes that live in the soil, like bacteria and fungi, help mobilize nutrients and extend plant roots to access these minerals, which encourages plant growth. Earthworms are nature's rototiller, pulling compost and other organic matter deep down into the soil so that fungi and bacteria can break it down and release nutrients. Furthermore, their castings help bind soil aggregates, or groups of soil particles, creating space for roots to grow and air to penetrate. So every time you dig or till the soil, you're killing these organisms by breaking them up or exposing them to the environment. Tilling makes it more difficult for plants to root, metabolize nutrients, access air, and hold water and brings new weeds to the surface.

Most gardeners don't realize the importance of air in soil, but it's vital. Soil aggregates, organic matter, and plant roots create air tunnels and hold them in place. Worms help perforate the soil with a network of channels for air, water, nutrients, and roots to move. Again, with every dig or till, these channels deteriorate, and depending on the extent of the damage, it can take years before they're reestablished. It's easy for the untrained eye to mistake firm, undisturbed, healthy soil for the compacted kind, tricking the most well-intentioned gardeners into rototilling. After rototilling, the soil appears "fluffy," and people think this is the same thing as having well-drained, open soil—it isn't. So unless you're reinvigorating a long-forgotten garden or beginning a new one, don't dig. Also, you may hear or read about a method called "double-digging." Don't get excited—this is the same as rototilling. Instead, apply organic matter and compost to encourage microbial activity and build soil structure.

COMPOST FEEDS SOIL; TILLING DESTROYS IT.

TOOLS OF THE TRADE

Most of my garden tools have been accumulated over time. I bought a few tools when my husband and I purchased our first home, "borrowed" some of the non-crucial pieces from my mom as needed, and inherited others from my grandparents when they passed. You certainly don't need an armory of tools to maintain a backyard garden, but a few quality pieces will make your work in the garden much easier.

Personally, I could not get by without a good, long-handled shovel, spade, fork, steel rake, a set of hand tools, and a wheelbarrow. Shovels and spades are different: shovels have a slightly rounded, pointed blade and are primarily used for digging holes and moving soil and compost. Spades on the other hand are flat and rectangular-shaped. I use these for edging and cutting in new beds. Additionally, they are ideal for turning green manures as they cut off the green growth easily at the root line, making it easy to turn and incorporate into the soil. Garden forks typically have four twelve-inch square prongs that are used to loosen soil and turn compost. Don't mistake a garden fork for a potato fork, which has flat, easily bendable tines. While you can choose tools with a T-shaped or Y-shaped handle, I prefer my long-handled tools have a D-shaped

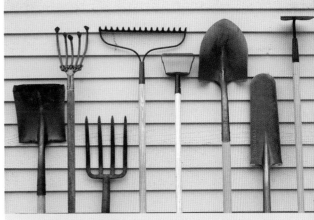

It's worthwhile to invest initially in quality tools that stand the test of time. Solid, forged heads are stronger than pressed steel, which are bent rather that heated and welded together. Left to right: spade, cultivator, garden fork, rake, stirrup hoe, shovel, transplanting spade, and Dutch hoe.

Wheelbarrows are key, especially if you have a large garden. Think of all the flats, plants, mulch, compost, and weeds you will be moving. Who wants to do that by hand?

hilt, as it is easier to grasp and manage. When it comes to a rake, not just any old rake will do. It should have a steel, bow-shaped hooped head with short, curved tines. I use this two ways: I use the tines to rake paths and soil and compost, and the back edge to smooth and flatten beds. And lastly, I could not get by without my wheelbarrow. Used to move loam, compost, and large shrubs about the garden and in garden cleanup, it makes short work of backbreaking and time-consuming garden tasks. In the absence of a wheelbarrow, an inexpensive large tarp can be used to drag soil and plant debris to and from the compost bin.

I have a tendency to leave my tools out and about in the garden, so my husband put up a pegboard to hold all my tools in the potting shed. It's so much easier to find and store them now, providing I remember to replace them when I'm finished in the garden.

My favorite hand tools include a trowel, fork, and weeder. I use these to transplant, garden in small spaces, and weed. Always test out how these tools feel in your hands as grips and sizes vary. There are a number of choices for handle materials, and you get what you pay for. Cheaper tools break readily, are poorly designed, and often hurt your hands and leave blisters. I prefer wood over plastic or metal because it holds up well over time, looks good, and doesn't tend to get too hot to the touch in summer or too cold in early spring or fall.

When it comes to harvest and pruning, invest in a pair of high-quality bypass pruners and lightweight fruit snips. Some gardeners prefer the anvil-style pruners with a sharp blade that cuts against a flat anvil, but I favor Felco bypass pruners for their scissor-like, sharp, clean cuts that rarely tear stems. Non-tearing cuts are important. If your cut tears, it invites disease, and plants are prone to damage. Snips are used to harvest stems from fragile plants like pea sprouts and sweet peas. Regardless of what types of pruners you select, I advise choosing ones with safety closures and bright-colored handles. I will often drop my pruners while I work, and by the end of the day I have trouble locating them—bright colors make finding them easier.

INVEST IN HIGH-QUALITY PRUNERS AND SNIPS.

WHAT'S IN MY GARDEN BAG?

Most girls keep an arsenal ready for a night out in their purse. I have a bag filled with my favorite goodies for when I'm out in the garden.

- Notepad and pencil – you may think you'll remember which variety is in each row, but good intentions are often forgotten. I've learned to write everything down.
- Gloves
- Hand trowel
- Hand fork
- Dandelion weeder
- Twine – I always seem to be running out. You can never have enough.
- Pruners and snips
- Labels and marker
- Small soil blocker (Hey—you never know when you're going to need one!)

Other tools that you might find helpful in the garden include hoes, hedge trimmers, hand shears, edgers, and lawn rakes. Hoes work similarly to brooms, and when dragged along the soil, cut weeds at their roots below the surface. They are available in many configurations, specific to various uses. Different types of hoes include the basic hoe; the Dutch hoe, which has an angled head and is used to cut weeds below the soil between rows and around plants with the least amount of damage to nearby plant roots; swan and collinear hoes, which have narrow, semicircular, and rectangular blades attached respectively; the stirrup hoe, which has sharpened edges on both sides of its blades, allowing you to cut weeds in the garden by both pushing and pulling; circle hoes, which are circular in shape and are excellent for weeding in small, awkward spaces and around nearby plants; and the cape cod weeder, which has a small blade at a 90° angle and can be held by a short or long handle.

Recently I discovered a new handheld weeding tool called a hori-hori. It is a Japansese knife with sharp, serrated edges that is used to pry and cut weed roots down to eight inches. Remember to be extra careful, as this tool can cause just as much serious damage to you as it does to weeds! Curved three- or five-tined cultivators can be used to incorporate air and compost into the soil and release nutrients. Hedge trimmers are typically powered and make quick work of the laborious task of pruning hedges, while hand shears should be used for short hedges and small shrubs. Hand shears also have a thick shoot-notch in the crux of the scissor-like blades for thick stems. Loopers and pruning saws are used to prune tall trees and large shrubs. Half-moon edgers are useful in bed preparation and lawn rakes for fall garden cleanup.

Some essentials that every gardener should have are a good pair of garden gloves, a watering can or hose and—don't laugh—a kneeling pad. I know it may seem like something only your grandmother would use, but your knees will thank you after a long day of working in the garden!

The hori-hori is my favorite new weeding tool. There is nothing this little guy can't do, just make sure to use it carefully—or with adult supervision!

While leather and cloth gloves protect your hands when pruning sharp, prickly, plants, they can be hot in the summer and uncomfortable when wet. Alternatively, you can use nylon gloves with a nitrile coating, which breathe easily, are flexible enough to facilitate fine motor movements, and keep your hands dry.

Water is an absolute must in the garden. Planning your garden close to a hose spigot is helpful, but if one is not at the ready, hoses and watering cans are a necessity. And while I adore galvanized aluminum or zinc watering cans, they are much heavier to carry than plastic, and thus I err on the side of comfort over aesthetic. It is also important to ensure your can includes a rose spout to break the stream of water into droplets, otherwise your seeds will swim and seedlings will bend under the onslaught of heavy water.

And finally one of my newest garden acquisitions is the Tubtrug, a flexible but sturdy bucket that comes in a variety of sizes. I use this versatile tub for everything and anything; it is with me all the time. I use it when weeding, transplanting, harvesting, and even carting my tools about the garden. Definitely worth the investment!

FEEDING THE SOIL

All living things need to be fed; the more nutrition an organism has, the more productive it is. Therefore, you want to enrich the soil such that both fertility and moisture retention increase. Compost is the ideal amendment, full of just the right amount of macro- and micronutrients. Leaf mold and cow, or farm animal, manure are also excellent soil conditioners. Develop your own stash of leaf mold by collecting and wetting leaves in either black plastic bags or wire cages for up to two years. Farm manure must be aged, well-rotted, or composted, as the nitrogen is not available in the first year. Nutrients, specifically nitrogen, must be converted into a form that plants can absorb, a process called mineralization. If the nitrogen isn't broken down, the manure has a good chance of burning plants' roots or foliage due to the high ammonia content. Mulch and other organic bulky materials suppress weeds and encourage earthworms and other beneficial microbes to tunnel to the surface to reach the new organic matter, thereby improving drainage, aeration, and soil structure.

I often hear gardeners talk about fertilizer as if it's a dirty word. You wouldn't expect to go through life without eating foods containing vitamins and minerals, so why would you deprive your garden of such nutrients—especially if they're from natural sources? Plants, particularly flowering ones, need to replenish spent or lost minerals, but as with any vitamin regimen, the right balance is critical. This is why soil tests are so important.

Macronutrients are three of the seventeen essential minerals that plants need in large quantities for optimum growth, and include nitrogen (N), phosphorus (P), and potassium (K), often referred to as NPK. Nitrogen is needed to synthesize amino acids, chlorophyll (particularly

SOIL TESTS ARE VERY IMPORTANT.

important for photosynthesis), enzymes, nucleic acids, and proteins, and responsible for lush, leafy green growth in plants. Phosphorus plays a vital role in strong root and stem development. It's integral to several crucial biochemical reactions such as photosynthesis, respiration, and energy storage and transfer that are necessary for all plants' normal life cycles. Potassium is important for many processes, including drought tolerance, water retention, and other regulatory functions, but is well-known for its critical part in bud and flower formation. Potash (K_2O), nitrate of potash (KNO_3), and sulfate of potash (K_2SO_4) are all good natural sources of potassium. Calcium (Ca), magnesium (Mg), and sulfur (S) are considered secondary nutrients, and you should pay attention to these levels on your soil test results. Trace, or micro-, nutrients like boron (B), chlorine (Cl), copper (Cu), iron (Fe), manganese (Mn), molybdenum (Mo), nickel (Ni), and zinc (Zn) are essential, but are required in smaller amounts. The remaining elements, hydrogen (H), carbon (C), and oxygen (O), are considered non-fertilizer minerals and are delivered through air and water.

Fertilizers are differentiated by varying amounts of nutrients, particularly macronutrients. This is clearly delineated by the three numbers listed on the packaging, each indicating the percentage of nutrients. These ratios are often referred to as NPK for their respective amounts of nitrogren, phosphorus, and potassium. So a 20-10-15 package is made of 20 percent nitrogen, 10 percent phosphorus, and 15 percent potassium. The remaining 55 percent of the bag is usually inert filler material. Balanced fertilizers, such as 10-10-10, have equal amounts of these macronutrients and are good general purpose choices for later in the season. Organic fertilizer options are often bulky, sloppy, smelly, and take time to work in your soil, but they provide natural, specialized amendments for your garden. Check out some of my favorites below:

Blood meal (12-0-0) is a highly concentrated nitrogen amendment, good for leafy vegetables and to replenish the soil after hungry brassicas have depleted the nutrient stores. Made of dried animal blood (typically cow), it is a powder that can be applied to the soil and worked in or dissolved in water or a liquid fertilizer. Since it quickly adds nitrogen to the soil, follow the instructions as the excessive ammonia can burn your plants if it's not used properly. Also be sure to bury it well as its smell can attract some unwanted critters like dogs, possums, raccoons, and other meat-eating animals. Alternatively, blood meal can be a deterrent for herbivores like deer, moles, and squirrels.

Bone meal (3-15-0), made of ground -up animal bones, is a well-known source of phosphorus. This fertilizer slowly releases its nutrient over time, and as such, I apply it to the hole directly at planting before my transplants or tubers are set in so my flowers and fruiting vegetable will have a reliable supply by the time they bud up.

Fish emulsion (5-2-2) is my favorite amendment, and I use it often. Derived from fish waste, it supplies a gentle dose of nitrogen with additional phosphorus, potassium, and other trace nutrients. I dilute it according to the directions and apply it to my crops at transplant and every few weeks afterward. Its foul smell is infamous, but it's well worth the effort of holding your breath!

Kelp meal, or **seaweed,** can be applied as mulch, in liquid or granular form. Obviously an ocean product, it is an excellent source of trace minerals rather than macronutrients. Liquid kelp has higher levels of valuable growth hormones than powdered or mulched forms. Many times you may even find fish emulsion and seaweed blends at the store, which provide the best of both worlds—the fish supplies your NPK and the kelp everything else!

Other meals like **alfalfa, corn gluten, cottonseed, feather,** and **soybean meals** are agricultural byproducts and available in granular or pellet form. They are wonderful sources of organic nitrogen as well as trace amounts of other nutrients, but be sure that you are purchasing organic varieties as those not labeled as organic may have been treated with pesticides.

Potash, the byproduct of burning wood, is high in potassium. So simply recycle your non-treated wood ash into the garden for your fruiting vegetables, being careful not to over-apply. As with any fertilizer, organic or not, too much of a good thing can cause imbalances that will do more harm than good. It is best to apply one-quarter to one-half pound of potash per one hundred square feet in the spring or fall so it has adequate time to be worked into the soil.

Lime applications are used in acidic soil to raise the pH to the optimal 6.5/7.0. Remember, if your soil is too acidic or too alkaline, it will lock up the nutrients. To ensure mineral availability perform a soil test and apply if needed. As a bonus, lime also contains calcium and sometimes magnesium. If your soil test shows an additional need for magnesium, select dolomitic lime.

Sulfur does the opposite of lime—it decreases your soils pH. If your soil is alkaline, it can bring the pH down to increase nutrient availability or create ideal conditions for acid-loving plants like blueberries, strawberries, and azaleas.

Rock phosphate is just what its name suggests—it is naturally occurring rock that is high in phosphorus, as well as a few micronutrients. Again, this is a slow-release amendment and thus needs to be added at time of planting or before in order to be effective.

Yummy, yummy worm castings. An excellent way to improve your soil structure and feed it some nutrients simultaneously.

You don't need to be a vermiculturist to have **earthworm castings.** You can build your own bin or buy the castings in a catalog and toss them into the soil. This biological batter is essentially worm poo—yes, you heard correctly—worm poo. It not only improves your soil structure, but is full of essential nutrients that are immediately available to your plants. Worm castings are a completely natural, organic fertilizer that can't burn your plants and add nothing but goodness to your soil!

PLANT CARE

Once your flowers and vegetables are growing, you want to keep them happy, and that will require a bit of your time to water, mulch, weed, fertilize, trellis, and prune. These simple tasks can quickly become overwhelming if you let them go. I know because I've gotten lazy a season or two and said to myself that I'll catch up on my weeding next week. By the following week, the weeds had gotten out of control. Now I spend at least ten minutes every day walking through the garden and keeping on top of my chores, and it helps tremendously!

Watering

Watering is vital. It is a requirement for photosynthesis and how your plants absorb nutrients. It is easy to take the mindset that once you've planted and initially watered-in your plants, Mother Nature will take care of the rest—not so. You will most likely need to water at least once a week, more in hot weather. It is best to water deeply, 6-8 inches, so it reaches the root zone and encourages deeper development, thus producing stronger, more productive plants. The rule of thumb is to ensure your garden is getting one inch of water per week between you and the weather. Watering will also depend on your soil. The more moisture retentive it is, the less often you need to water. If you have too much sand, water will drain away quickly, requiring longer watering. Most newly planted seedlings demand regular

Easy water access is crucial to your garden.

Keep kale and other brassicas moist and cool with soaker hoses.

waterings until they begin to mature, after which you should assess each plant and water accordingly. The key to good watering practices is to water infrequently but deeply, and to know your plants. For instance, leafy vegetables like lettuce and broccoli enjoy lots and lots of water throughout their lifetime, while too much water during fruit development can cause nightshades, like tomatoes, to split. Container plantings will likely need daily watering.

WATER FROM BELOW.

It is best to avoid watering during the heat of the day to avert leaf scorch and evenings so not to inspire root rot and disease. Cool early morning, late afternoon, and early evenings are best and give enough time for any water on wet leaves to evaporate and dry. Always water from below if you can. Watering from above gets the leaves wet, which opens you up to a host of issues by encouraging fungi, mildew, and blight with moist leafy conditions. When hand watering I use a shower wand. Its long handle allows me to direct a gentle flow to the base of the plants without wetting the leaves. Soaker hoses and drip lines are especially useful if you have a large area to water. Once planted, I lay my drip lines and mulch on top. This helps maintain soil moisture and keeps the roots cool.

Conserve water and collect rain in a stylish (and functional) rain barrel. The addition of the decorative rain chain helps guide the water from the roof's gutters into the collection basin for later use.

Mulching

Mulching is so much more than spreading wood chips for curb appeal. It holds a multifunctional role in the garden suppressing weeds, retaining soil moisture, preventing erosion, warming the soil, keeping the roots cool, retrieving and holding nutrients, and reducing soil-borne disease (but more on that in Chapter 4). Once you have your seedlings planted and watered in, you should mulch—don't wait to give your vegetables and flowers a good start to the season. Straw (or weedless hay) and seaweed teaming with minerals and nutrients are my go-tos for mulching, but compost, leaf mold, wood chips, cocoa hulls, and gravel or crushed shells work well also.

Weeding

Another crucial chore is weeding the garden. I don't think there is anything I loathe more than weeding. I know some people find it cathartic, the bending and pulling, and if you can find the Namaste in that, more power to you. For me, my entire goal in the garden is to weed as little as possible, and that means to weed as often as possible. So when I do my daily walk through to water and harvest, I make sure to pull and dispose of any weeds that I see. Weeds are not just unsightly, they compete with your garden plants for water, nutrients, and space, crowding out and setting seed. There are many vegetables like garlic that do not like to share their resources and will be less productive if faced with rampant weeds.

Annual weeds are typically quick growers and prolific self-seeders. Weeds have an uncanny ability to survive, and you don't want to make it any easier for them. Once they get a foothold in the garden, it can be time-consuming to get them out. Hoe and knock back any weeds as soon as they emerge, and try to remove as much of the remaining roots as possible. I use my fishtail (or dandelion) weeder to get out deeply rooted dandelions and

Running irrigation underneath your mulch (fabric, plastic, or organic) will help conserve soil moisture and keep your plants cool.

crabgrass. Once your garden is fully weeded, make sure to mulch to keep those weeds at bay and stay on top of any emerging weeds.

If an area is overwhelmingly infested with thugs like goutweed, I find it best to weed as much as I can, treat the area with vinegar, apply an organic mulch like grass clippings or straw, and cover with a hefty layer of wetted-down newspaper. Black plastic or landscape fabric will also do a decent job at weed suppression. I will do that for two to three years until most of the weeds have died. It is not foolproof but will do a more than adequate job of shading out the sun and killing the weeds without pesticides. A word of note, do not till this bed when ready to plant again. There are likely deeply buried weed seeds that, if tilled, will rise to the surface close to the sun and sprout, obliterating all of your hard work.

I've found that while organic herbicides work, their results are generally temporary and do not solve the problem. More often, time-consuming hand weeding will adequately handle your weed infestation if the weeds are tackled when young rather than mature. Additionally, pull deep, taprooted weeds after a rain when the soil is wet to reduce the chance of disturbing the soil, and hoe when the soil is dry, leaving the cut weeds to shrivel and die. And do not lose heart if you've let your weeding job get away from you. Just get on top of it before the plants start to flower and set seed—that is the worst thing you can let happen. If you don't have the time to weed, run around with some snips and cut off all the flower heads, disposing of them or composting them in a hot compost pile.

LANDSCAPE FABRIC

A few years ago I discovered the amazingness of landscape fabric. If you spend some extra time in the beginning of the season laying and securing the fabric, it will save you time later in the season by reducing the burden of weeding and watering. Once the bed is prepped with compost, I cover with landscape fabric and lay drip line over top. If your fabric is not permeable, lay your irrigation system underneath. I plant directly into holes that I cut into the fabric and voilà—no weeding, it retains moisture, and watering is easy as turning on a spigot! You can even cover the fabric with some wood chips or straw to camouflage the fabric. I reuse the fabric every year (it's rated for ten to fifteen years), and it makes garden life so much easier. I wish I knew about this technique years ago ... it would have saved me hundreds of hours!

Burning the holes into the fabric rather that cutting them ensures the edges of the hole do not fray throughout the season. Just make sure to do this outside to avoid inhaling fumes.

Fertilizing

I know we discussed fertilization earlier, but that was in relation to the soil and prepping it for plants. Now I want to talk about what to feed your growing flowers, fruits, and vegetables. Compost, fish emulsion, and kelp blend are always on hand. I use these at time of transplant as well as every few weeks through the season. But for my fruiting crops, I will alternate with my homemade comfrey "tea." Comfrey (*Symphytum officinale*) and Russian comfrey (*S.* x *uplandicum*) both produce effective natural fertilizers, but the 'Blocking 14' sterile cultivar of Russian comfrey is more potent—it is non-flowering, therefore putting all its energy into leaf development. This perennial herb is packed with high levels of nitrogen and potassium in its leaves, which are used to develop comfrey tea.

It is easier to start with a nursery-grown plant because its seed needs to be stratified before it will germinate, or alternatively you can simply ask a garden friend for a division in the spring or fall. Once you have one plant, you can divide it later if you want more. First year plants should not be cut to the ground, but established plants can be cut four times a year. Use a bucket with a lid, as this concoction will smell just as much as your fish emulsion, and fill it halfway with chopped leaves weighted down with

COMPOST AND FISH EMULSION ARE ESSENTIAL.

Comfrey is a beautiful landscape plant that also feeds your garden. But beware, it can spread unscrupulously, so cut back—never dig. I cut mine back up to four times a year to make comfrey tea or to toss the leaves into the compost pile.

a brick, then fill with water. Make sure to cover and leave out in the sun for three to four weeks. Some gardeners will use as is, but I dilute it down to 10 to 50 percent depending on what I am fertilizing; I'll use 10 percent to side dress garden plants and 50 percent for budded-up fruiting crops. Its leaves can also be buried at the base of plants under the soil as an organic mulch, or layered in your compost pile as an activator.

A little more complicated, compost tea infuses your plants with thousands of beneficial microorganisms. This recipe will require some beneficial bacteria and fungi inoculants such as

- worm castings and biologically active compost
- food sources like unsulfured molasses, fruit juice, humic acid (1 Tbsp.), fish emulsion, or seaweed to feed these microbes
- rainwater (dechlorinated), oxygen, and agitation.

Scarlet runner beans trained on a bamboo tripod save space and bring a bright spot of color to any garden!

Fill a five-gallon bucket with warm water, place an airstone on the bottom, attach the air pump, and let it begin to bubble. You should see a rolling bubble. If not, your pump is not strong enough and you will need to purchase a more powerful model that will both aerate *and* agitate. Then suspend a nylon stocking holding your inoculants (just like a tea bag) in the pail and add the food. Let it brew for twenty-four to thirty-six hours, no more. If it smells afterwards, you did not get enough air and agitation and should dump it out and start again. You know you are doing it right if it has a sweet, earthy scent.

Trellising and training

Trellising and training can also play a significant, and aesthetic, role in the garden. Vining crops like beans, peas, and cucumbers are especially happy when grown vertically. Not only does it save valuable real estate space, improve air circulation, and reduce disease and pest problems, but by keeping your vegetables up and off the ground they allow more well-formed fruit to develop without any white, blanched spots that are the result of sitting on the ground. Also, harvesting is easier.

There are a variety of trellising systems to choose from, but you should select the structure that works best for you and your garden. A-frame trellises are easy and

No matter how small or large a space, there is a trellis system for you. Trellises can be both functional and beautiful. Here are a few of my favorites (clockwise): Grapes on a wood arbor, bamboo teepee or freestanding wall made with recycled tree branches and strengthened with metal posts, fence carpeted with morning glories, and two large vegetable ladders for larger vegetables like pumpkin and squash.

A DIY A-frame made from wood and chicken wire.

invaluable. They can be constructed out of lattice, or from wooden frames with chicken wire strung across. Either way your peas, pole beans, or squash will be happy to run up them. Tall five- to six-foot teepees and tripods work well and add some architecture to your space. An interesting and productive way to create some privacy in the garden is to string netting between wood or metal T-posts. Your vertical supports can be as simple as a wooden stake inserted next to the plant, attached to each other with a soft closure or a long length of string dropped from a horizontal support and tied to the plant for it to grow up the twine. Even tomato cages do a decent job. Regardless of which method you use to train your vegetables, make sure to situate them on the north, or northeastern, side of the garden so they do not shade out your sun-loving crops.

Pruning

Pruning is a garden talent that only gets better with time and practice. You prune for a few basic reasons: to remove damaged, dead, or diseased plant material (known as the three Ds), manipulate the shape and/or size of plants, and to boost flowering or fruiting. Deadheading is especially important as some plants continue to produce new flowers during their bloom cycle as long as the spent ones are removed. Most pruning is done to maintain a full, healthy shape and control plant size, to keep it manageable and in proportion with the rest of the garden. Always err on the side of under-pruning, you can always cut more, but you can't glue the branches back if you've gone too far.

REMOVE DAMAGED AND DISEASED PLANTS.

As a rough guide, prune early spring-flowering shrubs immediately after they bloom and summer-flowering shrubs in the winter or early spring while dormant. If you wait till later in the summer to cut spring bloomers, you will be removing some of next year's buds and get a sad display the following spring. Many summer-flowering shrubs can be chopped down while dormant and still produce a significant wave of summer flowers since they flower on new growth.

When it comes to pruning, each crop is different. Fruit trees and berries typically require a midwinter pruning while dormant to keep them bearing the highest-quality fruit, to ensure strong branches, and to allow in adequate light and healthy air circulation, promoting production. Tomatoes on the other hand call for a more informal pruning during active growth, one that diminishes insect and disease pressure, and avoids tight, humid conditions that can lead to blight or rot and hasten ripening. Herbs such as bay, rosemary, and lavender can be pruned and trained into topiaries. Fruit trees such as peach and apple can be shed and trained into espaliers.

A classic espalier, apple trees trained against a lattice fence welcome visitors to the garden.

Among my gardening friends, I am known as "the pincher." I like my seedlings strong, compact, and bushy. Once a plant has three or four sets of true leaves (minus the two initial seed leaves), I use sharp snips or my fingertips to cut, or pinch back, to the central leader right above the lowest set of true leaves. This sends all the plant's energy back into the roots and lower growth, promoting more branching, vigorous side shoots, and a stronger, healthier plant.

I remember reading a British gardening magazine in high school and coming across what is known as the Chelsea Chop, named for the famous Chelsea Flower Show in London, and it stuck with me. This traditional technique involves a hard cutback in spring or early summer—just after the flower show in England, but in America planned around climate and zone system—a hefty dose of fish emulsion, and lots of water, resulting in overall stronger, fuller, and lusher plants later in the season. I pinch back all my seedlings hard, and use the chop on most things in the garden, particularly my sweet peas, dahlias, hollyhocks, and other flowering plants. The first time you test out this brutal chop is nail biting, but once you've seen the power of pinching you will be a believer!

PINCH BACK FOR BUSHIER PLANTS.

My dahlias are looking ready to be pinched back for stronger, bushier plants.

PESTS AND DISEASE

Bug off and keep those darn diseases away too! The most daunting and disappointing part of gardening is going to sleep when your beds are full of growing, tasty crops and waking up to see them infested or damaged from infection. The best defense against these nasty pests is to have a healthy garden. Give your plants adequate breathing room, just the right amount of water, lively soil, and nutrients, and you should have vigorous, healthy plants. The stronger your plants are, the less likely they will be to succumb to insect or disease pressure. Selecting resistant varieties will also improve the chances of your crops overcoming pests in the garden. Diverse plantings made by mixing vegetables, herbs, and flowers together in beds or rows draw beneficial insects to your garden and help keep the bad ones under control.

There is a big difference between good bugs and bad bugs in the garden (more on the good guys in Chapter 3). Correct identification of bad bugs is the first step in managing and controlling them. Here are some of the most common pests in the kitchen garden and how to deal with them organically.

Aphids

Aphids are the bane of every gardener's existence. These soft-bodied insects come in black, green, red, and white colors and suck the sap off young, fresh growth leading to a weakening of the plant, distorting and curling leaves, and transmitting

A tomato hornworm devouring a young tomato.

diseases. They also excrete a sticky "honeydew" substance that grows an unsightly black, sooty mold. The easiest way to rid yourself of aphids is to hose them off your plants with a strong spray of water, insecticidal soap, or Neem oil application. You can also attract or introduce a population of ladybugs or lacewing parasitic flies (aka "aphid lions") who naturally feed on aphids and control the problem.

Cabbage worms

Cabbage worms like your brassicas—anything from this family is susceptible to these green caterpillars that happily munch on and shred your leaves. They can be difficult to spot as they blend seamlessly with your vegetables' leaves and stems, but you will be able to notice the adult early in the season. If you see a white butterfly flitting among your cabbage crops, it is probably laying eggs, which are visible little black droppings in the leaf crotch. Remove and crush the eggs. Handpick any caterpillars you see. I drop the eggs and caterpillars into a mason jar of soapy water. Alternatively a lightweight row cover will keep the butterflies from laying eggs on the plants and caterpillars from developing. And if all else fails you can spray your crops with the naturally occurring, soil-borne bacteria *Bacillus thuringiensis* (Bt), which is toxic to these worms.

Adult Colorado potato beetle.

Colorado potato beetle

You're probably familiar with the Colorado potato beetle if you like growing potatoes or eggplant. This yellow and brown-black striped beetle and its red larvae are a serious pest and skeletonize plants' leaves quickly if left alone. Handpicking the hard-shelled beetles and their orange eggs can help control the population and should be the first line of defense since these pests quickly develop resistance to most insecticides. Ladybugs, soldier bugs, and parasitic lacewings are good biological control options with *B. thuringiensis* (Bt) 'San Diego' as a last resort as it is only effective when sprayed within a couple of days of larvae emergence.

Cucumber beetles

Cucumber beetles enjoy snacking on cucumbers, squash, and other cucurbit crops. Easily identifiable, these striped or spotted yellow and black beetles distort, stunt, and transmit disease. Though difficult to control, crop rotation, planting transplants, and utilizing insect barriers or floating row covers are good organic options. Edging your actual vegetables with "trap crop" planted along the perimeter is another way to entice these beetles from munching on your cucurbits. Pyrethrum, a natural broad-spectrum insecticide, or an organic spinosad, which acts as a deterrent and toxin, can also be used.

Cutworms

Fighting cutworms can be disheartening if you don't know how to deal with them. They live in the upper layers of your soil and attack young seedlings at night, particularly broccoli, cabbage, and cauliflower, cutting them off at the base and to the ground by morning. On the bright side, there is an easy fix—cardboard collars. To prevent cutworms from feeding and decimating your early spring crops, cut cardboard or toilet paper rolls to three inches tall, inserting the bottom one inch deep into the soil, with two inches above the ground around the stem. Some gardeners use newspaper as well. This will prevent these pests from attacking your seedlings. Once your seedlings have established themselves and grown, cutworms are no longer an issue.

Flea beetles

Flea beetles are small, black jumping beetles that feed on the leaves of a wide array of vegetables. They make their presence known by eating small, perforated holes in the leaves, which lead to defoliation and stunted growth in heavy infestations. Insect barriers installed early in the season do an excellent job of excluding these bugs. Radishes are a good, early trap crop, but once you have cornered the infestation to one plant, you still need to treat it with either insecticidal soap or pyrethrum.

Place a cardboard collar around susceptible brassica seedlings, like cauliflower, until they are established to protect against cutworms.

Japanese beetles

There are no words. Japanese beetles are simply devastating. Overwintering in the soil, emerging as grubs in spring, and developing into the loathsome metallic green and orange beetles by summer, they eat almost everything, but are especially drawn to grapes, raspberries, and roses. Proliferating rapidly and feeding voraciously on leaves, they are almost impossible to fully control. Floating insect or row covers are effective for your favorite crops, but you will no doubt be handpicking them throughout the season. I keep a jar of soapy water in the garden and each morning add to my collection of dead Japanese beetles. I read once that if you mix dead Japanese beetles with soap and water in a blender and use as a spray, it will deter new ones from feeding in a cannibalistic sort of way. Unfortunately I found that did not work. Some gardeners swear by hanging traps far from the garden, but that it not recommended; it simply attracts more (in droves) rather them leading them away. A more practical control is an

Japanese beetles defoliating a plant.

application of beneficial nematodes to control the grub population while still in the soil, or a milky spore powder (*Bacillus popillae*) that when ingested infects the grubs and kills them. You will most likely need multiple applications for milk spore to be effective.

KEEP A JAR OF SOAPY WATER IN THE GARDEN.

Leaf miners

Damage caused by leaf miners is easy to spot. White tunnels between the plant's leaf layers that run about the leaves in irregular patterns make it easily identifiable. Insect barriers are good at preventing these small, difficult-to-spot insects from landing. But if not, handpick any pests you do see, then remove and destroy any infected leaves. While infected leaves are still edible, you don't want to leave them on the plant to spread. Other controls include yellow sticky cards, beneficial parasitic wasps, and Neem oil.

Maggots

Maggots are fly larvae and are often found in apple and root crops. When apple maggots attack apple trees, the unfortunate result is deformed, wormy fruits. Apple maggot traps hung under the canopy are an easy fix, both trapping and killing this pest. Root maggots hatch from eggs that flies lay in the soil near vegetables like carrots, onions, and radishes. Once the larvae emerge, they burrow into the soil and begin tunneling through the crops within one to three weeks. Floating row covers or insect barriers installed at time of planting are an adequate control against maggots. Alternatively, lay heavy paper collars or cardboard paper on the soil around newly planted root crops so the flies lay their eggs on the paper and you can dispose of them easily.

HOMEMADE BEER TRAPS

- Fill a shallow bowl or jar lid with beer. Any will do, but draft beers have a higher yeast content, making them more attractive to destructive beetles.
- Sit the lid on the ground, at soil level near plants they are munching on. You can bury the bowl slightly to make it easier for slugs and snails to find their way to their alcohol-infused demise.
- Dispose of beer and drowned slugs in the morning.

Slugs and snails

Whether you have slugs or snails the result is the same ... snacked-on leaves, especially in cool, wet weather. You will often find these guys hidden in cool, dark crannies and crooks between leaves and stems. While you can handpick, the easiest way to collect snails is a beer trap. I remember the first time my mother suggested this and I didn't believe it would work, but it did! I set out a few shallow dishes and condiment lids in the garden, filled each with a helping of beer, and went to sleep. By morning the slugs, who are attracted to the yeast, were drowned in the deliciousness, and all I had to do was dump it and refill later that evening. Iron phosphate baits are also successful in ridding you of slugs. Copper strips adhered to container edges or sharp and salty organic mulches like eggshells or seaweed deter slugs and snails, keeping your crops safe.

Squash bugs

Squash bugs, sometimes called stinkbugs due to the putrid odor emitted when squashed, are detrimental but dealt with easily and efficiently with insect barriers or row covers. Be sure to cover the plants immediately after transplanting and keep covered until they flower and need to pol- linate. Primarily affecting squash, pump- kins, and other cucurbits, these flattened, gray or brown bugs fly, feed, and mate. Squash bugs suck the sap, causing the leaves develop yellow spots that eventually

A young squash bug that never had a chance to make it out to the cucurbit bed.

brown, causing wilting and even death for young plants. Wood boards placed at the base of infested plants are effective nighttime traps, or you can try a splash of diatomaceous earth to reduce the population. These guys will overwinter in garden debris, so fall cleanup is important. Insecticidal soap, Neem oil, and pyrethrum are all useful in controlling this pest.

Squash vine borer

The squash vine borer is a prominent pest to all cucurbits. Unfortunately it has usually done most of its damage before you see any symptoms. Adult flies lay their eggs on the stem, and when they hatch, the cream-colored caterpillars tunnel through the stems feeding on the interior tissues, causing the plant to wilt and often to die. The best way to prevent damage is to stop the borers before they enter the stem, as once they do almost all controls are inef- fective. Physical barriers like row covers and removal of autumn plant debris are the best ways to exclude this pest from the garden. Adventurous gardeners can attempt to deworm the stem. Look for sawdust-like frass below your squash stems. Make a slit above the debris and remove any borers, burying the now de-wormed stem to root. Some gardeners go as far as to suggest injecting Btk (*B. thuringiensis* 'Kurstaki') into infected vines.

Spider mites and whiteflies

Spider mites and whiteflies are small, more nuisance-like pests. Spider mites are usually found on the underside of leaves. They lay eggs and form a white webbing indicative of large populations. They favor dry, hot weather, so keep your garden well-watered. But if they develop into an issue, treat with insecticidal soap. Whiteflies are exactly what their name suggests—white flies. They lay their eggs on the underside of lower leaves and suck sap. Yellow sticky cards and leaf removal are useful in controlling adult populations, while ladybugs and lacewing larvae are excellent biological controls. Some simple ways to knock down any whitefly infestations include a heavy stream of water, insecticidal soap, Neem, and other horticultural oils.

Fungus

Anthracnose is a generic term used to describe a myriad of fungal symptoms ranging from leaf spot, blotches, or distortion, defoliation, and blight to sunken lesions on fruit and cankers. Many different crops are affected, including beans, cucurbits, cucumbers, eggplants, melons, peas, spinach, and tomatoes. This disease is most easily controlled with good air circulation, a mulching layer, watering from below, and keeping both fruits and leaves from touching the soil. Overhead watering and humid, cloudy weather create an inviting environment for over a dozen species of fungi to grow, so avoid if possible. Remove and destroy all infected plant residue, and do not compost unless you're practicing hot composting and your pile will reach over 120°F.

Blight

Blight is caused by a multitude of diseases, but regardless of which pathogen has infected your plants, it is characterized by a chlorosis, or browning and eventual death of leaves, and occurs most often in wet weather. The three most common types of blight are early, late, and bacterial. Peppers, tomatoes, and potatoes are common victims of early and late blight caused by fungi, but bacterial blight targets the legumes.

PLANT BLIGHT-RESISTANT CULTIVARS.

If infected, you will notice early to mid-season small, dark concentric circles on the stem and lower leaves, which will eventually drop, or on the fruit near the stem on plants with early blight. The best control is to plant blight-resistant cultivars, promote good air circulation and practice a three-year crop rotation plan as this fungi is spread by spores in the air and can overwinter in the soil. Potassium bicarbonate (baking soda) sprays are also useful when applied at least two weeks before symptoms typically appear in your region.

Late blight presents as bluish-gray splotches on leaves that drop, irregular brown, sunken spots on the fruit, and white mold rings developing around them mid- to late season. You can head off some issues if you can keep your plants' foliage dry and cut off and destroy any infected plant parts as soon as they appear. As with early blight, late blight overwinters in the soil, so it is still important to implement a rotation strategy and plant resistant varieties.

Bacterial blight is best managed with resistant cultivars, three-year crop rotation plans, destruction of infected plant debris, and ensuring that your beans and peas are not handled or disturbed when wet, as that often perpetuates the spread of this disease. You will know you have infected plants if you see water-soaked spots on pods and leaves or long, dark lesions on stems.

Gray mold

Botrytis, better known as gray mold, favors cool, moist weather, and is characterized by the presence of woolly or fuzzy growth on aging flowering and ripe fruit. You will often notice a gray sporey mist when infected leaves or flowers are handled. While people are most familiar with gray mold on their fruits and berries, your tomatoes and beans are highly susceptible as well. Avoiding overhead watering, maintaining good air circulation, cleaning up plant debris such as spent blooms, and keeping your leaves dry go a long way to preventing botrytis.

Clubroot

Clubroot is a soil-borne fungal disease that primarily affects plants in the cabbage family and is most common in cold, wet acidic soils. Brassica roots become swollen and distorted. Generally liming your soil to raise your pH to 6.5-6.8 is all you need to do to forestall this disease. Crop rotation and selecting resistant varieties are also helpful.

Damping-off

Damping-off, another soil-borne fungal disease, is responsible for killing your plants before they even get started. Here, your seeds rot before or soon after they've germinated. Simply don't overwater. Use a fresh, sterile soil mix with good drainage, keep your soil evenly moist but not soggy, avoid humidity, and water from below if you are starting seedlings indoors. Increased light exposure also reduces your chances of losing your plants to damping-off, and if you do start to notice some seedling death, slow or even stop your watering until they have rebounded.

Leaf blisters and curls

Vegetable leaves can show a variety of symptoms fluctuating between blisters, curls, and spots. Leaf blisters are characterized by raised yellow bumps, while curled leaves look puckered since the midrib doesn't extend in new pale or reddish leaves. Common in fruit trees, these diseases will damage your fruit. Both leaf blisters and leaf curls are caused by fungi. Leaf spot on the other hand can be caused by a bacteria or fungus, and results from cool, wet weather. Resistant varieties, air circulation, mulch, and a three-year crop rotation plan will help avoid these issues.

BLIGHT-CONTROL SPRAY RECIPE

Neem oil or a baking soda solution (1 Tbsp. baking soda, 2½ Tbsp. vegetable oil, 1 Tsp. of liquid soap [not detergent], and 1 Gal. water) applied every couple of weeks can help as a last resort. Be sure to test out on one plant before spraying your entire garden, as it may burn your plants.

Mildew

Caused by parasitic fungi, mildew is one of the most widespread diseases. There are two main culprits in the garden: downy and powdery mildew. Downy mildew is distinguished by white or purple fuzzy growth under the leaves and along the stems. The tops of the leaves fade, leaves can become distorted, and over time, the mildew turns black. Powdery mildew, however, is characterized by a white-to-gray growth on the upper side of the leaves and the development of small black spores that will spread. Leaves can die, flowers and fruit will abort, ripen prematurely, or taste poor on disease-ridden plants. Good spacing, staking, and air circulation are the best easy way to prevent mildew from becoming a problem. Besides a potassium bicarbonate spray, there is no treatment, and infected plants should be removed and destroyed as mildew is easily spread by wind and rain.

Nematodes

You know you have a nematode problem if your plants lack vigor, if growth has slowed, stunted, or begun to wilt. The best defense against these guys is high organic matter and plant resistance. Root knot nematodes can be particularly bothersome in the kitchen garden, attacking the root systems and producing stunted crops, distorted roots, and yellow leaves. Crop rotation, resistant cultivars, and marigold (*Tagetes patula* or *T. erecta*) cover crops, as well as solarization (excessive heating of the soil), will reduce the number of nematodes in your soil. To eliminate nematodes in plant roots, you need to dig them up and treat them to a hot water dip.

Rust

Rust is easily recognizable by the rusty, brown pustules (spore-producing structures) on the underside of plant leaves, but they can also be black, orange, white, or yellow. Some plants lose vigor, while others continue to thrive so long as you remove all affected leaves. Plants severely attacked may lose their leaves or die completely. There are not many organic controls besides removal, destruction of infected parts, and plant resistance. Good air circulation, sterilization of tools, rotation, and avoidance of high nitrogen fertilizers will help fend off rust colonization.

Viruses

Viruses affect flowers, herbs, and vegetables in the kitchen garden, and identification is usually the most difficult as it is a process of elimination. Symptoms can range from low yields, distorted leaves, spotting, and molting to deformed and stunted growth. The only ways to treat viral infections is with heat treatments and tissue cultures, which unfortunately are not available to the everyday gardener. So in the absence of these treatments, do your best by avoid viruses in the first place by planting healthy plants, maintaining clean tools, and keeping your insect population down with good garden practices and beneficial insects.

Wilts

Wilts are due to fungi or bacteria raid that clogs the water transmission system inside the plant, causing permanent wilting. The most common types of wilt are fusarium and verticillium, and they affect all garden plants. You may notice many of the symptoms mirror those of blight. To avoid your leaves wilting and turning yellow, start by selecting disease-resistant varieties, beware of overwatering, rotate your crops, and remove and destroy any infected plant parts.

Animals

And lastly, wildlife. Not all pests travel through insects, air, or soil—some walk right up to your garden and feast! Dogs, cats, birds, deer, raccoons, rabbits, rodents, and squirrels are just a few. The easiest way to keep these guys out of your garden is to fence them out. Whether it means a six-foot-tall deer fence, a netting over your crops to keep the birds from snacking on your growing veggies, or a fine metal mesh inserted at the base of your raised beds to keep rabbits and rodents out, barriers go a long way to relegating wildlife to mother nature, not your garden. Some gardeners have had success with animal urine, dried blood, garlic, hot pepper, human hair, or eggshells spread along the perimeter, but

At our last house this seemingly sweet groundhog and his family would decimate our garden haul regularly.

success seems to vary from one garden to the next. I swear by human hair, while my mother always used dried blood to keep the deer at bay. There are a number of organic repellants out there, so the best I can suggest is trial and error and see what works for you.

RECORD KEEPING

The more I grow, the more I learn that gardening is one giant experiment, and it is always good to have a record of what worked and what didn't. I learned to keep a garden journal a year after my first solo garden, when there was so much I couldn't remember. When did I plant my basil? Which week did I pinch the dahlias? How did I trellis my tomatoes? Keeping an accurate and detailed record of what you've grown, how you grew it, and your harvest is helpful in deciding what to grow and how to adjust things the following year. It can be as simple as a composition book in which you date and diary your plantings and observations, a Word document, or a slightly more complicated spreadsheet/chart where you detail dates and quality of harvest. Mark down and log weather patterns like rain, the date for first and last frosts, and average night and daytime temperatures. I also like to include notes on any soil amendments added, my favorite seed and plant sources, as well as photos from the garden from throughout the season. Alternatively, you can get a wall calendar and record your observations and notations each day, and keep it to refer to the following year. You'll easily be able to assess your seed starting, transplanting, crop rotation, irrigation, and fertilization schedules. Also keep track of any insects or diseases you ran into and how you handled them. Documenting whether the plant species you chose were tasty and successful will help you decide if you would rather try something new next year. It can also be devastating when you want to grow the same variety as you did the year before and you can't remember its name!

One of the most difficult things to navigate for the first-time gardener is all that garden jargon you see on seed packets or plant tags. Why can't we just call them cucumbers or sugar snap peas? Because there are lots and lots of common names among plants, and they vary by region and history, which can become confusing and supremely unhelpful when faced with the plethora of choices in catalogs. It's important to understand the basic structure of the universal Latin names so you can order the same delectable tomatoes or cosmos year after year.

Carl Linnaeus, an eighteenth-century Swedish scientist, created the classification system we use today. The descending ranks of family, genus, species, and variety or cultivar were derived from his love of order and organization. The Latin name is a combination of genus and species and always written in italic (or underlined if handwritten), with the first letter of the genus capitalized and species all lowercase. The variety is never italicized (or underlined) and is set within singular quotation marks. For example, what you might pick up and think of as white cauliflower is part of the Brassicaceae family, and its full Latin name is *Brassica oleracea* 'Denali.' Its genus is *Brassica*, species *oleracea,* and the variety Denali. Sometimes you may not be sure what specific species your plant is, and in that case the singular "sp." or plural "spp." is used. For example, if I were unsure of which species of cauliflower I was growing, I would indicate by writing *Brassica* sp. (Also, if you are talking about multiple plants with the same genus, you would write out the genus the first time, but only use the capital first initial ever after.)

You may see additional nomenclature on your packets or plant tags. Varieties and cultivars are similar in that they are a minor subdivision of a species (although not all plants have varieties, or cultivars) that have a particular difference in their structure or morphology. Varieties are naturally occurring, while cultivars are selectively cross-pollinated, bred, and raised and are often only able to reproduce vegetatively. Sometimes you will see the terms var. or cv. to delineate a specific variety or cultivar respectively.

Hybrid plants can be naturally occurring or man-made. They are a cross between two species and are represented with their genus, then an "x" and its given name. Heirlooms are a big buzzword today, but they simply refer to natural varieties that have been grown for 50 years or more.

All this botanical Latin actually means something. The language denotes a specific characteristic(s) and points toward a geographic region, growth form or habit, color, petal number, or the person who discovered the plant. But the overall point of all this nomenclature is to provide a universal taxonomy so no matter where you are in the world, you can find the exact plant you are looking for!

CHAPTER 2

PROPAGATION AND PLANTING TECHNIQUES

Propagating is my all-time favorite thing to do in the garden—it's like creating your own little bit of magic in the dirt. At its root, propagating is all about making new plants and increasing your plant stock. It can be achieved in one of three ways: by seed, through cuttings, or by layering. These simple techniques are fun, inexpensive, and rewarding. Certain plants respond better to one method over another. For example, French tarragon should be started with cuttings. It doesn't come true (or flavorful) to seed, whereas tomatoes and most vegetables grow readily from seed.

SOIL AND ITS MATERIALS

Regardless of which method of propagation you're employing, there are some materials you cannot do without. Soil, water, pots or trays, labels, a sharp knife, and snips are essential. In addition bottom heat can speed up germinating and rooting. Most gardeners swear by their secret soilless seed starting mixes, but oftentimes you will be able to find one of these mixes at your local garden center. Traditional all-purpose mixes are wasted on seeds, which carry their own nutrient supply with them. The additional fertilizers can actually inhibit germination and growth. Sterile, soilless mixes offer an economical space for water and air to go and roots to develop without squandering expensive food and fertilizer.

SEED-STARTING RECIPE

- 1 Part fine bark (or screened compost)
- 1 Part perlite or vermiculite
- 2 Parts coir or peat moss

To make your own seed-starting medium, toss a combination of compost, fine bark, topsoil, perlite, vermiculite, sand, coir, or peat moss into a large Tupperware bin, wheelbarrow, or dry sink, wet it down so it is the consistency of a wrung-out sponge, and mix. Many gardeners screen their compost, bark, and other materials to achieve a fine blend, but I've found that as long as my compost or fine bark is broken down enough (six to eight months), I don't need to use a sieve. It also ensures that the ammonia is decomposed enough that it won't harm or inhibit your seedlings' growth.

Fine bark is just what is sounds like—broken down bark—and you can either generate this on your own by shredding the bark before it's composted (speeding up decomposition) or purchasing it locally or online. It is light and improves drainage and air circulation. Perlite is expanded volcanic glass that is used for its aeration and drainage capabilities. Vermiculite, made from expanded mica, aids in aeration and drainage, but it is its high water-retentive qualities that differentiate it from perlite. Coarse sand is sometimes used when you want to improve drainage without the added aeration or water retention. Coir and peat moss are made of natural, fibrous material. But while coir is made of coconut hulls, peat is derived from decaying plant material in peat bogs. There is some controversy surrounding peat moss as it takes several millennia to develop and as such is a non-renewable resource. The ratio of ingredients varies from mix to mix, but coir or peat should make up one-third to two-thirds of the mix to make the most of its water- and nutrient-holding qualities.

SOWING SEED

Almost any plant can be grown from seed regardless of whether it's an annual, biennial, or perennial. And while there's nothing wrong with supporting your local garden center, it is substantially cheaper and abundantly more satisfying to grow your plants rather than buy them.

Seeds can be started indoors in trays and pots, or directly in the ground outside, also referred to as in situ. Seeds are programmed to germinate and grow; they come with their own food supply that lasts until they are established enough to produce their own food through photosynthesis. All you need to do is provide favorable conditions and let the

Sowing sweet pea (*Lathyrus odoratus*) seed in plug trays.

PLANT SEEDS ONLY AS DEEP AS THEIR DIAMETER.

seed do its thing. Seeds need water, light, and the right temperature to germinate. Water penetrates the seed coat activating all the metabolic activities inside, and the embryo busts out to release its roots and first leaves. The need for light varies depending on the seed. It's usually determined by planting depth and whether the seed is covered or not. Some seeds are buried deeper than others, some are scattered on the surface, others enjoy a thin layer of vermiculite over top. The directions for sowing are on each seed packet, but when in doubt the rule of thumb is to plant each seed only as deep as its diameter. Temperature is important for two reasons: it jump-starts germination and root development, and some seeds require a period of exposure to cooler temperatures before they will germinate.

HOW TO SANITIZE YOUR POTS, TRAYS, AND TOOLS

First, physically remove any dirt and scrub any salt spots. Mix a 10 percent bleach/90 percent water solution in a large tub or garbage can, submerge all pots, and let soak for approximately ten to fifteen minutes. Remove and rinse with water, then let them air-dry. For stone and terracotta pots, rinse and soak in a separate container of clear water for an additional ten to fifteen minutes to remove any remaining bleach from the pot's pores. Let air-dry.

When sowing indoors or early, I prefer to use soil blockers or plug trays to start most of my seeds. It just depends on my mood. Blocking is very soothing and Zen-like, but sometimes I need to sow too much seed, so out come the seventy-two-cell plug trays. If you are reusing pots or seed trays, you will need to clean them first to ensure there are no lingering fungi or diseases, otherwise your seeds will be dead before they begin. Also, all trays and pots should have drainage holes at the bottom. Using my favorite light seed-starting recipe, I firm-in the soil. Do not compact. (Loose soil provides good drainage and air space for roots to tunnel through and anchor to.) Compacted soil inhibits water intake, root development, and aeration. Then scatter or plant your seeds and cover following the instructions on the packet. Some gardeners like to use a dibble to create a planting hole, but a pencil will do the job just as well. To maintain soil moisture, cover each tray with a clear plastic dome; even some cling wrap from the kitchen will do. Additionally, I use heat mats under my flats until the seeds germinate. Consistent bottom heat results in seeds sprouting in as little as half the time! Just remember to remove flats from heating mats once seedlings have emerged, otherwise they can become leggy.

Sowing in situ isn't much different, but you are more restricted as to when you can plant due to cold temperatures. By using black or clear plastic

A happy lovage seedling in a soil block ready to be transplanted out in the garden.

SOIL-BLOCKERS

These handheld blockers come in different sizes: a large (two-inch) four-block unit and a small (three-quarter-inch) twenty-block unit. These blocks maximize space on your propagation tables and heating mats, in addition to saving money on all those plug trays and pots you won't be needing. Also, each block is automatically pushed with small depressions for easy sowing.

1. Mix soil until it has an oatmeal-like consistency.
2. Insert the blocker into the bin, filling the blocks. Twist against a hard surface until the water flows over the top of the blocker to ensure the blocks come out cleanly.
3. Press and discharge the blocker into a tray.
4. Rinse the blocker in a bucket of water between blocking to avoid jamming.
5. Start sowing!

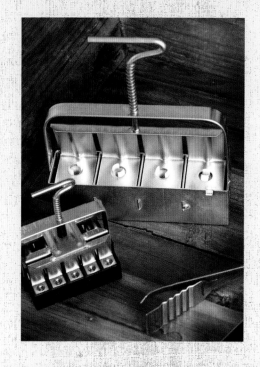

mulch for two weeks, you can heat the outside soil enough that you may be able to plant earlier if you plan on using some season extension techniques. But the the vast majority of gardeners begin planting once the soil has warmed to 55-60°F, waiting even a bit longer for warm-weather crops like cucumbers and melons. Contact your local agricultural extension office and find out your area's last frost date, and don't plant tender seedlings before. Otherwise you'll become obsessed with the weather forecast and will be running out to protect your new garden from surprise frosts.

It's common to plant in drills down a straight line. Use a pair of sticks and string to map out where you want to plant, then use a dibble, hoe, or shovel to make a shallow V-shaped drill along the line. Water down the new drill, sow seed evenly, space as per packet instructions, and cover with soil. Again, I cannot overemphasize the importance of labeling each drill.

HEATING MAT HACK

Bottom heat speeds up the germination process. A great garden hack is to use incandescent (not LED) outdoor Christmas rope lights under your flats! They will warm, but won't burn. Then, once germinated, remove your seedlings from the heat source. (Note: Seedlings don't require as much warmth as seeds.)

WAKE UP YOUR SEEDS

Some seeds need a little more TLC before they are ready to break dormancy and germinate. They may require exposure to cold temperatures (mix seeds in a zip lock bag with damp sand and pop in the fridge or freezer for a specific amount of time) or need to be overwintered in the ground to start growing. The latter is often the result of a tough seed coat. Either soak the seed overnight or scarify (scratch with sandpaper or nick with a knife), then soak. The seed should swell, taking in water, and be more likely to germinate once sown.

Seeds like baptisia, comfrey, and sweet peas have super hard shells or contain chemical inhibitors that make germination especially difficult. In those cases you will need to help the process along, and it can be done one of three ways: 1. Soak in warm water for twenty-four hours (no more). 2. Scarify. This involves either scratching the seed coat with sandpaper or nicking the corner before planting to allow water to penetrate. I've found that giving a soak after scarifying the seed speeds germination. 3. Stratification. Some seeds need

Sweet pea seed soaking in water overnight in mason jars. The labels help me remember which variety is which!

exposure to cold temperatures before they will sprout. To trick the seed into thinking it's experienced winter, toss the seed packets into a sealed zip lock bag or glass jar, and stick in the refrigerator for a prescribed amount of time. It's so important to label the bag or jar with the removal date, because as much as you think you will be able to remember when you started the process, you may not. Stratification can last anywhere from two weeks to six months, and the only danger is in removing the seeds from the chilled environment too soon. It never hurts to chill longer. Some seeds will perform even better in the process if mixed with damp sand in the zip lock rather than just the seed packet.

TESTING SEED VIABILITY

Unused seeds should be stored in a cool, dry, dark place if you want to reuse them, as old seed has lower germination rates, or may not germinate at all. To avoid wasting your time and resources, perform a seed viability test in the spring. Place a few seeds on a damp paper towel in an open zip lock bag and expose to the light. Make sure to label which seed is which, and watch over the next couple weeks. You will be able to see if they sprout or not. If you do have success, you can plant the sprouted seeds in pots.

Overwatering is the number one cause for seeds not germinating. Too little water isn't good either, which is why I find it's best to water from the bottom. This also helps the seedlings develop strong root systems. The tendency to overwater is not the only reason for poor germination. It can also be the result of seeds being buried too deep, the air temperature being too cold, or just impatience. Parsley takes an exceptionally long time to germinate, and every year I question whether it's going to come in. Of course it always does. So keep the faith!

Once your seedlings are growing, at some point you may see some leaf discoloration and flopping over at the base. This is an indication that they've caught a

BOTTOM HEAT WILL SPEED GERMINATION ALONG.

fungal disease, broadly referred to as damping-off. Unfortunately there is no cure, and you should cut your losses immediately. Do not compost these seedlings—trash them. The best defense against this type of disease is cleanliness. Use clean pots and fresh soil mixes, sow thinly to improve air circulation, and don't overwater.

SAVING SEED

Collecting and using your own seed is so easy it can become addicting! Let the plant go to flower and wait until the seed head starts to dry (wet seed rots). To harvest, place a paper bag over top of the dried seed head, secure at the base, and cut the stem farther down. Then hang upside down in a cool, dry, dark place for one to two weeks. Once the seed heads are sufficiently dry, take down the stems and shake. You should be rewarded with the sound of delightfully dry seeds puddling at the bottom of the bag. Clean the chaff off any seeds, label, and store in airtight jars, paper seed packets, or envelopes. Keep in your fridge or a cool, dry spot until next year.

As I mentioned earlier, my garden friends know me as "the pincher." I am ruthless in my thinning and pinching of seedlings. Both of these practices result in healthier, stronger, and more productive plants. Typically you plant more than one seed per pot, cell, or garden bed, and if you're lucky, more than one will grow. The drawback to keeping all seedlings is overcrowding, which encourages disease and damping-off. It's vital to remove the weaker seedlings, allowing air to circulate and giving them more room to spread out. I'd suggest thinning in increments, as you'll find some seedlings naturally die off, are attacked by a pest, or are nibbled on and carried off by a neighboring critter. Cut back at soil level. Once your seedlings have four to six sets of true leaves, it is time to pinch back. You can either use your fingers or some sharp snips to cut out vigorous, center stalks of your plants just above a node and set of leaves. Plants send most of their energy into the development of the main stem and terminal bud, so by pinching it out, all that energy is being redirected back to the roots. This selective pruning encourages branching and side-shoot development, creating a bushier, compact plant that is more productive. You can pinch back multiple times for an even stronger plant if you are feeling adventurous. Once you see the benefits of pinching, you'll be a believer!

If you've raised your seedlings indoors or in a greenhouse, they need to be hardened off before they can be successfully transplanted. This means a gradual exposure to cooler temperature than the seedlings are used to. Place your pots and trays on your porch or deck for a few hours for a couple days, bringing them in at night. Slowly elongate the time spent exposed to the outside temperature, wind, and elements. After two to three weeks the plants should be acclimatized and ready to live outside.

PROPAGATION BY CUTTINGS

Cuttings are underrated as a propagation method. It's as natural as breathing for some plants to root—they'll do it without any help from you. Have you ever put mint or basil in a glass of water only to see white hair roots develop within a week? Other plants need a bit more inducement to root. The primary motivation for taking cuttings over seeding is to preserve the exact characteristics of a plant that does not comes true to seed. Or, if germination is particularly spotty, it's often easier to take cuttings as a little extra insurance so you don't lose any of your favorite performers. Sometimes this practice is referred to as vegetative, or asexual, propagation because there is no seed making involved in creating offspring. Cuttings are like cloning—you're using one piece of a living organism to make an identical replica. For herbs like French tarragon and lavender, this is the only way to get true plants, but for others like bay leaf it is a shortcut. Bay takes three to twelve *months* to germinate and another two to three years growing in a pot before it can be planted out, but a cutting will root in three to six months ... it's really a no-brainer which method to use.

For the best chance of success, always choose shoots from thriving, healthy plants with fresh growth and use clean, sharp snips or knife. You can take root, leaf, or stem cuttings, but the most common is stem. Then there are softwood, semi-ripe, and hardwood type cuttings,

but this refers more to when the shoot is being cut rather than the part of the plant being used. Softwood cuttings are taken from new growth in spring through early summer and are the easiest to root. They are your "most likely to succeed" type of cutting, but you have to be aware not to let them dry out. When taking cuttings, I carry a large zip lock bag that I periodically mist and keep closed to keep the cuttings moist. Semi-ripe stems look as if their growth has begun to slow—the stem is becoming more woody. Cut this in late summer, keeping in mind that these will take longer to root than fresh softwood cuttings. Hardwood cuttings taken in late autumn through winter off deciduous trees and shrubs should root by the following spring.

CUTTING MIX RECIPE

Moistened 50 percent perlite (or coarse, builder's sand) plus 50 percent peat and/or coir with seaweed meal (or liquid seaweed).

Softwood and semi-ripe cuttings are taken the same way, cut four- to-six-inch lengths with four to six sets of leaves at an angle from the stem tip, carefully removing the lower two-thirds leaves so as not to exhaust your new roots. If you tear or squish the stem, it may make rooting difficult and invite disease. Then make a new cut just below a bare node near the bottom. Shaving a sliver from the side of the bark of semi-ripe cuttings can stimulate the rooting cells when the wound calluses over. Dip the bottom and barren nodes of the cutting into rooting hormone to promote root development. Just be sure to pour the powder you're using into a separate dish and discard afterward to avoid contamination with your supply. Use a soil mix similar to what you used for seed starting—garden soil is too heavy. Also, mixing a few teaspoons of seaweed meal and bonemeal into the soil will get your cutting off to a good start without generating too much top growth from nitrogen fertilizers. Gently insert the cutting into your soil blocks, seed trays, or cells until the remaining leaves sit above the soil and then firm at the base.

Rooted scented geranium cuttings

TIPS FOR FASTER ROOTING

- Choose thinner stems—they root more quickly than thicker stems.
- Take cuttings in early morning when the plant is still turgid and less likely to dry out.
- Select young, strong branches.
- Side shoots root better than terminal.
- Remove any flowers.
- Cut any large leaves in half. They will still photosynthesize but won't exhaust the roots to do so.
- Use a root hormone powder, particularly for semi-ripe and hardwood cuttings.
- Employ a heating mat underneath for more rapid rooting.
- Cut the base at a slant to expose more stem surface for root development.
- Dip your cutting tools in 10 percent bleach solutions to avoid disease transmission.

Keep the soil moist and use plastic bottles, clear domes, plastic bags, or kitchen cling wrap to maintain the humidity, venting daily. Do not let the plastic touch the leaves. Heat mats are useful in accelerating rooting. Most cuttings will root in three to six weeks, sooner if kept in a greenhouse. You'll know when your cuttings are rooted by lightly tugging on them; if they resist being pulled, they are rooted.

Hardwood cuttings are typically six- to-eight-inch, pencil-thin lengths cut at an angle below a node at the bottom. Make another cut at the top, this time straight, above a node. The straight and slant cuts will help you differentiate the top from bottom of the cutting. Wrap branches in damp paper towels to maintain freshness until you're ready to plant. Smother the bottom of each in rooting hormone and insert two-thirds to three-quarters inch deep into a pot filled with soil mix, water, and place in a cold frame or greenhouse over the winter. Remember to check periodically to ensure your cuttings are moist throughout the cooler weather. For gardeners in warmer climates (zone 8+) you can keep your cuttings outside until the spring, but they may take longer to root. Over the next six to eight months you should see new growth. Tug to make sure they are rooted, and it's now time to transplant into the garden.

Check regularly for water and moisture. The soil medium should be moist, not wet; otherwise you will see a disease called Black Leg. Basically this is rot, starting at the base and going up. You will know you have this if you see the bottom of the stem turn black. It is important to maintain humidity, hence the plastic domes or bags, but if the plastic touches any leaves it will invite mildews, rots, and disease. Also, you should vent periodically to prevent condensation buildup on the interior of the plastic.

Leaf cuttings are typically successful for tropicals and houseplants. Similar to softwood and semi-ripe, cut one leaf with a one- to-two-inch long stem and stick it into a moist potting medium at an angle until the leaf is above the soil line. Cover with clear plastic to maintain humidity as you would with other cuttings.

Root cuttings are different because they are taken when the plant is dormant. At this time of year the roots are full of food and carbohydrates. Dig up one side of the plant, exposing the roots (this won't disturb the parent plant), and cut two- to-six-inch, pencil-thick lengths close to the plant base. Cut the top straight across and the bottom at an angle, so you can easily find the top. Bundle and store the roots in moist potting soil or coarse sand in a dark spot at 40°F for three weeks. Once removed, use a dibble or pencil to make a hole in your potting mix, planting the slanted end down such that the top is just covered with soil. Store in a cool location where they won't freeze until spring, then harden them off and plant once they are rooted and have formed leaves.

Layering

These are the lazy gardener's cuttings. Essentially you train one or more stems to root while still attached to the plant, then separate them using a sharp knife or pruners. The best time to do this is while the plant is actively growing.

You will need some open garden space around the plant you want to layer. Loosen the soil nearby where a flexible stem will come in contact with the soil. Find one or more long, healthy stems and strip the leaves where it meets the ground, leaving a significant amount of leafy growth so the plant can continue to photosynthesize. Using a sharp knife cut the underside of the stem below a node one-third of the way through. Situate the stem such that the wound stays open when buried under the soil. Anchor with landscape staples, pins, or a heavy rock. You can stake the green stem/growth to help the plant grow upright if you like. Water regularly and keep an eye out for new growth. Sever the new plant once it's thriving on its own, This can take time—anywhere from a few weeks to a year. Although you can leave it in place for another season, I prefer to dig it up and move it to another spot in the garden so the roots don't get intertwined with its parent's. Another quick layering method is to insert the growing tip of a branch into some bare adjacent soil. Bury the tip and secure. Again, you can sever once the new plant is growing vigorously.

Dividing

Perennials come back year after year, but oftentimes if they are not divided periodically, their roots get congested, resulting in a weaker plant and reduced flavor. Dividing gives these plants the room to grow, flourish, and extend their lives. The general guideline is to divide every three to five years, replanting the newest, hardiest sections and ensuring that each division has at least one growing point and its own root system. Dividing works for plants with fibrous root systems and should ideally be performed in the spring or fall. Woody plants cannot be divided. I prefer to wait for a cool day after a rain so the soil is a little looser and the plant is less likely to dry out. Prepare clean one-gallon pots or make a hole in the ground, depending on whether you plan to share and swap plants with friends or transplant divisions in the garden. Then you need to dig up the plant, making sure you get the entire root ball. Give yourself plenty of space and take your time.

After you dig the plant up, lift it using a fork and divide. You can separate your herbaceous perennials a few ways. Smaller plant roots can be teased apart with your fingers or hand forks, but some of the larger ones I find easier to slice through using a spade or saw. When my husband and I were newly married, his grandmother offered to share her lovely, but way overgrown, hosta collection with us. The crowns were so tight that it took an ax to separate them. So if you need to, think outside the box. (By the way, our hostas look beautiful!)

Replant your divisions in the garden immediately to avoid drying out, or with some loam and compost in a pot. Water-in well and maintain steady moisture until the plant is established. Your old plants will look much happier and appear rejuvenated.

Transplants

Planting out is the most exciting day of the season! Using my local agricultural extension's last frost date as a guide, I spread a few inches of compost over my garden beds two to three weeks before. If possible, I like to schedule my first big day in the garden after a rain so the soil is more workable. Then, using my overly detailed garden plan, I begin planting seeds and my hardened off seedlings using my favorite transplanting trowel and kneeling mat. I know a kneeling mat doesn't sound very sexy, but after a few hours on your knees bending over delicious compost planting, your body will thank you! Don't forget to label as you plant.

Lettuce seedlings needing to be thinned.

Time can get away from even the most diligent of gardeners, and before you know it, the time to sow tomato seeds has passed and the only way to have fresh tomatoes is to purchase some seedlings. Off to the garden center you go! There's nothing wrong with having someone else do all that seeding and nurturing for you. And while you may have more choices for novelty varieties in seed catalogs, the most

Healthy basil seedling ready to be planted and thinned.

popular varieties should be available at the garden center. When purchasing seedlings always check your plant labels to ensure you are getting the correct variety. You don't want to grow one type of cucumber only to find out later they are for slicing, not pickling.

Whoever said money can't buy happiness has clearly never been to a garden center. I can easily get carried away purchasing things I didn't know I needed. Some items just hop into my wagon. Once the overwhelming sense of euphoria from being surrounded by all my favorite things fades, its time to get down to business. You need to inspect everything you buy. First, there should be no bugs. Look at the leaves—they should appear green and healthy with no curling, black or brown spots, or singed tips. The plant should be full—avoid those with bare stems. I will often pop the root ball out of the pot and check the roots. Healthy roots should be white and fibrous. If you see any girdling, or circling, the plant is rootbound. Don't buy it unless you plan to do some root pruning. Do not be seduced by plant size or number of flowers. I always prefer to buy the smallest, tightest plant on the table. Let it grow and prosper under your pruning hand, because unless it has been properly pinched back it will be leggy and require more work to get into good shape.

I am a huge bargain hunter and am not above shopping at the clearance table, local hardware store, or community plant sale. When buying discounted plants, you need to be especially careful to avoid insects and disease so that you don't bring them back home to your own garden. Discount plants may require a little tender loving care, but can often be brought back to health quickly.

Garden clubs, Master Gardeners, and agricultural fairs will often advertise their sales in the spring. As most of the plants are divided and harvested by a savvy gardener, the selection is usually in excellent health and out of this world. You can even shop from your own living room—mail-order nurseries are wonderful resources for your favorite plants and varieties, and many can be found online.

ROOT PRUNE ROOTBOUND PLANTS

1. Lift the plant from its pot.
2. Slice one-half to one inch off the bottom.
3. Make three or four vertical cuts into the sides.
4. Butterfly the roots and repot or plant in the ground.

USE STRING TO PLANT NEAT, STRAIGHT ROWS.

CHAPTER 3

ORGANIC GROWING PRACTICES

There's a personal satisfaction in growing a bountiful harvest using nature as your guide. When planning and growing a garden, there is a wide array of tools we can use to strengthen plants' health, success, and productivity. Today, there are all sorts of buzzwords like organic, sustainable, ecological, natural, biodynamic, and permaculture to describe how to grow plants without the use of synthetic chemicals and pesticides. And the best part is, most of these methods are free!

Unsustainable garden practices like the overuse of fertilizers, tilling, herbicides, and pesticides deplete the soil of its inherent goodness. The goal is to use the following techniques in combination with one another to restore your soil to its rich, natural state, thereby boosting the quality and yield of your vegetable harvest.

CROP ROTATION

One of the easiest and cheapest ways to a healthy and productive garden is to implement a crop rotation strategy. This is an essential technique with many benefits that should be implemented in every kitchen garden. Cycling vegetables around the garden improves soil fertility and reduces weed, insect, and disease problems. While all plants require a hearty dose of macronutrients, nitrogen (N), phosphorus (P), and potassium (K), each will benefit from a heightened application of one or more depending on the type of crop. For instance, cabbage—a leafy vegetable—enjoys a bed with an abundance of nitrogen in the soil, which it uses to make full, generous heads. However, if potatoes were grown in such a bed, you would be disappointed with the size and amount of spuds, since the extra nitrogen would result in

Rotate your vegetables throughout the garden to prevent any one crop from depleting the soil of any one nutrient.

more green growth rather than potato production. By moving your vegetables throughout the garden, you prevent any one crop from depleting the soil of any one nutrient.

Weeds are not fans of this approach. Planting a timely sequence of vegetables with diverse characteristics and needs diminishes the tendency for specific weeds to adapt and become problematic. Also, steady sowings and harvesting stop weeds from gaining a foothold in the garden.

ANNUAL CROP ROTATION USING FOUR PLANTING BEDS				
	Bed 1	**Bed 2**	**Bed 3**	**Bed 4**
Year 1	legumes	brassicas	root/cover crops	nightshades
Year 2	brassicas	root/cover crops	nightshades	legumes
Year 3	root/cover crops	nightshades	legumes	brassicas
Year 4	nightshades	legumes	brassicas	root/cover crops

Without regular rotation schedules, insects and disease can overwinter in your soil and create even bigger problems than you had the previous season. If you change vegetable placement from year to year, when insects emerge from the ground in spring, they'll be disappointed to find their food source gone and move on to a more fruitful hunting ground. Diseases can overwinter in your soil as well, and you certainly don't want them to wake up and infect your new seedlings just as they are establishing themselves.

There are many ways to plan your crop rotation; you can group them by edible parts, nutrient demands, plant families, or a combination thereof. Related annual vegetables should never be planted in the same location for two or more years in a row, so a three-year cycle (legume and fruit; brassicas; root, shoot, onion, and leaf OR leaf, fruit, and root crops) should be mandatory. It is the simplest to manage and ensures that no single crop will exhaust the soil of its nutrients. Four- or five-year rotation plans are ideal, as the more you move vegetables through the garden, the more each crop uses the soil's fertility efficiently while simultaneously making it a difficult place for weeds to establish and preventing insect and disease buildup.

I prefer employing a combination of nutrient demands and plant familial relationships in my rotation strategy, with an annual application of compost being the only amendment added. My first kitchen

Legume crops like snap peas are nitrogen-fixing crops, adding nitrogen to the soil rather than draining it of this macronutrient.

Carrots and other root crops not only till and break up the soil with their roots, but they primarily use phosphorus to establish strong, tasty crops. Alternatively, you can grow deep-reaching cover crops like alfalfa to draw up trapped nutrients.

Tomatoes are in the nightshade family.

garden had four raised beds: legumes, brassicas (cabbage family), root crops, and nightshades (Solanaceae family). I started with peas and beans (legumes) since they are amazing soil boosters, followed by the heavy feeder brassicas, who thrive on the newly added excess nitrogen. Then the root crops like carrots, celery, onions, beets, and garlic break up the soil. They are particularly happy that the brassicas ate up all the nitrogen, as too much results in abundant leafy top-growth and small roots. Next in the bed are the nightshades, which do not have a particularly high nitrogen demand, but benefit from the previously unused phosphorus and potassium that strengthens bud and fruit development. Over the years I've expanded the garden to include additional beds for the gourd (Cucurbits), onion (Alliaceae), and carrot (Apiaceae) families.

There are precious few vegetables that don't circle through the garden. Perennials like asparagus, artichoke, and rhubarb shouldn't be moved. It typically takes them two to three years until they are established enough to have a steady, tasty harvest. So be sure to think ahead and consider where you plant them, since they are going to be there for the long haul.

The key to a successful crop rotation plan is making sure that related vegetables—with the exception of perennials— are not planted in the same spot more than once every three years at a minimum.

Arugula, endive, lettuce, onions, radishes, spinach, and swiss chard are a few vegetables that do not suffer from lack of movement in the garden and can be planted in whichever bed you have room. They are remarkably forgiving, and neither quality nor yield is sacrificed. And, as a bonus, many of these vegetables are quick to mature and do not take up a lot of space. Also, keep in mind that kitchen gardens are dynamic, meaning that you may need to change or alter your strategy based on insects, disease, or space.

SUCCESSION PLANTING

"Sow little and often" is a phrase you've probably heard gardeners chant during the growing season. This practice enables you to have an endless supply of fresh vegetables, which is especially important in a backyard garden where space is at a premium. Quick-to-mature, cool-season crops are ideal candidates for succession sowing. You can go about this one of two ways: you can sow seed every two to three weeks, or sow a mix of early-, mid-, and late-season varieties at one time so they will mature at different points in the season providing you with a staggered

"SOW LITTLE AND OFTEN."

harvest. There is nothing sadder than having thirty tomato plants ready to harvest at once. You can only eat so much fruit in a week, and if you're planning on canning or freezing your crop, you'll have a long night ahead of you. Growing a blend of early, mid, and late tomatoes ensures that you'll be rewarded with ten plants to prune and harvest at any one time while maximizing the production from one month to two or three depending on your climate.

You can replant successions using the same crop, or replace them with another as the weather turns. This is especially true for quick-to-mature crops like salad greens, bush beans, radishes, carrots, and beets. It's better to sow and plant frequently so a few plants are ready to pick at their peak every week rather than all at once.

New lettuce seedlings (left) are planted after the first harvest of salad greens. When planning to succession sow throughout the season, it is important to remember to leave enough open space in the garden for those new additions.

It's important to leave space in your garden bed, or rows, for the next crop sown. Every few weeks you'll plant a new row and harvest from the previous. By the time your first crop is depleted, you can begin harvesting from your second. To maintain high yields, work in an additional one inch of compost between successions before replanting. Raking in a slow-release, complete fertilizer wouldn't hurt either.

SUCCESSION SOWING

My favorite quick-succession crops are carrots, beets, kohlrabi, radishes, lettuce, and other salad greens. You can sow most seeds directly in the ground, but I like to start a variety of leaf crops in trays in the greenhouse every two weeks for an endless summer supply.

INTERCROPPING AND CATCH CROPPING

In the backyard garden, space is a high-value commodity. To avoid waste I like to employ some intensive planting techniques similar to succession planting and companion planting: intercropping and catch cropping. Both methods involve planting on unused, bare soil to take advantage of time and growing space. Intercropping involves multiple crops growing together over the same period of time, whereas catch cropping uses the open area between the harvest of an early crop and the sowing of a later crop to sow, grow, and harvest a third. These strategies can be used whether you are planting in a mixed bed, alternating rows, or along edges and borders.

Intercropping combines plants with different maturity rates, growing patterns, and requirements. Pairing vegetables by plant shape is very useful—mixing tall with short, or spreading with upright—maximizes the entire growing space. The classic combination of corn, pole beans, and squash is known as The Three Sisters. The tall corn acts as a trellis, supporting the pole beans that crawl up it, while the beans enrich the soil. The nutrient greedy corn flourishes in this nitrogen-rich soil, and the squash acts as a living mulch, shading the root systems and keeping critters away with its spiny leaves and stems. When partnering vegetables by maturity rates, you don't have to pick between the tortoise and the hare. Take advantage by planting quick arugulas and lettuce among your slower growing cabbage or cauliflower. The brassicas won't fill out for at least six weeks, and by that time you'll have already harvested and enjoyed your salad greens. Grouping plants by their cultural needs is by far the easiest way to interplant. Lettuce planted under an A-frame cucumber trellis enjoys the summer shade, extending the harvest season beyond the spring and fall. Not only are these cropping mixes an efficient use of space, but they also minimize weeds and add visual interest with texture, scale, and structure to the garden. In addition, these combinations often attract pollinators.

A catch crop is a crop that's grown during the open period between an early harvested vegetable and the planting of a later one. Think of it as a bonus crop. Typically these are rapid growers like radishes, salad greens, and leaf crops, but they can also include bush beans, baby beets, or baby carrots. Growing crops on these bare patches is also a good way to keep the space from turning into weed city.

Remember to add a few inches of fresh compost after every harvest of intercropped vegetables before sowing or replanting.

COMPANION PLANTING

Diverse plantings grow better than identical ones. It's that simple! Companion planting has been practiced for centuries, but the technique has seen a comeback in the past fifty years. Gardeners suggest that combining two or more different vegetables in close proximity creates mutually beneficial effects, such as improving health and flavor, attracting pollinators, and deterring pests and disease.

There is a lot of debate over how accurate the advantages of these pairings actually are, as much of the information is passed down through folklore and our grandparents. However,

Borage is considered the magic bullet of the garden. It is known to attract beneficial bugs and repel damaging pests.

today we know that plants are much more likely to flourish in gardens that mimic the diversity seen in nature. The practice of polyculture (planting different crops in the same area) improves crops' ability to resist disease and insects. If a single species field—or monoculture—is infected, pests will feast on its ample food source and continue to do so for multiple seasons. Think about it—why would they want to move? Similarly, disease pathogens are much more likely to remain in soil that supports a large population of desirable host plants. By comparison, diversified plantings offer limited food/hosts sources to lingering pests and disease.

PERMACULTURE

Designing your garden to mimic nature is the essence of permaculture. Integrating vegetables, flowers, and wildlife to create a living ecosystem—one that requires minimal involvement from the gardener while still producing high yields—is the goal of this age-old

LASAGNA GARDENING

Also called sheet mulch, a lasagna bed is made up of different layers of organic material in the fall. The pile mimics nature, and over the winter these layers break down, essentially composting in one (permanent) place, to create a new no-dig bed. Simply dig right in and plant!

Perfect sheet mulch recipe

Layer 1: Adjust the ground pH with lime or sulfur and amend with one-half to one inch of manure.

Layer 2: Add one-half inch of newspaper or corrugated cardboard.

Layer 3: Apply another one-half to a couple inches of manure layer or several inches of dried leaves.

Layer 4: Pile on eight to twelve inches of bulky organic matter or other green material (I usually use straw).

Layer 5: Another one to two inches of compost or manure.

Layer 6: Heavy layer of seed-free organic mulch (straw).

Layer 7: Optional: secure with row covers, newspapers, or heavy cardboard (remove these in the spring).

practice. Using these ecological, commonsense principles, it is easy to construct a sustainable and self-sufficient garden.

It's easy to create a sustainable garden.

There are entire books devoted to the practice of permaculture, but you don't need to be a certified permaculturist to apply these fundamental principles and reap the rewards of a beautiful, nutrient-rich, low-maintenance, high-yield garden. First, you must observe nature. Look at what plants are native and thriving in your area. This will help you choose the right plants for the right place and succeed without much work. Along these same lines is the concept of community, locally sourced food, and economy—for example, focusing on eating locally grown food like heirloom carrots from your backyard rather than exotic mangos shipped in from South America. Using only what is needed, energy awareness, conservation, and preventing waste are also key. Reciprocity (using the product of one process to aid in another) is a tenet of the permaculturally inspired garden. This is as simple as using a large barrel to collect rainwater to water your tomatoes. Then, once you harvest the tomatoes, compost the stems and foliage to be added to the soil the following spring to feed your snap peas. At its core, reciprocity is recycling, and the cycle could go on and on as nature does. Understanding the relationships between different plant species—how they are stronger when planted together, using resources efficiently and wasting nothing—is crucial.

STRAW BALE GARDENING

Straw bale gardening is just a new, innovative way to container garden. There are entire books dedicated to this practice. The bales are sterile (no pests or disease), retain moisture well, heat up quicker in spring, keep the roots cool in summer, and are weed-free—what's not to like! Purchase an organic bale from a local farmer to ensure it is weed- and chemical-free. Site and position the straw so the strings constraining the bales are on the side, not on the top where you will be planting. First, you need to "condition" your straw bales two weeks before planting. Fertilize and water them on alternate days to stimulate natural decomposition and composting. After fourteen days, make a hole and sow or insert your rooted seedling. Lay a soaker hose over top and it will almost grow by itself.

PLANT STACKING IN THE GARDEN

Save space by growing quick, cool-weather crops under your heat-loving cucumbers. The vines on the trellis shade the tender butterhead lettuce underneath. Then to make the absolute most of the space, I plant onion sets along the edge. Three vegetables, one footprint.

Diversity is key to creating sustainable, edible landscapes. Have you ever heard the saying, "The whole is greater than the sum of its parts"? Well, this adage applies in the garden. Polyculture, the practice of growing many different crops, results in stronger, healthier, and more productive plots than a large, single species planting. Growing a variety of different plants together imitates the diverse and efficient ecosystems in nature. These varied plantings reduce the chance of your entire garden being taken down by pests and disease, as well as maximizing wasted space that is a byproduct of monoculture.

Finally, choosing multifunctional plants that work together to solve multiple problems is an essential permaculture technique. These are also known as stacking functions. Growing pole beans or cucumbers on an arbor or trellis on the south side of your house over a window underplanted with lettuce and broccoli tackles numerous issues in a very small footprint. During the heat of the summer the trellised vine will shade the window to the living room keeping your house cooler, while in the winter the annual creeper will die back to let a maximum amount of sunlight into the home, reducing your need to heat. Also, since beans and cucumbers have a moderately shallow root system and are being grown vertically, another shallow-rooted crop such as broccoli can be grown below in the same space. While the broccoli is developing, sow some quick leaf lettuces around the base. The lettuce serves as a living mulch, keeping the broccoli and vining plants' roots cool, and will be harvested before the broccoli needs the space to grow. Another perk is that the trellis will shade the cool-weather brassica and greens. Permaculture at its best.

SOIL BUILDING AND COMPOST

Keeping your garden fertile and soil rich is the key to growing hearty, delicious vegetables. Decomposed or well-rotted compost is essential to every garden. The easiest way to achieve the almighty "black gold" is with a backyard compost pile. It can be as simple as a freestanding 3 x 3 x 3-foot mix or a homemade weekend project using wood, chicken wire, or plastic. While you can compost anything that was once alive, some materials break down slower than others. If you are anxious like me to use your compost sooner rather than later, you'll want to use materials that decompose more quickly. The crucial element to quick, healthy compost is using the correct proportions of carbon and nitrogen—the ideal C:N (Carbon to Nitrogen) ratio is 30:1. This sounds complex, but to simplify, I use the recipe of two parts carbon to one part nitrogen. Think of it in terms of buckets: for each bucket of nitrogen-rich green material, use two of carbon.

When you imagine carbon, think "brown material." The best and easiest sources are dried leaves, pine needles, and cardboard. Since dry leaves are only available in the fall, it's a good idea to bag up about four or five bundles and keep them for the following garden season. This is the most important component of compost. Not having enough dry, brown material results in a slimy, smelly pile where nothing will break down. The bacteria in your compost needs the carbon to work and decompose your pile into the yummy, organic material your garden loves. Wet "green material" makes up the nitrogen element in your bin. Grass clippings, fruit and vegetable scraps, farm animal manure, and fresh leafy materials that rot quickly are ideal sources.

It's important to keep in mind that compost takes time. The speed at which your compost breaks down is dependent on four principles: oxygen content, water, temperature, and the right mix of ingredients. Turning your compost one to four times a month helps incorporate air into your pile and encourages

This is what it looks like when you're done.

COMPOST BIN BILLBOARD

It's amazing what you can come up with when you're resourceful. All you really need to compost is a large (ideally 3 x 3 x 3-foot) pile of the right mix of organic matter. Here are some great ideas from some savvy gardeners.

- Rot-resistant, non-pressure-treated wood bin
- The three-bin wood pallet system
- Three-foot tall wire cylinder
- Plastic tumblers
- Wood and fencing

The backyard gardener has many options for compost structures: A three-bin system made from wood pallets (top), non-treated wood (middle left), wire fence or chicken wire tied in a cylinder (middle right), from the garden store plastic tumblers (bottom left), and a wood and chicken wire design (bottom right).

I prefer to compost in batches, using a multiple bin system like the one shown here. This scheme allows me to have different piles at various stages of decomposition, so I always have a good source of ready-to-use compost.

decomposition to speed up. Oxygen is essential for the aerobic bacteria to break down the organic material into compost. Moistening your pile until it has the consistency of a wrung-out sponge will help the bacteria decomposing your heap.

Most compost piles will take an average of six months to one year to ripen, but they will break down quicker if the temperature generated by the pile gets hot enough. To heat up to 135-160°F, apply your brown and green materials in multiple, thin layers, and turn every two to four days from the outside in and from the bottom up. You should monitor your pile with a thermometer, making sure to wet and turn if the temperature drops below or exceeds 160°F. The hot temperatures will destroy any lingering disease, fly larvae, and weed seed. You can use your compost in the garden when it crumbles between your fingers and smells earthy, like a woodland forest. If anyone claims that you can compost in as little as a few weeks, *don't* drink the Kool-Aid. If your compost hasn't broken down enough and you use it, the high nitrogen content will burn your plants. If you're not sure it's ready, put a handful in a closed jar or zip lock bag for a week. If it smells woodsy, you're good to go, but if it's slimy and smells unpleasant or like ammonia, give it some time. I prefer to compost in batches, using a multiple bin system. This scheme allows me to have different piles at various stages of decomposition, so I always have a good source of ready-to-use compost.

WHAT TO ADD TO YOUR COMPOST PILE	
Carbon Sources	**Nitrogen Sources**
leaves	grass clippings
shredded newspaper	vegetable scraps
pine needles	coffee grounds
cardboard	manure
paper bags or towels	fish or seaweed
mulched non-treated wood	garden waste
sawdust or straw	hay or alfalfa

Compost is not only an excellent source of nutrients to feed your plants, it also improves your soil...for free! Providing both macro- and micronutrients that are often absent in most fertilizers—organic or synthetic—compost releases these elements slowly over time as crops need them. It also promotes good soil structure by making it less likely for soil to erode or splash up onto plants, loosening tightly bound or clay soil, and boosting water- and nutrient-holding capacity. A 5 percent increase in organic material *quadruples* the soil's water retention! And the added diversity of bacteria, fungi, worms, and microorganisms supports a thriving ecosystem that results in happy, healthy, thriving plants.

MULCH AND COVER CROPPING

Mulch is a newly planted garden's best friend. So simple, yet so often overlooked, a layer of mulch goes a long way to keeping your plants healthy and productive. Whether organic or inorganic, a generous blanket of mulch helps retain soil moisture, suppresses weeds, protects plants from soil-borne infection, insulates plant roots from extremes in temperature fluctuations, and adds curb appeal. I like using mulch because it acts as a barrier between your soil/compost and the stems and leaves of your crops. It also protects them from soil-borne diseases by stopping water from splashing up from the soil onto the plant. There are plenty of choices, including weedless straw, seaweed, grass clippings, wood chips, compost, shredded leaves, pine needles, pebbles/gravel, or plastic. One of the benefits of using organic mulch is that it will eventual decompose over time, thereby improving soil structure and fertility.

An autumn mulch application is an excellent way to prevent weeds from getting a foothold in your garden beds between the seasons, but using a living mulch, or cover crop, is even better. These green manures go a few steps further than simply safeguarding the soil against weeds and disease while conserving moisture; they prevent erosion and enrich your soil with organic matter and nutrients that would be lost over the winter, and act as a frost blanket, allowing the soil to warm faster in the spring. Normally, rain during the winter months and mud wash away nutrients that plants need stored in the soil. But fast-maturing cover crops planted in the fall will lock in those nutrients. Stored in the roots, the nutrients are held there until the spring when they are released by turning crops, further improving the soil's fertility.

TURN COVER CROPS UNDER BEFORE THEY GO TO SEED.

Nitrogen-fixing clover grown in the front bed is prepping the ground for its next resident.

Late summer or fall planted cover crops are the organic gardener's secret weapon. They bulk up the soil, enhancing its structure with their fibrous root systems, and incorporate air once dug under. These plants do the work for you by tilling the soil with their roots. I prefer annual cover crops as they are typically quick growing, establish readily, and last a single season, whereas perennial crops are often slow, root deep, and run the risk of becoming a weed if left to flower and go to seed. Some of my favorite green manures include Dutch white or crimson clover, winter rye, and alfalfa. I favor winter rye because it is quick to grow and can be sown in the fall and dug under in spring. Clover and alfalfa both decompose readily and are nitrogen fixers, providing more nutrition than other cover crops. But I like clover primarily due to its shade tolerance and alfalfa for its ability to tap and bring up nutrients trapped deep underground. I also like buckwheat, as it's a super fast cover crop that can be turned in as little as six to eight weeks! But beware of letting it go to seed. It's a perennial and could become invasive in the garden if you are late in digging it under. These green manures can be planted anytime from spring through fall. If you have room in the garden, it is a good idea to leave one vegetable bed empty and grow one of these living mulches in its place as part of your crop rotation.

Whether growing annual or perennial cover crops, it is critical to mow down and dig under before the plants flower or go to seed, otherwise you will be "blessed" with new weeds to contend with. Once dug under, it will take time for the living mulch to decompose and break down into the soil, thereby releasing precious nutrients, so wait approximately two to three weeks before replanting. Cover crops also act as excellent underplantings with vegetables like cucumbers and cabbage. They truly become a living mulch, conserving moisture, keeping the roots cool, discouraging weeds, and confusing pests, all while improving the soil structure and fertility once turned under. See the cover crop comparison chart in the appendix.

INTEGRATED PEST MANAGEMENT

Throughout the summer, the garden pumps out plenty of delicious fruits and vegetables, but you may be dismayed to discover that you are not the only one enjoying its fresh snacks. While it can be tempting to run out and grab some off-the-shelf pesticide from your local hardware store, don't! Many garden pests and diseases can be managed organically with a little tender loving care from beneficial insects and an integrated pest management (IPM) approach. Without resorting to chemicals and pesticides IPM uses a combination of cultural, mechanical, and biological controls as a way of dealing with pests and disease. Start by keeping the garden clean. Cultural controls are primarily preventative. Maintaining healthy soil with a pH around 6.5, amended with compost and organic matter, and full of active microorganisms is essential to avoiding pest and disease. You can also avoid many issues simply by keeping your plants strong and healthy. Good garden practices like even moisture, mulch, and water at the base of plants, choosing the "right plant for the right place," and avoiding overfertilization will go a long way to helping plants fend off unwanted predators. Crop rotation and plant selection are also important. Selecting resistant varieties, choosing the right spot with the right conditions for the plant to thrive, and only using healthy seeds and compost will help prevent the invasion of hungry insects and disease. And by moving plants throughout the garden, overwintered pests emerge the following spring to find their food source gone.

When working in the garden, monitor your plants for pests. If it's early enough, you can handpick and destroy visible pests. Japanese beetles can be a serious issue in the kitchen garden. I carry around a mason jar filled with soapy water and

Do not harvest all your lavender—let some flower. They attract many beneficial insects to the garden that keep detrimental pests under control.

knock them off into the jar, drowning them. There are a number of ways to treat pests with natural, do-it-yourself recipes from the kitchen. Aphids will decimate your crop quickly, but a heavy spray of homemade insecticidal will kill those that come into contact with the non-toxic spray. Other homemade remedies include skim milk to treat powdery mildew, a splash of diatomaceous earth for earwigs, slugs, and snails, and a baking soda mix for fungal diseases. But what about the pests you don't see? What about insects that bore into the stems of your squash and cabbage? The best defense against these intruders is a good offense. Insect barriers or row covers placed over vulnerable crops at time of sowing or transplant keep destructive insects out. And netting or fencing will also keep scavenging birds and other critters away from newly planted seed and vegetables that might otherwise be gone by morning.

HOMEMADE INSECTICIDAL SOAP RECIPE

Mix the ingredients together in a spray bottle and shake thoroughly to mix. Spray infected crops in the morning to avoid leaf scorch, while being sure to thoroughly cover all plant surfaces including the undersides of the leaves for maximum effect.

- One-and-a-half tablespoons of pure, biodegradable liquid soap.
- One quart of water (tap is typically fine, unless you have hard water which should be evidenced by soap scum floating at the top. If that is the case, use bottled water.)
- A few drops of citrus essential oil (Acts as a natural insecticide while helping the blend cling to the plant.)

Modifications:

- ~ One-half tablespoon of light cooking oil (canola, olive, or safflower) to help the mixture linger longer on the plants.
- ~ One-half tablespoon of light cooking oil and one tablespoon of baking soda to remove powdery mildew.
- ~ One-quarter teaspoon of cider vinegar to tackle powdery mildew.
- ~ One-quarter teaspoon of chili powder, red peppers, or garlic to repel chewing pests such as borers and Japanese beetles.

DROWNING IN JAPANESE BEETLES

Don't want to touch those nasty Japanese beetles? Don't worry. Fill a mason jar halfway with soapy water and go out to the garden. Instead of handpicking these gangsters, hold the jar up and knock them into the soapy cocktail. I'll cover the jar and leave it in a corner of the garden so next time I'm in the garden it's easy to stay on top of these pests.

Beneficial insects will eat and take care of problematic spiders and insects if you create a hospitable habitat and offer them something to eat. Biological controls encourage good bugs to make a home in your garden by increasing plant diversity and providing a multitude of flowering plants whose continuous supply of pollen and nectar lure in these natural enemies.

Whether you attract beneficials or ship them in—yes, you can now buy bugs by the pint in catalogs and have them mailed to your house—inviting good bugs to make a home in your garden will benefit any vegetable plot. One of my favorite natural enemies is the green lacewing bug, which in larvae form attacks and consumes huge amounts of aphids, earning its moniker the "aphid lion." These little guys gobble up other soft-bodied insects, including mealybugs, leafhopper nymphs, scale bugs, spider mites, whiteflies, and caterpillar eggs. You can also attract the adults by planting nectar-producing flowers throughout your patch. The illustrious ladybugs, or lady beetles as some know them, are not only pretty and thought to bring luck, they are workhorses in the garden eating aphids, asparagus beetles, chinch bugs, Colorado potato beetle larvae, leafhoppers, mites, scales, thrips, and other soft-bodied insects. Each adult will devour fifty to sixty per day and as many as five thousand aphids in their life, so interplant pollen-producing flowers in your garden to encourage these ladies to hang around. Parasitic wasps are a bit devious and go about destroying agricultural pests in a different way. They lay their eggs on the back or within the eggs of their prey, killing the host when hatched. There are many different wasps that cover a multitude of insects including aphids, beetle larvae, cabbage worms, Colorado potato beetle, corn earworms, cucumber beetles, cutworms, gypsy moth caterpillars, Japanese beetles, leaf miners, mealybugs, Mexican bean beetles, moth and tent caterpillars, scales, squash vine borers, tomato hornworm, and whiteflies. Encourage parasitic wasps by planting flowering herbs that provide both nectar and pollen. The trichogramma wasp is the most popular and among the smallest of the group and particularly good for controlling cutworms, cabbage worms, and various borers. Other beneficial hustlers in the garden are assassin bugs, damsel bugs, ground beetles, hoverflies, parasitic flies, predacious stinkbugs, and mites.

Overall, the goal of using IPM and beneficial insects is to emphasize good growing techniques and prevention with chemical control as a last resort.

SEASON EXTENSION

When living in colder climates, season extension is a must. Luckily, there are a plethora of tools to help gardeners achieve a longer growing season than they would normally have.

Row covers are the most economical way to extend the season and, as a bonus, they are also multifunctional. Whether floating or supported by small hoops fashioned out of PVC or old closet hangers, they can extend the season by several weeks in both the spring and fall. Row covers exclude pests, warm the soil, speed up germination, and protect seedlings and tender crops from cold temperatures while allowing water, air, and light to pass through. When it comes to material—polyester (Reemay)

EXTEND THE SEASON WITH ROW COVERS.

Hoop houses and quick tunnels are a great way to extend your season in cold climates.

or polypropylene—I prefer the latter as it is more durable and reliable, and available as an insect barrier or in a variety of weights (low, medium, and heavy). The assorted densities offer different amounts of light transmission and frost protection. The varied thicknesses allow temperature gains between 4° and 6°F, and down to 24°F depending on the rating. When using row covers as a physical barrier against insects and hungry rodents, be sure to secure and seal the edges with rocks or water jugs, or by burying the edges beneath the soil. If using row covers with crops like cucumbers, squash, or tomatoes, keep in mind that they need to be pollinated to produce. Therefore, you need to remove the row covers before the flowers bloom or you'll be penalized with a lack of fruit and vegetables. It's also vital to vent during warm weather.

The easiest, cheapest, and most portable tool in the gardener's tool box is the **cloche,** or bell jar. This is a smaller, more compact version of a row cover, in which a clear jug acts as a mini-greenhouse and covers a single seedling. When sunk into the soil a few inches, it heats up the ground underneath, speeding germination and protecting tender new

ALTERNATIVE CLOCHES
& THE WALL O' WATER

Glamorous glass cloches are not readily available—and they're certainly not bargain-priced. Large clear glass or plastic salad bowls from Goodwill or Salvation Army work great for small seedlings early in the season. The Wall o' Water is a good alternative for getting your seedlings off to a good start early in the season. Open the plastic so it encircles your seedling, then fill each vertical pouch with water. During the day the sun will heat the water, reradiating it back to the plant and soil, keeping them warm into the night. An advantage the Wall o' Water has over the traditional cloche is its open top—it doesn't need to be vented when the temperature heats up. You can also replicate this idea by recycling two-liter plastic soda bottles. Once you have enough bottles to connect in a circle, use duct tape to secure them and voilà! Homemade wall o' water.

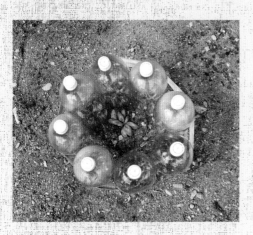

seedlings from prowling critters. Bell jars are often temporary, used for a few days and on cold, frosty overnights, and can be used to cover plants up to four weeks (providing the plants do not outgrow the space). It is important that the plant leaves and stems do not touch the edges, otherwise they are susceptible to damage. Cloches are especially useful in small gardens where there isn't enough space for tunnels. The best part is that they are made from a variety of materials, ranging from plastic milk jugs, used soda bottles, recycled glass, or clear plastic bowls to professionally produced hot caps, "wall-of-water," and glass jars. Some cloches will have small holes at the top to vent the excess heat, but if not, you may have to prop up the bottom with a small block of wood. If you forget to vent, the cloche could create ideal conditions for unwanted diseases, or you may find your plants looking scorched.

Another easy and inexpensive tool to get your plants started early is the **cold frame.** This term breeds a bit of confusion among new gardeners as some books and articles will

Venting the row cover on a warm day.

Glass cloches create microclimates, warming the air and soil in early spring thereby allowing seedlings to get off to an early start.

Homemade cold frames with a 10-15° transparent cover, facing south maximize the solar capture.

refer to hoop houses as cold frames, but traditionally they are square or rectangular boxes with a transparent top. A cold frame is a box with a clear, sloped cover that traps solar energy and protects seedlings and plants from temperature fluctuations and weather. It is comparable to growing one more zone south than you typically can grow. Whether made of wood, aluminum, polycarbonate, cinderblocks, or straw bales, the back should be raised an extra three to six inches to create the 10-15° slant. Recycled windows and doors make excellent tops, but polycarbonate or clear, heavy greenhouse poly will do just as well. Cold frames are portable, but if you intend to site yours facing south, where it gets the greatest sun exposure and have no plans to move it, sink the box into the ground. Doing so will increase the insulation for those crops grown inside. I like to insert a fine wire mesh at the bottom of mine to keep greedy critters from snacking from below, and I fill the top six to ten inches with a combination of potting soil and compost, leaving room for plant growth.

Cold frames perform a slew of garden tasks, including acting as a seed and/or crop bed, a place to harden off seedlings, or a spot to grow heat-loving crops like sweet potatoes. During the winter, I make sure to leave any snow on the top of the cold frame to help insulate whatever I have growing inside. However, once you start your seedlings, brush the snow off to let light in. It may seem counterintuitive, but when the outside temperature reaches 48°, you need to prop the cold frame open to keep the interior at an optimal 40-50°; just don't forget to close it in late afternoon before the chill of the night touches your seedlings. During the summer, you can remove the cover completely and let your plants grow up and out. Painting the exterior black, or lining the exterior of the box with black-painted, water-filled soda or milk jugs, maximizes the heat retention of the cold frame. Other ways to intensify and trap heat include backing your cold frame against a north-facing structure; using snow, dry leaves, mulch, old carpets, and blankets or straw bales to border and insulate the box; or using row covers inside. Additionally you can paint the interior white to reflect light within the box to enhance plant growth. Constructing a polytunnel over your cold frame will also move your zone *two* zones south.

The first time I heard about gardeners using plastic in the garden, I was thrown for a loop. Aren't we supposed to use organic materials for everything? But that was before I learned about the many advantages of **plastic mulch.** The chief benefit is that it warms the soil. Yes, it still suppresses weeds, conserves moisture, helps prevent soil-borne disease, and keeps the roots cool, but the main reason to use this material as opposed to other mulches is that is heats the soil so seeds can begin germinating and plants can establish themselves earlier. Even though

Red plastic mulch radiates the red wavelength back up into the tomato canopy, stimulating fruit production.

Clear plastic mulch gives warm-season sweet potato crops a well-needed start in cooler regions.

plastic mulch is often used in commercial-scale growing, it is just as effective in the backyard garden.

Once you've come to terms with and become excited about using plastic mulch in the garden, you have to make some decisions, as there are plenty of types to choose from. There is black, clear, IRT solar mulch, SRM red, white-on-black, and metallic silver, and they all have their purpose. Black plastic is the predominant color for vegetables; it's economical, increases the soil temperature, and does everything else a good mulch should. But some of the other mulches simply warm the soil better. Clear plastic does a super job of warming the ground, but because it's translucent, it lets in every light wavelength and stimulates weed growth rather than suppressing it. IRT (infrared transmitting) solar mulch comes in a brownish-green, allowing infrared wavelengths to pass through and heat up the soil while visible light is blocked for maximum weed suppression. Solar mulch increases the soil temperature on average between 8-10°F, which is optimal for heat-loving plants like cucumbers, melons, and squash. SRM (selective reflecting mulch) red mulch is primarily used for tomatoes and strawberries, and was developed by the USDA and Clemson University. It performs similarly to black plastic with its soil-warming and moisture-retentive properties, but what sets it apart is the reflection of far-red light up into the crops' understory, stimulating photosynthesis, rapid growth, and development. USDA tests show a dramatic increase of 12 to 20 percent in marketable tomato production. Meanwhile, white-on-black mulch is particularly potent with cool- and cold-season crops, including many of the brassicas. This mulch is applied black side down for weed suppression and white side up to reflect light and keep the roots cool in warmer weather. Metallic silver mulch, on the other hand, has a very different goal. It keeps the soil 2-6°F cooler and its reflective surface disorients and repels pests like aphids, Colorado potato beetle, flea beetles, and whiteflies, which often carry and spread disease. As the inherent reflective nature of this mulch cools the soil rather than warming it, northern gardeners should expect slower plant growth. Therefore, it makes much more sense to use metallic silver mulch in warm climates, where gardeners will see an increased yield in specific crops like peppers.

Plastic mulch can be used in open fields, tunnels, or raised beds. Lay the fabric two to four weeks ahead of time to give the soil enough time to heat up. To anchor the plastic to the ground, use metal landscape pins or bury the edges under the soil. I've found that if I overlap the edges when installing, I can keep the rows between my crops weed-free. Once the soil had been sufficiently warmed and you're ready to sow or transplant, use a sharp knife and cut small Xs into the plastic and plant directly through. Depending on the quality of plastic you purchase, you may even be able to get more than one season. To double up your winter protection, combine plastic mulch with row covers, cold frames, or tunnels.

Low tunnels, or **mini tunnels,** are similar to row covers, but rather than warmth being the sole priority, light is. Low tunnels are basically smaller versions of the semicircle, or arched, tunnel hoop houses that run along crop rows or beds in your garden. It is the plastic coverings that are important, transmitting the maximum amount of daylight, rather than the insulating nature of the covers that differentiates them. Constructed out of PVC or heavy-duty wire/pipe, these tunnels can be eighteen to forty-eight inches tall at the apex, with the taller versions best suited for colder climates. Spaced every four feet, on average, they are not tall enough to walk under and offer little in the way of cold protection, but let in significantly more light. Tunnels can be more labor intensive, requiring you to go out and vent daily if the temperature is expected to reach 90°F. Cut slits in the plastic to help air circulate and escape. Because rainwater can't permeate through the plastic, drip tape or soaker hoses will easily solve that problem.

Raised beds are the most common season extension device, though many gardeners are unaware of the fringe benefits associated with growing above the soil level. While they can be any shape, triangles and rectangles are the least painful to construct. Lengths vary,

Mini tunnels connected to a raised bed base to keep tomatoes warm and productive.

Homemade greenhouse built completely with recycled materials. The wood was collected from lumberyard scraps, and the plastic was previously used to overwinter a boat.

but most beds are three to four feet wide so you can access the center of the bed with ease. If you have to step into the bed to reach your crops, you are defeating half the purpose. My beds are approximately one foot deep and constructed with non-treated two-by-four-inch

Garlic growing in a raised bed.

cedar boards, but they can be anywhere from six inches tall to three feet. Taller, waist-high beds are particularly useful for gardeners with disabilities or those who have difficulty bending. The beds can be made of anything, including rock, cinderblocks, or even mounded soil. The only caveat is, do not use pressure-treated lumber. One of the great things about raised beds is you can control your soil. Fill it with high-quality potting soil, loam, and compost, and with some good crop rotation and planning your soil will be the envy of the neighborhood and a feast for your plants. The nutritious soil often results in better root systems, which translates to improved crop yields. And because the beds are above the soil line, the soil tends to warm a few weeks faster than traditional gardens. For a two-for-one deal, you can even insert slots of PVC into the corners and sides of the bed so you can effortlessly attach low tunnels over your raised beds.

NEVER USE PRESSURE-TREATED LUMBER IN THE GARDEN.

Hoop houses, also called **polytunnels** or **high tunnels**, are larger tunnels that you can walk under. They extend the growing season up to eight weeks on either end (that's four extra months of growing!). These tunnels are particularly useful for early sowing, late harvesting, and overwintering hardy crops while offering plenty of light. Quick and easy to build, their frames can be constructed from one-half to one-inch PVC piping or square, metal tubing to form semicircular or gothic points in the center to better cast off snow.

I use the Hanley Hoop House design (http://kerrcenter.com/organic-farm/hoop-house) on my farm and secure the polytunnel using eighteen-inch rebar stakes hammered into the ground. Then we slide the square, bent arches over the rebar pins to hold up and form the frame, or backbone, of the tunnel. Next, fasten the four or six mil greenhouse poly by lacing quarter-inch rope over the top with snap carabiners at each footing. The anchoring is especially important to ensure both the frames and the covering stay put. To secure the sides, bury the edges of the plastic twelve inches deep. If possible, orient your tunnel north and south to maximize its sun exposure and site such that the wind hits the side so it rolls over the hoops. Some gardeners opt for a hard polycarbonate

This is the fifty-foot tunnel my husband and I put up using rebar stakes, one-inch square metal tubing, greenhouse film, string, and carabiners—in less than four hours!

BUILDING A ONE-FOOT-TALL RAISED BED

My husband is truly a saint. Every time I come to him with an idea to expand the garden, usually involving more work than I imagine, he goes along with it (almost) no questions asked. These raised beds are simple to make and last a long time if you use rot-resistant (cedar or oak), non-pressure-treated wood. I like eight-by-four-foot beds, so we purchased:

- Six (6) eight-foot, straight five-and-four-quarters-by-sixes (5/4"x6"x8')
- Three (3) four-foot two-inch cedar stakes (2"x2"x4')
- Box of wood screws

Directions:

For each level use two eight-foot boards for the long sides and two four-foot boards (eight-foot board cut in half) for the short sides. Note: You can alter the dimensions to your own preference, but do not make the beds any wider than four feet, otherwise you won't be able to reach the center without damaging your plants.

1. On a flat surface, like a garage floor, position two sides such that they make a 90° angle and fasten together with two wood screws after drilling pilot holes.
2. Continue screwing at the corners till the first level is complete. It should look like a rectangle.
3. Repeat, creating a second rectangle.
4. Cut the four-foot two-by-two wood boards in half, so you have six two-foot stakes.
5. Lay one wood rectangle on top of the other and sit the first stake tight to the corner, pointed end up. Drill through both upper and lower boards on two sides to secure.
6. Repeat with the other three corners.
7. To prevent warping and better hold the raised bed together, measure to the middle (4') along the long side and screw another stake. Repeat on the other side.
8. Flip over and bury the stakes in the garden. Fill with loam and compost and plant!

system without hoops. Regardless, ventilation is just as important when it comes to high tunnels as it is with low tunnels, but in this case, it's easier to roll up the sides than to cut the plastic to let the hot air escape.

There are a variety of ways to modify high tunnels, making them especially useful. If you combine row covers, mulch, and tunnels, the result is equivalent to moving your garden *two* zones south. Just imagine all the wonderful vegetables you can grow in this structure!

Or, if the summer heat gets to be too much for your crops, cover the hoop house with shade cloth. Available in a variety of sizes and materials, they come in an array of shade densities, just like row covers. During warm summers, a 30 percent shade cloth is ideal for tomatoes and peppers; 40 to 50 percent is optimal for cool-weather crops like salad greens and brassicas; and shade-loving plants require 63 percent shade. I personally prefer knitted, polyethylene covers as opposed to woven, as they are easier to maneuver over the hoops and do not unravel when cut.

While similar in construction to hoop houses, **greenhouses** are more elaborate and oftentimes much more expensive. Typically they have a wood, brick, or stone base and sidewalls with polycarbonate or glass sides and roof. Though they don't have to be, most greenhouses are heated, four-season structures used to start seeds on tables, overwinter plants, or plant directly into the ground. Also, because greenhouses are made with heavier materials with more thermal mass, they retain the heat better than a simple hoop house.

Growing in a polytunnel with mulched raised beds is like moving your garden *two* zones south!

Black landscape fabric and drip irrigation cover an herb field surrounding the four-season greenhouse.

CHAPTER 4

SOWING AND GROWING

LEGUMES

These nitrogen-fixing crops aren't only high in protein; they're workhorses—infusing your soil with plenty of nitrogen, which is responsible for the lush, green shoots and leaves plants need to thrive. When beans and peas grow, their root nodules below the surface fill with good bacteria called rhizobia. Living symbiotically in the roots, the rhizobium takes the gaseous nitrogen from the air, mineralizes and converts it into useable ammonium that plants can absorb through their roots (unfortunately, plants cannot use nitrogen from the atmosphere or convert it into a useable form). To get a head start and ready your soil for the next crop, at the end of the season cut off all the green growth above the soil, leaving just the roots. You can also let the plants die back to the ground then

Sugar snap peas growing vertically on a net trellis.

turn over in the spring when these overwintered root nodules will release this fixed nitrogen into the soil.

Beans (*Phaseolus vulgaris*)

Family: Fabaceae (Legume)

Plant Type: Tender, warm-season annual, zone 3–11

Light: Full sun

Soil: Rich, well-drained. Nitrogen fixer, soil builder

pH: 6.0–6.8

Height x Width:

Bush: 10–24" x 6–8"

Pole: 8–15' x 8–12"

Sow: Direct seed 1"deep, 2" apart, thin to 4–6" apart

Succession:

Bush: Every 10 days through midsummer

Pole: Every 3–4 weeks until 2 months before first expected frost

Days to germination: 5–10

Days to Maturity: 45–60 for bush, 60–85 for pole

Water: Low at planting, moderate until flowering, and heavy through harvest

Feed: Low N, moderate PK

Friends: Carrots, celery, chard, corn, cucumber, eggplant, peas, radishes, rosemary, potatoes, tomatoes, and summer savory

Foes: All brassicas, beets, onions, and shallots

A common misconception about beans is that they need lots of space. Not true! They can be grown in containers, scramble up fences or bamboo stakes, or be planted out in the open. They are an easy, dependable warm-weather crop. You can't compare the taste of fresh beans to the ones you buy in the supermarket. The ones in the supermarket don't have bright, beautiful flowers either. As a member of the legume family, beans—like peas—are soil builders with their nitrogen-filled nodules that release this macronutrient into the soil for greedy feeders like cabbages or brussels sprouts to consume the following season.

When I first started thumbing through seed catalogs, I didn't realize how many different types of beans there were: broad beans, French, runner, fava, bush, pole, dry, green, snap, wax, shell...the list goes on and on. It can be confusing to understand all the classifications—at first. To break it down, there are two major types of beans: shell and snap, which can be further divided by growth habit: bush or pole. Shell beans, also called "shellies," are eaten fresh or dried and are grown for their protein-rich seed. Azuki, butterbean (lima), chickpea, cranberry, fava (broad beans), flageolet, kidney, pinot, soybean (edamame), winged, white, and the yard-long bean (asparagus or Chinese bean) are all shell beans. Fresh shellies taste best around sixty to seventy days when their seeds are plump—right before they begin to dry. Shell beans left to mature on the plant until pods are withered, about eighty-five to one hundred days, are referred to as dry or soup beans. They're typically shelled first and soaked in water before cooking. Snap beans, or green beans, are eaten whole in their young pods. Most snap beans mature within forty-five to sixty days and if left to mature, can be shelled. French (haricot vert), scarlet runner bean, winged, yard-long, and wax beans, which can be yellow or purple, are all considered to be green beans. Although there are still a few string beans that have a fibrous string that runs along one side,

The bright red flowers of the scarlet runner bean draw your eyes up while adding a nice pop of color to your kitchen garden.

most modern beans are derived from "stringless" cultivars developed in the 1890s, which negates the need to strip the strings before they're eaten.

The secret to a long bean harvest is to grow a combination of bush and pole beans. Bush beans are usually self-supporting, less work, and do exceptionally well in containers. They are harvested in as little as six weeks, significantly earlier than pole types (which take eleven weeks), and if you sow them successively every ten days, you will have a continuous harvest. Pole beans may take longer to develop but they also have a longer harvest (six to eight weeks). Since pole beans are twining vines, they require some structure to crawl up. Simple stakes, lattice, A-frames, string, wire trellises, or tripods and teepees made of bamboo or long tree branches make exceptional supports, draw the eye up, and look lovely in the garden. Pole beans do not have tendrils to grab the trellis, so gently twist the stems if you see them flopping aimlessly to help them bend toward and around the support.

Scarlet runner beans are similar to pole beans, only they're more flavorful and grow better in cooler climates. These beans have attractive, edible red flowers offering the best of both worlds. You can eat the young pods once they grow three to four inches or wait a bit. If you leave them to mature, your patience will be rewarded with red and black-speckled seeds to enjoy fresh or dry.

As a warm-season crop, beans like a sunny spot with well-drained, fertile soil. They will not tolerate shade and will rot under wet conditions. That's why it's important not to water too much during planting. Once seedlings emerge, provide even moisture until the plants begin to flower, then water well until harvest for full, flavorful pods and beans. You can start sowing seeds one-inch deep once the soil warms. For best germination, beans should always be direct seeded, with the eye pointed down. To accelerate germination, give the seeds a quick twenty- to twenty-five-minute soak in diluted kelp or compost tea and warm the soil for one to two weeks with black plastic prior to planting. Once sufficiently heated (60-70°F), cut holes in the fabric and plant directly into them. Use additional row covers to trap heat for overnights and maintain moisture. Doubly helpful, row covers protect seeds and seedlings from being scooped up by ravenous birds. Also, quick-growing salad greens and radishes are great interplant buddies for newly sown seeds. By the time your beans need the space, they will be harvested and gone.

Whether you're growing bush or pole beans, they all adhere to the philosophy "the more you pick, the more you get." When in season, expect to harvest at least every other day. Snaps should be slender, about the diameter of a pencil, when you harvest them. Pods should be crisp when snapped, and the seeds shouldn't bulge. Grow shellies just as you would green beans, but instead of composting them, allow their seeds to swell and develop. Fresh shell beans are ready to harvest when they feel round, firm, and fleshy. Dried beans should be left to develop on the plant until fully dehydrated and shriveled. Allow the entire plant to turn brown and dry. If you're unsure, press your fingernail into the bean. If there is no mark, they've sufficiently dried and are ready to harvest.

Even though beans are a warm-season crop, extreme high temperatures can cause flowers to droop, which means you will have minimal or no beans to harvest. I mulch with a few inches of straw or weedless hay to keep the roots cool and maintain soil moisture. Aside from that, once established, beans generally take care of themselves. There's no need to fertilize. The most you should do is side dress with compost mid-season and avoid any high nitrogen fertilizers. If you feed your plants, you'll see lots of lush, green growth, but you'll also have a disappointingly small harvest. As

THE MORE YOU PICK, THE MORE YOU GET.

Once you show the pole beans the support, they grab hold and twist themselves up.

mentioned earlier, beans are nitrogen fixers, and as such need to be rotated every three years at a minimum. The rotation puts extra nitrogen into the soil for hungry brassica crops, but it also helps protect against mosaic disease. Good spacing and air circulation also help prevent infection. Water in the morning under the leaves so they can dry by evening and do not harvest after a rain or early when wet, as it may invite and spread diseases like mosaic, rust, blight, and anthracnose. Selecting resistant varieties will also go a long way to sidestepping many issues. While insects rarely bother with beans, row covers or insect barriers prevent cucumber beetles, Mexican bean beetles, and aphids from gaining access to your crops. Ladybugs and lacewings are good candidates to release in the garden as they are natural predators and feast on beetle eggs. Slugs like to munch on bean seedlings, but a splash of diatomaceous earth deters them.

Peas (*Pisum sativum*)

Family: Fabaceae (Legume)
Plant Type: Cool-season annual, zone 2+
Light: Full sun, tolerates part shade with reduced yield
Soil: Loose, rich, well-drained. Nitrogen fixer
pH: 6.0–7.0
Height x Width: 2–6' x 6–10"
Sow: Direct seed ½–1" deep, 2–4" apart
Succession: Every 3 weeks until late spring, start again in late summer
Days to germination: 9–14
Days to maturity: 55–70/100
Water: Moderate until blossoming, then low
Feed: Low NPK, none
Friends: Beans, carrot, corn, cucumber, radishes, salad greens, and turnips
Foes: All alliums: leek, garlic, onions, and shallots

There's nothing quite like the snap and crunch of fresh-off-the-vine sugar snap peas. Easy to grow from seed, all you need is a sunny spot and rich soil for peas to flourish. The only fertilizer required: a hefty two- to three-inch supply of compost or well-rotted manure dug into your garden the previous season. Once your plants reach five weeks, their nitrogen-fixing root nodules will take over the job from there. Follow the old adage and direct sow your pea seeds "as soon as the soil can be worked" in the spring, which is typically four to six weeks before your last frost. However, if you live in a place where you get a lot of snow, you may want to tweak this timing. While peas are generally tolerant, they do not like weather extremes, and if you live in a place like I do where it snows a lot, it's better to wait until mud season has passed so the waterlogged soil does not rot your seeds. If you're eager for an early start, sow them in a cold frame one to two months before your last frost, covering the plants with an extra sheet of plastic or a vinyl tablecloth to protect your plants against a surprise cold snap. The plants themselves are hardy, but the developing pods aren't and can be damaged by freezing temperatures.

Snap peas on a chicken wire A-frame trellis.

Peas are divided into three classes: shelling, snow or sugar, and snap. Shelling, also known as English peas, are grown for the individual peas, not the pods. Those are then further separated into two groups: round, smooth peas, which are hardier, and shriveled peas, which are more sweet. Harvest shelling peas when their pods appear round and plump. I toss the pods in the compost bin and enjoy the peas raw in salads or cooked in soups and side dishes. Snow, or sugar, peas are meant to be eaten whole and taste fantastic whether fresh or cooked in stir-fries. You can tell it's time to harvest when the pods are flat and the peas are still small. My favorite—and probably most people's favorite—is the snap pea, which can be eaten whole or shelled, raw or cooked, and is a blend between the sweet juicy shelling peas and the crisp snow peas. Like shelling peas, it's best to harvest snaps once the peas are full and round. Good luck making it from the garden to the kitchen without sneaking a handful!

If you're anything like me, there are never enough peas in the garden and harvest time comes and goes too fast. To get the most out of the season, grow a mixture of early (seventy days), mid (eighty days), and late (one hundred days) season varieties and grow successive crops of each. I plant a new crop every three weeks, or as soon as the recent crop has emerged, until mid-July, harvesting that last summer crop in late September or early October. Although early spring crops are more productive than later crops, fresh-from-the-garden peas beat frozen, store-bought peas any day.

Sugar snap peas.

The night before I plant my seeds I soak them in lukewarm water with a bit of seaweed fertilizer. The seaweed doesn't do anything to help my seeds germinate, but it does help to deter mice and rodents. Pea seeds are especially delectable to mice, rabbits, and even birds, so even if you plant plenty in the garden, you may be surprised to see few seedlings. Another way to keep these critters away is to cover seeds and seedlings with a row cover or bird netting until your seedlings are a few inches tall, at which time they become less appetizing to grazing birds and rodents.

Although not required, inoculating your seeds with rhizobacteria before you plant can be especially useful in boosting and maximizing plant growth and yield. Even though this bacteria is already present in your soil, using an inoculant will give your plants a little extra boost by increasing root growth and improving your plant's ability to reach, grab, and use nutrients and water. Inoculant can be a little pricey, so I like to pool some resources with my garden friends and then split the bacteria.

Peas will perform okay under glass, but they really shine when planted out in the open in the garden. You can transplant seedlings after three weeks or direct sow your seeds two to four inches apart (two inches for shorter and four inches apart for taller varieties) in one-inch deep, V-shaped drills. If planting in rows, it is especially efficient to grow two rows six to ten inches apart. This way you can place a trellis between the rows and get twice the bang for your buck. When your seedlings are two to three inches tall, you will see their tendrils start to develop, which means it's time for some support. I like to use natural materials like birch, hazel, or willow branches from the yard to form a trellis, but plant netting, tomato cages, and galvanized chicken wire work just as well. Once the peas reach one foot tall, mulch. A nice layer of weedless straw helps prevent weed infestations as well as maintain moisture. And if you choose black plastic, which you can cut holes in and plant directly into, it will also help warm the soil. Remember to keep your variety's height in mind and make sure your trellis is tall enough to support your peas straight to the top. I usually have to add a new strand of garden twine every twelve inches to hold the billowing pea stalks to the trellis.

To keep their roots cool, I lay a thick, four-inch layer of weed-free straw or hay as mulch. This not only protects the roots from the summer heat, but it also keeps the soil moist. Stimulate pod development by pinching off the top of each plant vine as soon as the first pod is ready for harvest. Not only does it make the plant stronger, it also increases pea production! Once your plants start growing, they'll require very little attention aside from weeding, trellising, and water. I've found that by increasing the amount I water my peas when they start to flower, I'm rewarded with a boost in sweetness. Remember, when harvesting, hold the plant stalk with one hand and use the other to pull the pod and harvest regularly from the bottom up to encourage pod development.

If you're short on space or are moving, don't worry—you can still grow peas. For those whose garden is on the smaller side, you may want to choose one of the taller varieties as they are typically the most productive. However, if you live in a condo, apartment, or home with no outdoor space, just grow your peas in pots! I recommend planting dwarf or bush varieties like 'Dwarf Grey Sugar' or 'Maestro' in containers just as you would in the garden. These shorter peas grow one to three feet tall and typically don't need support. If you find your peas billowing off to the side, stick a tomato cage in the pot and twine your peas through. Just be sure to use good potting soil, water regularly, and maybe even give them a side dressing of fish emulsion once they are a few inches tall. Another way to enjoy peas in pots is to grow them for their shoots. Harvest the top two inches once the plant reaches six to ten inches tall. Select taller varieties for reliable, decent shoot lengths, and you should be able to harvest weekly until the heat of July kicks in.

The harvest might be finished, but your legumes aren't yet. Cut them down to their roots and gently fork them into the soil. I compost the vines, but by the next spring the roots will have broken down and released extra nitrogen into the soil for the following crop to use. This is the main reason I always plant brassicas after my peas: the more nitrogen, the better.

Pests and disease plague peas just as they do other vegetables. Avoid beetles by covering young plants with row covers, pinch off aphid-infested foliage, hose off plants to get rid of any remaining pests, and fence out other critters to keep them from nibbling on your peas. Aside from preventing birds and rodents from eating seeds in spring, keeping your plants well-watered, mulched, and healthy will make them less prone to mildew and disease. Pea mosaic usually occurs when gardeners fail to rotate their garden beds. The only solution to blight is to destroy the infected plant and sterilize, or solarize, your soil with clear plastic. If you see evidence of downy or powdery mildew on your plants, treat your foliage by spraying them with a baking soda solution (1 Tsp./1 Quart of water). The best way to prevent these diseases is to choose disease-resistant varieties. And remember, don't jostle or harvest from wet vines. Always dig up and destroy disease-infected plants.

BRASSICAS

The cabbage family is greedy. Brassicas suck up nutrients like a leech, exhausting the soil of its nitrogen. I find brassicas easiest to start from seed and transplant (some carefully) into the garden a few weeks before my last frost. Get them off to a good start in beds amended with aged manure or compost. A slightly lower soil pH (6.5–7.0) also reduces the chance of the fungal disease clubroot. Just as thirsty as they are hungry, brassicas need to be watered regularly to grow tender, succulent leaves. Drip irrigation or soaker hoses are worth every penny! A few inches of mulch help keep weeds down as well as maintaining soil moisture while keeping the roots cool. Because brassicas have an army of nasty pests, crop rotation is a must. This planting strategy serves two purposes. First it confuses the pests and prevents diseases. By removing desirable food and susceptible plants, many of these problems can be avoided. Second, it allows different crops to nourish and replace those nutrients that the brassicas just depleted. I always follow my legumes with the brassicas. As nitrogen fixers, legumes infuse the soil with the nitrogen the brassicas crave to be highly productive. Once the season is over, use a nitrogen-fixing green manure like clover or buckwheat to replenish the soil's fertility for the next crop. Also, as cold-weather crops, their flavors usually improve with a little frost and benefit from a little shade in the hot weather.

Broccoli (*Brassica oleracea* 'Italica')

Family: Brassicaceae
Plant Type: Hardy, cool-season biennial, grown as annual, zone 3–10
Light: Full sun, tolerates partial shade (but will slow growth)
Soil: Fertile, well-drained
Height x Width: 2–3' x 2–3'
pH: 6.0–7.5
Sow: ½–¼" deep, 12–20" apart
Succession: Plant early-, mid-, and late-season varieties or plant a second crop one month after the first
Days to germination: 4–7
Days to maturity: 78–98
Water: Moderate and consistent, avoid overwatering (heavy)

Feed: Heavy feeder
Friends: Artichoke, beet, carrot, celery, chard, cucumber, herbs, lettuce, nasturtium, onion (alliums), pea, potato, spinach, and tomato
Foes: Beans and strawberries

My personal favorite of the cabbage family, broccoli is easy to grow and quite a faithful producer. There are two main types, big head (calabrese) and sprouting. I grew sprouting the first year because it was described as a short-season, cut-and-come-again crop with smaller heads on several stems and steady production; it seemed perfect for me. Many of the white cultivars have a slightly better flavor, and the purple are hardier. As with legumes, harvest regularly—it stimulates growth and produces more spears, sometimes up to six weeks! Over time I've come to appreciate the other types as well: the large head, which looks exactly what it sounds like; Romanesco, a long-season, lime-green broccoli with spiraled fractals around

A typical brassica, broccoli is rapacious in a nitrogen-rich bed, so plant seedlings in a bed a legume has recently vacated and you will have some very happy, highly productive broccoli plants.

its tightly bound head; and their distant cousin, broccoli rabe, another quick, cool-weather, sharply flavored crop favored for its tender buds, leaves, and stems.

Like all brassicas broccoli is a greedy feeder and savors well-drained, fertile soil.

Because broccoli welcomes as much nitrogen as it can get, I plan my crop rotation so that it follows my legumes or a planting of a nitrogen-fixing green manure such as hairy vetch (*Vicia sativa*), field peas (*Pisum sativum* var. *Arvense*), or clover (*Trifolium* spp.), and work in two to three inches of compost, leaf mold, or aged manure. To get a jump on the harvest I sow my broccoli one-quarter to one-half inch deep six to eight weeks before the last spring frost in flats, fertilizing with half-strength fish emulsion once the first true leaves emerge. While you can practice succession and plant a second crop one month after the first, I prefer to use the staggered harvest technique. Starting early-, mid-, and late-season varieties all at the same time at the start of spring is less work, and you don't have to worry about planting your second crop when it's too hot. For warm-region gardens, select quick-developing varieties to avert bolting. Once done planting, I don't have to think about any more sowing and still benefit from an elongated harvest. For an autumn harvest, sow seeds twelve to fourteen weeks before the first expected fall frost.

Once hardened off for five to ten days, broccoli transplants well. When it has four to six leaves, this brassica is ready to go in the ground, which should be about two to four weeks before your last frost. I always sink my six-inch-tall seedlings one to two inches deeper and remove any leaves below the soil line to encourage sturdier plants and a healthier, more extensive root system. Keep in mind not to plant too soon or too late in the garden, as extended exposure to cold or hot temperatures at this stage results in smaller, "buttoned" heads that will bolt. Use cloches, row covers, or low tunnels to protect new seedlings against unpleasant weather or unexpected frosts. Just remember to remove them as the weather warms. Interplant with quick-maturing salad greens and radishes. They don't require much room and flourish under the shade provided by broccoli. If you only have a patio or small garden, an alternative to growing in the garden is to grow broccoli in containers. Just be sure the pot is large enough, at least twenty inches deep with drainage at the bottom, and has plenty of compost mixed in. You can also protect your pots from adverse weather by bringing them indoors.

If you've prepped your bed suitably the previous season with a living mulch, practiced crop rotation, and applied a healthy amount of compost, your broccoli should not need much in the way of fertilizer. Unless you see leaf yellowing indicating nitrogen deficiency, a side dressing of compost or fish emulsion application is all you need to reinvigorate your plants. Too much nitrogen can cause hollow stems. Broccoli likes lots of sun and water. It thrives in full sun, and will still produce in part shade, just at a slower rate. Ensure continuous moisture by using soaker hoses, drip tape, and a healthy dose of mulch to cool roots, maintain soil moisture, and reduce weeds. Slow, deep watering is most effective. But no matter what, avoid overhead watering, especially if the heads are maturing, as it invites disease and rot.

Broccoli is best harvested in cooler weather, when you see the head developed fully into a dark green (or other color) firm mass of tight buds. Harvest in the morning to maintain sweetness. Cut the stalk four to six inches below on a slant, or water could pool at this wound and rot the plant. To guarantee your broccoli keeps producing, harvest heads and side shoots with a sharp knife as long as they appear. Again, this is an example of the more you cut, the more broccoli you get. It should last until the first frost kills the plant. You do not want any of the yellow florets open as they signify to the plant it is time to wind down for the season, although they are edible.

Flea beetles, slugs, cutworms, cabbage worms, cabbage loopers, maggots, and aphids are some of the most common brassica pests. Three-inch-tall cardboard collars sunk one inch into the soil protect against cutworms, and floating or supported row covers sealed along the edges to exclude destructive beetles and worms are inexpensive and effective ways to control these bugs. Handpicking caterpillars is time-consuming (and gross), but adequate. Or you can purchase green lacewings, trichogramma, and other predatory wasps to release into your garden. Clubroot manifests itself with the general weakening and yellowing of the plant and the presence of malformed roots. As the primary disease broccoli faces, the easiest way to prevent this fungal disease is to practice crop rotation and select disease-resistant varieties. Lime your soil to raise the pH to 7.2 to kill any lingering disease.

Brussels Sprouts (*Brassica oleracea* 'Gemmifera')

Family: Brassicaceae
Plant Type: Cold-season biennial, grown as annual, zones 4–7
Light: Full sun, tolerates partial shade
Soil: Well-drained, fertile
Height x Width: 2–3' x 1½–2'
pH: 6.0–7.5
Sow: ¼" deep, 18–24" apart
Succession: Plant a second crop, 4 months before first fall frost
Days to germination: 5–8
Days to maturity: 90–110
Water: Moderate and even
Feed: Moderate nitrogen, high phosphorus and potassium

Friends: Beet, carrot, celery, cucumber, onions, spinach, and herbs
Foes: Pole beans, kohlrabi, strawberries, and tomatoes

While brussels sprouts may be easy to grow and survive through frost and snow, not everyone is a fan. They're very polarizing, eliciting strong love or hate reactions from almost everyone I know. But if you want to give them a go, wait till they've had ample time to grow and experience a few hard frosts—that's when they're at their sweetest! As sprouts are an acquired taste, don't be tempted to eat them in summer unless you enjoy gnawing on cardboard. In my opinion it is best to wait till autumn for a fair shake.

Super hardy, brussels sprouts are a late fall and winter crop—they thrive and are most flavorful after the onset of cold. Sprouts grow best in cool, evenly moist soil. Start them off right with a sunny spot and moist, well-drained soil improved with forked-in compost, aged manure, or leaf mold. Brussels sprouts grown in warm climates have a tendency to "blow," appearing like a loose, open cabbage, and lack the sweetness brought on by frost. Blown buds can also indicate a nutrient deficiency during the growing season. To avoid these miniature-cabbage looking sprouts, select hybrid varieties that are less likely to blow. Brussels sprouts are a long-season crop. You can direct seed or grow transplants— either way they need at least four months to develop before fall's first frost. I sow two

Brussels sprouts in the garden can become top-heavy. Either stake plants or mound the soil at the base a bit for more leverage.

Lower leaves are removed to encourage the ripening of sprouts.

seeds per cell and thin to the strongest. After a week of hardening off, space seedlings approximately two feet apart when four to six inches tall (four to six weeks old). Plant your seedlings deeply, such that the first true leaves are level with the soil and heel in, or firm, the soil about the base. This helps anchor your plants once they become top-heavy and laden with sprouts. Brussels sprouts are sensitive to root disturbance—avoid later damage and blown buds by inserting stakes or extra support when seedlings are young. As the plants grow, tie them to the stakes to prevent them from swaying and blowing over in heavy wind or on exposed sites. I also like to earth up about the stem as the plants develop and become heavier.

Water thoroughly and give brussels sprouts a monthly dose of fish emulsion or aerated compost tea as they are a heavy feeders. Side dress with a dose of blood meal and mulch once plants reach twelve inches tall to retain moisture, keep the roots cool, and moderate soil temperature.

My favorite interplanting candidate is looseleaf lettuce. As a rapid growth crop, leafy greens will bask in the shade provided by brussels sprout leaves. And for those gardeners without yards of space, you too can grow sprouts if the container is large enough. Short season and early to mature, dwarf varieties such as 'Jade Cross' or 'Oliver' are particularly good for pot cultivation.

Although sprouts have a bad reputation of not being the tastiest vegetable, reserve judgment until you've tasted them after they've experienced a few frosts—you will be amazed at their sweetness!

You can begin harvesting sprouts when they reach the size of a one-inch marble and feel firm. However, they will still lack the nutty sweet flavor the cold weather adds. Many of the older heirloom varieties develop from the bottom up, while newer cultivars mature evenly. Remove lower leaves once lower buds show signs of growth, and continue to remove a few leaves each week. You should "top off" plants if you discover that they are slow to develop and are about one month away from a hard freeze. Topping is a technique in which you pinch out the growing tip when the bottom sprout is about three-quarters inch in diameter, helping advance bud formation by redirecting the plants' energy into the remaining buds, similar to the removal of lower leaves. Once your brussels sprouts have reached the desired size and experienced a few frosts, it is time to harvest. You can cut the buds away with a knife, twist until they separate, or snap them to remove from the stem. If nighttime temperatures dip to 25°F or you see a decline in sprout quality, cut the entire plant, discard any remaining leaves, and hang in a cool, dry garage, basement, or root cellar. They should last at least three weeks.

To extend your brussels sprout harvest beyond December in colder growing zones, mulch around the entire stem with straw or shredded leaves using a row cover to hold the mulch in place. Low or high tunnels also offer additional protection, but a greenhouse will extend your sprout harvest for another six weeks.

Brussels sprouts are a card-carrying member of the cabbage family, and as such suffer from all the same pests. If slugs present an issue, set a beer trap in the evening and discard your slimy collection the following morning. Cardboard collars deter cutworms, and row covers implemented at planting exclude cabbage worms, cabbage loopers, and slugs from taste testing. Good crop rotation practices are also an effective way to discourage these destructive bugs.

Cabbage (*Brassica oleracea* 'Capitata')

Family: Brassicaceae

Plant Type: Cool-season biennial, grown as an annual, zone 3–11

Light: Full sun

Soil: Rich, fertile, well-drained

Height x Width: 12–15" x 24–42"

pH: 6.0–7.0

Sow: ¼–½" deep, 1" apart, thinning to 12–24" apart

Succession: 3 harvests; early spring, mid-spring, and late summer

Days to germination: 4–7

Days to maturity: 70–120 from seed

Water: Heavy until head formation

Feed: High NPK

Friends: Beets, bush beans, carrots, celery, cucumbers, lettuce, nasturtiums, onions potatoes, spinach, and many herbs

Foes: Pole beans, strawberries, and tomatoes

Grab your cloches, row covers, low tunnels, and get sowing! Take advantage of the cool weather and plant a combination of early-, mid-, and late-season varieties. You'll be harvesting heads of cabbage from early summer until late fall, filling your root cellar or basement to its brim. With so many choices, there is a cabbage for everyone. All you have to do is pick between smooth, savoy, and Chinese types; rounded, flattened, or upright-shaped heads; and green or reddish-purple cabbage. All are super easy to grow. The most familiar is the smooth head. Sweet and crunchy, it's firm with tightly wrapped, fan-shaped leaves and available in green or reddish-purple. Savoy, the prettiest, and my personal favorite, has a mild, earthy flavor with deeply wrinkled leaves. Not as tightly bound, their rumpled leaves have a bit more give than smooth heads due to the crinkly texture. Chinese, or Napa, cabbage is a cousin of the traditional cabbage, with its romaine-like, cone-shaped leaves on white stalks, and slightly softer and sweeter than smooth.

The key to good cabbage production is getting your plants established before the summer heat sets in. Four to six weeks before your last frost are plenty of time to get your seedlings established, unless you're growing in a tunnel. In that case start your seeds twelve weeks before your last spring frost and transplant at six weeks. Remember if you're stretching the season, vent the tunnel during the day so the temperature doesn't exceed 40°F and close again at night. A good year-round vegetable, cabbage can yield three ample

A mature head of savoy cabbage ready for harvest.

harvests in a single year. Your first crop in early spring should be started four to six weeks before last frost, a second sown when the first is planted out, and the third about ten to twelve weeks before first fall frost. Alternatively you can sow a mix of early-, mid-, and late-season varieties in early spring for a staggered harvest from late spring through late fall.

Preferring full sun and rich soil, well amended with compost, cabbage should follow beans and peas for optimal fertility. After a week of hardening off, plant transplants twelve to twenty-four inches apart. Seedlings should be six inches tall and have several true leaves. Cabbage has a very shallow root system, and thus is easily damaged. If not direct seeding, be careful handling transplants. Any stress or disturbance to the root ball will slow growth and head formation. Due to its shallow root system, you can grow cabbages in containers providing they are at least twelve inches deep with an eight-inch diameter. Weed competition inhibits growth, especially if sown in situ. Mulching goes a long way to addressing many of these issues. A thick layer of seaweed or straw helps control weeds, maintain moisture, and keep the shallow roots protected and cool.

Cabbage is a heavy drinker and feeder. Provide ample, steady water during growth and give them a balanced dose of liquid feed or fish emulsion once seedlings have been in the ground for approximately four weeks and again midway through the season. You may notice some splitting on your heads as they develop. This is caused by stress to the roots or too much water as the heads mature and grow too large. There are a few things you can do to prevent your heads from splitting. One, plant split-resistant varieties. Two, curtail your watering once heads begin to mature. Planting cabbages closer together results in smaller but more flavorful heads that are less likely to split. Or you can prune the roots with a sharp shovel or spade. Wait until your cabbages are round and firm. Then, using a shovel, slice into the soil about six inches off one side of the plant severing half the roots, thereby restricting water uptake.

You will know it's time to harvest by the "feel" of the heads. Squeeze once, and if firm, use a knife to cut as close as possible to the head. I suggest cutting high on early and mid-season cabbages, because you will be able to grow and harvest up to four more smaller cabbages from the stalk. Once the main head is severed, leave the stalk and as many leaves as possible and cut an X about one-half inch deep into the tall stump. Water well with fish emulsion, and you will soon see four new mini cabbages growing, each a perfect single serving! Fall- and winter-harvested cabbages are more flavorful and keep better when the entire plant is harvested, roots and all. Simply loosen the soil and pull the entire plant from the ground, roots and all. Then remove large leaves, leaving a few wrappers, and bundle up in newspaper, and you should have cabbage that will store until spring.

Since cabbage is a brassica, it's affected by all the same bad bugs, including cutworms and cabbage worms. I wrap three-inch cardboard collars around the base and add row covers immediately at time of planting to exclude these pests as well as cabbage loopers, root maggots, slugs, and aphids. Clubroot stunts growth and can eventually kill the plant. Healthy seedlings are less vulnerable to this disease, but if infected, destroy and do not compost. Clubroot prefers a pH less than 6.5, so lime your soil to raise pH to 7.0–7.2 to stop disease reproduction, and use a three- or four-year crop rotation plan to prevent it.

Cauliflower (*Brassica oleracea* 'Botrytis')

Family: Brassicaceae
Plant Type: Cool-season biennial grown as annual, zone 3–11
Light: Full sun, tolerates light shade
Soil: Fertile, well-drained
Height x Width: 18–24" x 18–24"
pH: 6.5–7.5
Sow: ¼–½" deep, 3" apart, thinning to 15–20" apart

Succession: Every 4 weeks or staggered harvest

Days to germination: 4–6

Days to maturity: 70–120 from seed, 55–80 from transplants

Water: Moderate and even

Feed: High NPK

Friends: Artichoke, bush bean, beet, carrot, cucumbers, celery, lettuce, nasturtium, garlic, onions, peas, potatoes, and herbs

Foes: Pole beans, strawberries, and tomatoes

Notoriously one of the most challenging and difficult crops to grow, cauliflower can be finicky. These cool-weather curds will button and not develop properly when planted too early, too late, or if stressed by damage, being rootbound, drought, or early warm

Even self-blanching cauliflower will taste better once blanched.

temperatures. Planting at the "right" time becomes crucial for this crop. Spring and autumn crops produce the best cauliflower. Although cauliflower is temperamental, if it's grown quickly and matures under consistently cool (less than 70°F), moist conditions, you will be rewarded with a happy, large, nutty-flavored curd. For gardeners short on space, cauliflower will thrive in twenty-inch deep, self-watering containers.

Available in cream, white, purple, orange, or green, cauliflower needs to start off right. You will have better success with transplants than by direct seeding. Work an ample compost or aged manure into your soil and scratch in a granulated balanced fertilizer to ensure steady growth. Transplants should be started six to ten weeks before your last spring frost and planted out four to six weeks later when seedlings have four to six true leaves. Do not plant too early or too late.

CAULIFLOWER TASTES BETTER BLANCHED.

Early frost causes young plants to bolt and older plants to become "checked," or so rootbound that they will only produce tiny heads. Plant deeply such that the first leaves are even with the soil line and space two to three inches apart, thinning to eighteen to twenty-four inches. Insect barriers and cardboard collars used at time of transplanting are the best defense against flea beetles, cabbage worms, slugs, and cutworms, which can be particularly bothersome to young cauliflower seedlings. Just remember to vent on warm days!

Cauliflower has a delicate, shallow root system, which if damaged results in "buttoning," or small, undeveloped heads. Additionally this brassica despises extreme temperatures, hot or cold, and abhors dry conditions. Curds require a copious amount of water for vigorous, healthy growth. Make sure your plants get plenty of consistent water, as inadequate hydration can also cause your curds to bolt or button. A few (three to four) inches of straw or seaweed mulch suppress weeds and help maintain an even moisture and soil temperature. Like any vegetable that belongs to the brassica family, cauliflower likes lots of nutrition, so I give a few additional applications of kelp or fish emulsion, starting once the plants have been in the ground for at least four weeks.

Once your cauliflower has been growing for about a month, start checking it daily to determine how large the head has grown. When the curd is the size of an egg, between two and three inches in diameter, you will need to start blanching. Blanching is a technique used for white varieties. Simply bend the large surrounding leaves over top of the head and secure with twine or a rubber band to shield from the sun. If you fail to blanch your white cauliflower it, turns yellow and flavor diminishes. Self-blanching varieties' leaves naturally curl over heads, but your crop will still benefit, and taste better, after blanching.

Harvestable cauliflower heads should be fairly regular and compact. Separated curds, referred to as "riciness," indicate that the head is overly mature and will taste strong and tough. Use a knife to cut the head from the stalk when it is about six to eight inches wide, or five to fourteen days after you started blanching white varieties. Unlike their cabbage relations, cauliflower is a one-trick pony—there are no side shoots, it produces a single head and no more. Once your early and mid-season varieties are harvested, you can follow with a catch crop of beans, a few quick successions of radishes and lettuce, or a nitrogen-fixing living mulch like clover or alfalfa. Late varieties won't be ready until late fall, and while young cauliflower will tolerate frost, mature heads will not. Use row covers or mini tunnels over the crop when the danger of frost creeps up in fall.

Along with its unforgiving nature, cauliflower is haunted by the same culprits who attack broccoli and cabbage: aphids, cabbage root maggot, cabbage loopers, cabbage worms, cutworms, flea beetles, slugs, and snails. Rotate every three to four years to avoid clubroot and select resistant varieties to avoid fusarium wilt and black rot. Heat-tolerant varieties are a great option for gardeners with warmer summers.

Collard Greens (*Brassica oleraceae* 'Acephala')

Family: Brassicaceae
Plant Type: Cool-season biennial, grown as an annual, zones 3+
Light: Full sun, tolerates light shade
Soil: Fertile, well-drained
Height x Width: 24-30" x 24"
pH: 6.0–7.5
Sow: ¼–½" deep, 6" apart, thinning to 18–24" apart
Succession: Every 2–3 weeks
Days to germination: 4–7
Days to maturity: 60–70
Water: Moderate
Feed: Low NPK
Friends: Tomatoes and peppers
Foes: Celery, potatoes, and yams

Traditionally a southern favorite, collards are making quite a name for themselves in northern gardens. Their flavor improves with frost. While their leaves are loaded with nutrition, they need to be cooked to taste their best. Raw they are rather tough and chewy. These "headless cabbages" are an easy-to-grow crop and one of the most heat-tolerant brassicas. They look great as edible ornamentals in borders and perform well in ten-inch-wide containers that are at least twelve inches deep.

Start spring transplants about six to eight weeks before your last frost, planting out eighteen to twenty-four inches apart six weeks later after the standard hardening off period. You can plant successively every couple of weeks to keep your kitchen full of fresh greens all season. Fall crops can be direct seeded one inch apart three months before first frost. Thin plants to twelve to eighteen inches apart and throw the leaves in your stir-fries. Tighter, intensely planted collards produce better than ones that are more loosely spaced. As a non-heading, leafy brassica, collard greens adore and can never have enough nitrogen. Prep your beds and dig in two to four inches of compost or well-rotted manure before planting. If possible, follow a fall-planted legume crop or living mulch. Collards are an undemanding crop; just water well, keep soil consistently moist, and mulch for high-quality, flavorful leaves. They can tolerate drought, but their leaves may become tough and unappetizing. Generally they taste better in cooler weather. I apply fish emulsion periodically throughout the growing season, tapering off at the end of summer for lush, vigorous growth.

Treat collards as a cut-and-come-again crop. New leaves form from the center, so harvesting outer, bottom leaves first encourages steady, uninterrupted production. You can begin harvesting leaves for the kitchen once the leaves are large enough to eat. If grown in tunnels or cold frames, mulch overwintering plants heavily and you can enjoy your fall crop late into the season after they've been sweetened by cooler temperatures. Leaves will toughen up once they're past maturity, so as your plants reach their peak, harvest the entire plant.

While collard greens are a brassica, they are an anomaly within the family. Keep an eye out and monitor for conventional pests, including cutworms, slugs, and cabbage worms, but they don't seem to trouble these greens. Besides a crop rotation schedule, the use of insect barriers, floating row covers, or collars to protect against early infestations is all that is required to maintain a healthy crop.

Kale (*Brassica oleracea* 'Acephala')

Family: Brassicaceae
Plant Type: Cold-season biennial grown as an annual, zones 3–11
Light: Full sun, tolerates part shade
Soil: Fertile, well-drained

Height x Width: 18–36″ x 12–36″

pH: 6.0–7.5

Sow: ½″ deep, 1″ apart, thinning to 12–24″

Succession: Autumn/winter crop tastes best

Days to germination: 5–7

Days to maturity: 55–75 for seed, 30–40 for transplants

Water: Heavy

Feed: Heavy, moderate NPK

Friends: Artichoke, beets, bush beans, celery, cucumbers, lettuce, onions, peas, potatoes, spinach, and herbs

Foes: Pole beans, strawberries, and tomatoes

Baby kale ready to be planted.

Kale is the northern counterpart to southern collards. They are both non-heading, easy to grow, nutritious, and look amazing in borders. But whereas collards flourish in the summer heat in the south, kale performs and tastes better after a frosty kiss in northern gardens. Grown for their foliage that ranges in color from an array of green tones to red and purple, they can be intensely ruffled and frilly or flat and coarse. Whichever you prefer, young leaves are the most tender, and their sweet flavor is only enhanced by frost and cold weather. There are two main types of kale, Scotch and Siberian. Scotch is the traditional intensely curled kale known for its cold tolerance and ornamental value in the garden. Siberian, or Napas, is flatter and particularly tasty in salads. I sow these thickly, then thin when the baby greens are two to three inches tall, and again when six inches high. Leaving appropriate space for the remaining seedlings to develop, I toss my "thinnings" in with my mixed greens.

Plant kale transplants once a legume crop is finished in summer. Kale is a cool-weather crop and tastes better after a light frost.

Almost everyone agrees that the Italian heirloom 'Lacinato' is the tastiest. Also known as 'Tuscan' or 'Dinosaur' kale for its large, dark blue-green leaves, it may not be the most uniform or cold hardy, but it is the most sought after for its culinary advantages. Thriving in cold weather, varieties with blue-green leaves are the hardiest and can withstand temperatures down to -10°F when protected!

Transplants tend to do better than direct sown, and if my early peas are finishing up, I'll plan to follow them with my kale. Before planting, dig in plenty of compost, well-rotted manure, or leaf mold. Or you can use a nitrogen-fixing green manure the previous season instead. You can sow in early March and transplant mid-April for a baby green crop in May, but since there are so many quick and easy greens for the spring, it's better to wait until summer and start your autumn crops. Sow a couple of seeds three months before your first fall frost, thinning to the strongest seedling and transplant twelve to eighteen inches apart when four weeks old. Since kale is quite large, it can become top-heavy. Heal, or firm-in, seedlings well, and consider staking. If planning to support your greens, insert the stakes at time of planting so you don't disturb developing plants later on. A row cover over early transplants will help keep out flea beetles, white butterflies, and other pests. As with all brassicas, keep weeds under control, mulch to keep the soil moist and cool, and water moderately. Kale typically doesn't need much water unless you're experiencing drought conditions. In fact, aside from a monthly feed of fish emulsion, this is one of those "plant it and forget about it" plants.

Although kale gets quite tall and spreads out, it is well behaved in containers eight inches wide and deep. Potted-up kale is attractive, long-lasting, adds curb appeal as other plants are dying off and still provides food for the kitchen. So by the time your garden is winding down, your kale should be gearing up! Begin harvesting the super nutritious outer leaves as the weather starts cooling off, leaving the center to keep producing new and tender leaves. Treat kale as a cut-and-come-again crop that sweetens up after a few frosts. Don't worry about losing leaves to the frigid temperatures—it is nearly indestructible. With a combination of mulch, row covers, or tunnel, you can continue harvesting well into winter and through the snow until it turns bitter and goes to seed. If it does survive into the spring, compost it.

Unlike most brassicas, kale isn't as affected by pests as others. Cardboard collars and barriers or row covers are still the best defense during early sowing or transplanting against troublesome insects. Clubroot and other fungal diseases are rarely an issue as long as you're rotating your vegetable beds every three to four years.

Kohlrabi (*Brassica oleracea* 'Gongylodes')

Family: Brassicaceae
Plant Type: Cool-season biennial, grown as an annual, zones 3–11
Light: Full sun, tolerates light shade
Soil: Rich, well-drained
Height x Width: 9–12″ x 9–12″
pH: 6.0–7.5
Sow: ¼–½″ deep, 9–12″ apart
Succession: Every 2 weeks
Days to germination: 5–10
Days to maturity: 45 by seed, 20–25 after transplant
Water: Moderate and even
Feed: Heavy, moderate NPK
Friends: Bush beans, beets, celery, cucumbers, lettuce, herbs, nasturtiums, onion, and potatoes
Foes: Pole beans and strawberries

Quick and unusual, kohlrabi is grown for its baby greens and curious bulb-like stems that sit above the soil. Looking more alien-like than vegetable, this cool-season

Harvest fresh swollen kohlrabi stems when they are two to three inches wide in cool weather.

crop is ready for harvest in just a few weeks and an excellent candidate for interplanting, particularly with brussels sprouts. Tucked among your other, slower brassicas you'll be able to cut fresh salad greens and then the turnip-flavored swollen stem before anything else in the garden begins to spread out. White varieties are the best option for a catch crop as they are the fastest growing, whereas purple stems are slower but hardier, and thus a better choice for late summer and fall harvests.

As with any vegetable in the cabbage family, they grow best in full sun with rich soil improved with compost or aged manure for fertility. For early spring crops I suggest starting your seed early and transplanting nine to twelve inches apart once the soil has warmed. Kohlrabi is temperature sensitive and does not like cold soil. If you do wait until the soil has warmed to 65°F, it is better to direct sow your seeds. Even though kohlrabi is a cool-weather crop, it is the least hardy, and if the temperatures dip below 40°F, it will run to seed before developing its swollen, ball-like stems. Row covers and insect barriers are very useful in protecting young seedlings from the cold and destructive pests like flea beetles and white butterflies.

The secret to sweet and tasty stems is rapid growth and getting established without any interruptions. So make sure to keep it weed-free, water regularly, and ensure the soil stays evenly moist, otherwise it will become woody. Kohlrabi appreciates a layer of mulch to maintain these conditions. If established before the summer heat, the stems will be sweeter and more tender, but grow slower due to the warmer temperatures. A side dressing of leaf mold when stems begin to swell is all the feed you need if you amended your soil properly. For new beds or container plantings, fertilize every two to three weeks with fish emulsion or a balanced organic fertilizer. Kohlrabi does well in pots, just requiring ample water, full sun, and liquid feed every fourteen days, making it a great conversation piece on a deck or patio. Because they are such a quick crop, start new seed every two weeks for a consistent summer supply.

Harvest kohlrabi leaves when young and tender, leaving enough so it can develop good-sized swollen stems. Once the bulb-like stems reach one to two inches in diameter, typically about seven to eight weeks after seeding, pull the entire plant from the ground. Trim the leaves and roots for better storage. If they are forgotten in the garden and grow beyond three inches, they may lose their taste and become tough, requiring you to peel the skin.

Overall, kohlrabi handles non-ideal conditions like drought and high temperatures better than other brassicas, as well as being less susceptible to pests and diseases. Clubroot and black rot are the most problematic diseases kohlrabi faces, but a smart three- to four-year rotation plan will alleviate much of this danger. And early insect barriers or row covers used at planting will keep most troublemakers like aphids, cabbage worms, and flea beetles out until plants are established and less vulnerable.

NIGHTSHADES

Known for its heavy hitters like tomatoes and peppers, the Solanaceae, or nightshade, family is diverse. Categorized by their alkaloid content, some are highly toxic. However, nightshades such as eggplant contain small amounts of the chemical compound and are often safe to eat. These warm-season vegetables like high potassium fertilizers, so potash and comfrey tea are ideal as they promote flowering and fruit development. Due to their nutrient requirements, nightshades grow best in a minimum three-year crop rotation schedule, but four is better. Not only does this ensure that there are enough nutrients, it also stems issues with bothersome pests like the Colorado potato beetle or verticillium wilt.

Eggplant (*Solanum melongena*)

Family: Solanaceae

Plant Type: Annual, zone 5–12

Light: Full sun

Soil: Fertile, well-drained

Height x Width: 24–30" x 24–36"

pH: 5.5–6.8

Sow: ¼–½" deep, 6–8 weeks before last frost

Succession: n/a

Days to germination: 10–14

Days to maturity: 100–140 from seed, 50–75 from transplants

Water: Deeply, regularly

Feed: Every 3–4 weeks with fish emulsion

Friends: Beans, greens, peas, peppers, tomatoes, basil, dill, marigold, tarragon, and thyme

Foes: Corn and fennel

Although eggplant can be a bit fussy, it is well worth the effort. One of the prettiest vegetables, eggplant is glossy and available in a myriad of shapes, sizes, and colors. I'm a big fan of the white and purple streaked Fairytale variety. Consistent warmth is the key to growing plump, juicy eggplants, which grow best at temperatures above 70°F. Sow six to eight weeks before your last frost and do not let your seedling dry out or become rootbound. Once your seedlings have two sets of true leaves, repot them into four-inch pots. Keep in mind that germination can take up to two weeks, so be patient. Add bottom heat and cover them with clear plastic domes to net fast, strong starter plants. Feed your seedlings twice a week with a half-strength dose of fish emulsion and seaweed. Harden off your

Get a jump start on the season by planting eggplants in coldframes.

eggplant for at least a week before you plant out. This is the time to add a few inches of compost and warm your beds by tacking down black or IRT plastic mulch for one to two weeks. Raised beds and containers (minimum twelve inches deep) filled with rich compost are great alternatives to the garden as they warm quicker. Transplant when nighttime temperatures are consistently above 60°F and the danger of frost has passed.

Once planted, fertilize once to twice a month. Fish emulsion mixed with seaweed works well, but avoid high nitrogen feeds, which results in more leaf growth and less fruit. I like to use homemade comfrey tea to infuse my fruit crops with much needed potassium, keeping fruit production high. Make sure your eggplant beds stay moist, getting at least one to two inches of water a week. Too little watering leads to water-stressed plants, which taste bitter. It may seem counterintuitive, but once the buds begin to form, pinch off all but six to eight. This will decrease the number of eggplants you get, but the ones that are left to mature

For sweet and tender eggplants, harvest when they're young. Here are a few just-picked traditional, black Italian 'Nadia' and oval, pink and white Asian type 'Orient Charm' eggplants.

will be large and flavorful. I also pinch back the central leader to the next set of branching leaves twice, once when it's six inches tall to encourage branching and again when plants are twelve to twenty-eight inches tall to promote fruiting. This also strengthens the plant, negating the use of stakes. Harvest your eggplants once they're bright and glossy. Dull eggplants are usually dry, with seeds and tough skins. To check whether your eggplants are ready to harvest, press your finger gently on the skin. If the flesh springs back, it's ready. To avoid breakage, use a knife or snips to cut the fruit off tough stems and branches. Young eggplant tends to be sweeter and more tender. Hard fruit indicates that the eggplant is still developing and isn't ready to be picked yet. Check and harvest regularly to keep production high. Do not wait too long to harvest, otherwise your eggplant parmigiana will be dry and bitter.

Since eggplant needs the long hot summer to ripen, cool-climate gardeners need to help them along. Like tomatoes, they enjoy high-intensity light and perform exceptionally well in tunnels and greenhouses. Cloches, row covers, and mini tunnels are great tools to get them started earlier. You'll also want to leave them in the garden longer. Remember to vent on warm days and remove when night temperatures reach 60°F.

One thing eggplants have is pests, particularly the Colorado potato beetle. The easiest way to deal with them is to handpick the mature yellow and brown striped adults before they defoliate your plants. Check under the leaves regularly for their orange or yellow eggs and crush them to prevent them from developing. Ladybugs and stinkbugs are also natural predators. While they enjoy munching on potatoes, they actually prefer eggplant. I usually plant one sacrificial eggplant at the end of each potato bed as a "catch plant" to tempt the beetles. Eggplants are also susceptible to flea beetles, which leave tiny pin holes in the leaves, and spider mites. Lightweight insect barriers used early in the season are a great way to shut out these insects, just be sure to remove them when the flowers open for pollination. Soil-borne verticillium wilt can also kill your eggplant. Fast-growing, healthy plants are more resilient and handle both insects and disease better. A three-year (four- or five-year is better) crop rotation plan, well-spaced plantings, good garden cleanup practices, and resistant varieties will go a long way with pests and other problems.

WATER-STRESSED EGGPLANTS TASTE BITTER.

Peppers (*Capsicum* spp.)

Family: Solanaceae

Plant Type: Annual, zone 4–12

Light: Full sun

Soil: Light, well-drained

Height x Width: 6–48″ (dependent on variety) x 12–24″

pH: 5.5–6.8

Sow: ¼–½″ deep, 8 weeks before last frost

Succession: n/a

Days to germination: 7–10

Days to maturity: 60–95 days from seed, 55–80 days from transplant for green, 15–20 more days for mature, ripened peppers

Water: Regular and even until buds appear

Feed: Medium-heavy feeder, avoid high nitrogen

Friends: Basil, carrots, eggplant, onion, parsley, parsnip, peas, and tomatoes

Foes: Fennel, kohlrabi

Growing peppers is just like growing eggplant, but with closer spacing. Peppers are a warm-season crop that shouldn't be rushed; they need hot air and warm soil temperatures before they will flourish and mature. Classified into two groups, sweet and hot, peppers vary widely even within these classifications. Sweet peppers are typically mild—and obviously—sweet. The scoville scale measures a pepper's "hotness" from the sweet bell at zero, to verde chilies at 500-1,500, to habaneros at 200,000-350,000, and beyond. Besides differing in heat and taste, they also come in a variety of shapes, colors, and sizes.

A mixed harvest of early and late peppers.

Young, green peppers taste milder than those left to ripen to their mature colors.

Start seeds eight weeks before your last frost date, using grow lights and bottom heat (peppers germinate best at 80°F). After four weeks, repot into four-inch pots, and harden them off after another three to four weeks. At the same time, lightly amend your soil with compost, potassium, and calcium depending on what your soil test suggests. Potassium and calcium are essential for flavorful, meaty peppers, and help protect against rot. A good, organic source of calcium is ground eggshells, but if you don't eat enough eggs to spread in the garden, limestone and bonemeal are great alternatives. If you have heavy clay soil, incorporate bulky organic matter such as straw to loosen it up. Then cover with black or IRT plastic to warm the soil. You don't need to do this, but it will speed up your plants' development. Transplant directly through the plastic by cutting Xs into it and plant twelve inches apart in rows, fourteen inches in raised beds. Some taller varieties benefit from staking, as the peppers can become top-heavy. I like my plants strong and bushy, so I give my seedlings a good pinch off the top when they reach six inches tall.

Peppers are happy in the polytunnel or the garden as long as they have full sun, nutrients, and a steady supply of water. Cool evenings (below 60°F) can set them back, so season extenders like low tunnels and row covers can be useful in cold climates. Again, remember to remove any devices once you see flowers so they can pollinate. Containers are a wonderful alternative for small-space gardeners and simplify rotation plans. The heat from black pots placed on black asphalt can make a remarkable difference in your pepper development. If the leaves are losing their bright green color by midsummer (July), give your plants a hit of a nitrogen feed like fish emulsion. Be careful not to overfertilize with nitrogen, or else you will have lush, green plants and very few peppers. Once the first blossoms appear, pinch off the lower buds to fend off rot, sending energy back into the plant, and irrigate with comfrey tea to stimulate fruit development.

Peppers can be harvested early or mature. Young peppers are green and taste milder than fully grown peppers. I like both and harvest a few immature fruits—when they're big enough—once a week in midsummer. Harvesting continuously encourages the plant to keep producing buds and fruits. Peppers left to ripen on the plant turn vivid colors like red, orange, yellow, and purple, while their flavors (both sweet and hot) become deeper and more complex. Chili peppers left on the plant get hotter and their flavor richer. The downside: bud production decreases, resulting in smaller harvests. Heavy watering right before harvest produces milder peppers, while withholding water right before harvest will increase spiciness. Peppers contain capsaicin, which is a skin and eye irritant, so I suggest wearing rubber gloves when harvesting and prepping these peppers. Don't tug the peppers either, as this often causes branches to break and the loss of other ripening peppers.

As with eggplant, the secret to most pepper problems is a good three- to four-year crop rotation strategy, good air circulation, and disease-resistant varieties. Row covers are great tools for preventing pests like caterpillars and European corn borer. Aphids and flea beetles are easily handled with insecticidal soap or dislodged with a strong stream of water. Other issues include blossom end rot and flower drop. Blossom end rot is caused by a calcium deficiency and inadequate or sporadic watering. Extreme low and high temperatures (below 60°F and over 90°F) can stress the plant and cause the flowers to drop. And if the buds fall, you won't have any peppers. Row covers, cloches, and tunnels are good protection against the cold, and mulch helps keep the roots cool in warm weather.

Potatoes (*Solanum tuberosum*)

Family: Solanaceae
Plant Type: Annual, zone 3–11
Light: Full sun
Soil: Loose, well-drained
Height x Width: 24–30" x 24"
pH: 5.0–6.5
Sow: 2–4" deep, 2 weeks before last frost
Succession: Early-, mid-, and late-season varieties
Days to germination: n/a
Days to maturity: 90–110 days (early), 100–120 days (mid), 110–140 days (late)
Water: Moist, not waterlogged
Feed: High, avoid high nitrogen
Friends: Beans, brassicas, corn, eggplant, and marigolds
Foes: Cucumber, fennel, kohlrabi, pumpkin, squash, sunflower, and turnip

In the mood for a treasure hunt? Try growing potatoes, one of the most productive—and easiest—crops to grow. While you can start them from seed, it's significantly quicker to use seed potatoes. Catalogs offer an expanded selection of seed spuds. From the thumb-sized, skinny fingerlings to medium and large, rounded potatoes available with blue, purple, red, white, and yellow skins and flesh, you'll be surprised at the wide array of choices of shapes and colors. Use the whole seed potato or cut into smaller pieces—but they have to have at least two eyes, or sprouts, and enough flesh to feed the growing potato until the root system has developed. Some gardeners say they should weigh two ounces, but as I don't often have a scale handy, I just make sure that none of my cut seed potatoes are smaller than one-and-one-half to two inches. To avoid rot and disease, allow cut potatoes to "heal" in the sun or in a cool, dry spot before planting unless the soil is warm, then plant away! If your spuds haven't grown eyes yet, they need to be chitted. Simply lay them out indoors on a bright windowsill and leave them for a week at room temperature till the

Remember to really root around when digging potatoes. Every year I think I've got them all, but inevitably the following season I always see a leftover potato plant pop up.

sprouts are one inch long. Sometimes I set them in an old egg carton until they sprout. Don't let the shoots get too leggy, and be careful not to damage them when planting.

It may seem economical to chit potatoes from the grocery store, but resist the impulse. Most of those spuds have been treated with sprout inhibitors and might even carry disease. Neither are desirable traits in seed potatoes, even if they have sprouted.

You'll want to perform a soil test before prepping your bed. A low pH (5.0–6.5) and compost—not manure—will reduce the risk of potato scab. This disease doesn't affect the yields or taste, but the potatoes won't be as pretty with brown, pitted lesions. To reduce pH and start your spuds off right, add a few inches of compost, and potentially sulfur. Kelp meal or mulching with seaweed will increase micronutrients for the tubers. If you've had problems with scab in the past, start with certified, disease-free seed potatoes from a reputable supplier and use a three- to four-year crop rotation.

Hilling and mulching potatoes keep them from becoming green and toxic.

When your potatoes start to flower, increase your watering—your spuds are swelling.

Plant potatoes eye up, four to six inches deep in trenches or holes in bright sun two weeks before your last frost and cover with two inches of soil. I've found that trenches work better for large areas, but if space is limited, a bulb planter is just the thing. I start off planting shallower and hill as they grow, since the soil is warmer and encourages accelerated sprouting. Hilling, or earthing up, is the process of gradually covering the shoots with more compost and mulch as they mature. This is especially important because tubers exposed to sunlight turn green, taste bitter, and become toxic. I hill my potatoes a few times a season, mounding up the soil when my potatoes are four to six inches tall, and then again every three weeks until the mound is twelve to eighteen inches tall, mulching more heavily, as needed.

Growing spuds in potato bags is a great way to save on space, and it makes harvesting easy—simply pull them up or tip it over.

You can sow early potatoes in succession from mid-spring to midsummer if you buy enough, but it's more practical and less work to purchase and plant a mix of early-, mid-, and late-season tubers. Planting a blend of potatoes with different maturity rates ensures that they all won't be ready for harvest at the same time, elongating the season significantly.

Mulch with straw or seaweed once spuds are an inch tall. This shades the roots, conserves moisture, and blocks light from the growing potatoes, which like to be kept moist but not soggy. Waterlogged conditions invite rot and disease, while reducing quality and yield. Feed with bonemeal or another high phosphorus fertilizer after about a month. Once flowers develop, boost irrigation as your potatoes are now beginning to set and swell. After six to seven weeks, your buds will open, signaling it's time to "steal" some new potatoes from the bottom or side of your bed. Carefully dig one foot off to the side of the plant, and if the potatoes are large enough, clip a few off the root and rebury the rest. The term "new potato" generally refers to any potato variety that is harvested when young. Sometime small, full-grown potatoes are also called new, or baby, potatoes.

Harvesting is when the fun begins. You can harvest potatoes at any size, but cut back on watering two weeks beforehand. This toughens the skin and improves storage quality. Whether you decide to dig new, six-week-old potatoes or wait until the first frost has killed the top growth, it's easiest to harvest when the soil is dry. A potato fork is particularly useful, as its flat tines bend around the tubers rather than spearing them when digging through the soil. Start about a foot away from the plant, loosening the soil and pulling up the plant. I've found that unless you get down and root around on your hands and knees you will miss potatoes. Every year I'm amazed at how many wind up growing far off to the side or super deep. If you miss these spuds, don't beat yourself up. They will be volunteers in next year's garden. Brush soil off the potatoes, but do not scrub or wash. Washing invites rot and reduces storage quality. Leave the harvested spuds in a warm spot for four to six hours so their skin hardens. Store in hessian or brown paper bags in a cool, dry, dark basement if you don't have a root cellar. Only store solid, healthy tubers; compost or eat any damaged from the harvest immediately.

Container plantings work similarly to the garden. First, make sure you have drainage holes at the bottom. If not, drill baby, drill. The minimum pot size for potatoes is twelve inches deep and wide, but I'd go with something larger to allow for more potatoes. Fill your container with five to ten inches of compost—more if you have a larger container—and plant your seed potatoes eye up. Cover and mulch. In a few weeks you should see your shoots growing tall. Hill, just as you would in the garden, only this time add another few inches of compost to your container—just enough to cover the shoots, allowing the leaves to stick out the top. Add mulch, and if you have room in your pot, hill again in another couple weeks. When it comes time to harvest, you can either pull the plant and its attached potatoes or tip it over and collect your new spuds!

PLANT POTATOES EYE UP.

Always buy certified, disease-free seed potatoes for a quality harvest.

Some gardeners who favor rare heirloom varieties will save a few potatoes wrapped in straw or newspaper for the following spring. I suggest using a basket or wood crate to store them in to ensure they are well protected and have good air circulation. However, after a few years, you may find that the quality has declined or they may be more susceptible to pests or disease. That's when you know it's time to order fresh seed potatoes.

Aside from scab, the potato's number one pest is the Colorado potato beetle. Handpick the yellow and brown striped adults and check the underside of the leaves regularly for their yellow-orange eggs. Crushing any visible eggs will prevent them from hatching. Insect barriers and row covers are effective against aphids, beetles, corn borers, flea beetle, leaf miners, and worms when their edges are sealed. Insecticidal soap and a direct stream of water from the hose will handle aphids and other virus-transmitting insects. Blight can also be a problem in the late summer, leaving small brown-black splotches on the foliage and stems. If damaged, remove and destroy. Good garden cleanup, soil fertility, bed rotation, and disease-resistant varieties will reduce these problems significantly.

POTATO TOWER

Potato towers are super easy to make and can be constructed out of an old Tupperware tub, compost bucket, or chicken wire. Not only do I enjoy the rustic look of the chicken wire, it's cheap and practical. Best of all, it's easy to harvest—simply cut the chicken wire apart, knock it over, and voilà! Potatoes!

1. Choose a flat, sunny spot in the garden, close to a water source.
2. Cut enough three-foot-tall chicken wire to form a cylinder—as narrow as eighteen inches in diameter to three feet—and secure with zipties. Use a metal post hammered into the ground to help stabilize the tower.
3. Pack the bottom and sides with a thick layer of straw and shovel in a mix of compost, loam, and bonemeal.
4. Add a layer of seed potatoes around the sides of the tower and a few in the center.
5. Pack more straw against the sides and shovel in another layer of soil mix.
6. Continue layering with seed potatoes, straw, and soil mix until you reach the top. Add more straw to the top to cover the soil/last layer of potatoes.
7. Water well and regularly. Potatoes love water! And as soon as flowers begin to appear you can "steal" new potatoes from the bottom or wait until they're more mature to cut the wire and tip your tower to harvest.

Tomatoes (*Lycopersicum esculentum* or *Solanum lycopersicum*)

Family: Solanaceae

Plant Type: Annual, zone 3+

Light: Full sun

Soil: Fertile, well-drained

Height x Width: 24+" x 18–24"

pH: 5.5–6.8

Sow: ½" deep, 6–8 weeks before last frost

Succession: n/a

Days to germination: 5–7

Days to maturity: 50–90

Water: Moderate-high, deep, tapering off as fruit develops

Feed: High potassium (P)

Friends: Asparagus, basil, brassicas, bush beans, carrots, celery, chives, cucumbers, garlic, lettuce, marigolds, melon, mint, nasturtiums, onion, parsley, peas, and peppers

Foes: Corn, dill, fennel, kohlrabi, and potatoes

Tomatoes are the heart of every garden. Used fresh in salads and sandwiches, roasted or cooked in sauce, they're a summertime staple. There are too many varieties and flavors to mention, in fact there are entire books dedicated to the subject of tomatoes. But they all need lots of sun, rich soil, water, support, and, last but not least, patience, because you can't rush perfection.

The first time you open the tomato section of your seed catalog, it's easy to feel overwhelmed. Options include: maturity dates (early, mid, and late), habit (determinant or indeterminant), size (small, medium, or large), shape (round, oblong, pear, heart, ribbed), color (red, pink, orange, yellow, green, purple, black,

Heirloom tomatoes come in various shapes, colors, and sizes. The 'Costoluto Genovese' is one of my favorites with its deeply ribbed shape, but my garden would not be complete without 'San Marzano' plums with their traditional Italian heirloom taste.

white, bicolor), flavors (sweet or acidic), and uses (fresh, cooked, dried, frozen, or canned). Because I enjoy growing a variety of tomatoes and it can be costly to buy ten or more seed packs, instead my gardening friends and I pool our wish lists and swap seeds. Who needs fifty 'Sungold' seedlings when two or three will do?

Tomatoes are most often described by their habit, and this determines how they are grown. If you grow them incorrectly, you will be penalized with weak, unproductive plants and small fruit instead of plump tomatoes. Determinant tomatoes resemble a bush and are shorter (three to four feet), growing to a predetermined height. Because of their small stature, they're easy to control, and tomato cages offer sufficient support. Flowers and fruit develop at branch ends and are spaced close together, generally bearing fruit within four to six weeks (much earlier than indeterminate types). Since most determinant tomatoes mature early, they often ripen at the same time, which is perfect for canning. This is also a boon for cool-climate gardeners who must contend with shorter growing seasons. Determinant tomatoes are excellent candidates for container growing, including specialty pots like topsy-turvy planters and earth boxes. For best results, use pots with a diameter of at least twenty inches, fill with compost, and top off with a tomato cage.

Vining, or indeterminate, tomatoes could grow vertically in perpetuity as long as they have enough room and favorable weather conditions. They require staking or more elaborate trellising to keep them growing up and their fruit off the ground. Unlike bush types, vining tomatoes produce flowers and tomatoes on lateral shoots. Their central stem, sometimes referred to as a cordon, typically grows seven feet or more unless pinched off. Indeterminate tomatoes produce longer, owing to the fact that they can continue growing if left unchecked—so long as all their needs are met. Fruits are spaced a bit farther apart, and are typically larger and taste better. Their superior flavor can be attributed to the fact that bigger, taller plants with more foliage are able to photosynthesize more sunlight to produce more sugar. And being an heirloom variety doesn't hurt either.

A cross between indeterminate and determinant, 'Celebrity' tomatoes are one of the few varieties considered semi-determinant, sharing characteristics of both.

The type doesn't just determine how they're pruned, but how they are held up as well. Supported plants are healthier, easier to pick, and ripen faster. Although they will still produce fruit, bushes should be kept off the ground. An alternative to the tomato cage is galvanized four-inch square fencing, bent into cylinders around the plant. Indeterminate tomatoes are more complex, and there are more choices on how to train them vertically. The traditional stake is easy, clean, and works well. Insert the pointed end of a six-foot wooden stake into the ground at the base of your seedling when planting (doing this later can damage the root system, foliage, or both) and secure the stem to the stake using a soft piece of fabric or tie periodically to keep it upright. Suspension trellises can be erected with a wood or metal frame above your tomato bed or hung from a purlin, or brace, in a greenhouse. Attach a piece of compostable jute string to the top, and as it dangles down gently twist it around the top of the tomato plant stem and secure. The vine will continue growing up the twine producing tomatoes. For a more advanced system, install a rollerhook for a longer growing season. It works the same way, except instead of tying the string to the top of the frame, there is a spool of string. Once the vine reaches the top and you have harvested most of the fruits along the stem, you can lower the string, allowing more vertical space for the plant to keep growing. My

TRELLISED PLANTS ARE MORE PRODUCTIVE.

personal favorite trellis method is the basket weave. Insert cheap wood or metal stakes at three- to four-foot intervals along your bed and use string to weave in between the plants and their branches. Repeat this weave every six to ten inches to hold the plants and their fruits upright, making it easy to harvest and for air to circulate. Regardless of which staking method you use, check your plants every few days to see if they need any training before they get out of hand.

A few words on pruning—less is more. Determinant tomatoes shouldn't be pruned at all except for base suckers to improve air circulation. However, vining fruits can benefit from a light pruning. Cut back to one to two stems. Pinching out thin, pencil-sized suckers keeps plants from becoming unsightly and crowded. Packing plantings also greatly increases the chance of disease. As the season draws to a close, cut back the terminal growing bud on indeterminate plants. This "topping" will redirect all the plant's energy into fruit development and ripening rather than new flower buds that will never have an opportunity to grow into a tomato. Prune based on the support technique used; prune only bottom growth from bush fruit, lightly prune staked plants, and moderately prune trellised plants to direct growth vertically and control overcrowding. Staked and trellised plants should be pruned to a single stem.

Warm weather is a requirement for successful growing. Seeds need to be sown eight to ten weeks early under glass or lights so they have enough time to grow and produce, particularly in cold climates where the growing season is shorter. Seedlings germinate best at 70-80°F, and bottom heat is helpful in getting them started. Suspend supplemental

TOMATO TRELLIS IDEAS

Keep your tomatoes happy, healthy, and upright. Your trellis can be as simple as a tomato cage or hand-made frame. They all work!

1. Wood Stake or T-Posts
2. Twine and Boxed Frame
3. Traditional Tomato Cage
4. Tomato Ladders
5. Branch Obelisks
6. Curved Metal Stake
7. String-Trellised in a Polytunnel
8. Basket-weave

1.

2.

3.

4.

5.

6.

7.

8.

lighting one to two inches above seedling to prevent them from becoming leggy. Maintain a moist soil medium, taking care not to overwater, which results in damping-off. Thin to the strongest seedling per soil block and repot into larger four-inch pots once the first set of true leaves develops. Harden off for ten to fourteen days before planting out once the danger of frost has passed. While I don't recommend succession sowing for tomatoes since they are a long-season crop, starting a second crop four to six weeks after the first as a backup can be useful if something goes wrong with the first.

If you decide to buy your seedlings, get to the garden center early. You will have more choices and plants will still be young. I look for small, compact seedlings whenever I purchasing my plants, because they're typically the healthiest and the least stressed. Stay away from leggy or flowering plants unless they are on the clearance table and you plan to give them some TLC before planting in the garden.

RED MULCH

Black or IRT plastic will warm your soil, but recent USDA research has proven that SRM red mulch increases tomato yields in cooler climates. As with other plastic mulches it suppresses weed and warms the soil an average of 4–6°F. But the key is in the reflection of the sun's far-red wavelengths back up into the plants' canopy, stimulating photosynthesis and rapid growth. Penn State has reported a yield increase of 12 to 20 percent over black plastic in their studies.

Prep your beds with a few inches of compost and check your soil test to determine whether you need any additional potassium or nitrogen. Nitrogen is required in smaller amounts, as too much results in lots of lush foliage with few or no tomatoes. Many years ago a friend suggested that before I plant, I remove the lowest set of leaves and bury the stem deeply. This strengthens the plant, which develops roots at the point the leaves were detached making it more drought tolerant and helping prevent blossom end rot.

Protect crops early in the season from cool night temperatures and surprise frosts with row covers, cloches, and mini tunnels. Remember to vent on warm days, or you run the risk of wilting and frying your plants.

Tomatoes enjoy a slightly higher pH, between 5.5 and 6.8. Regular watering is crucial. Drip tape or soaker hoses make watering almost effortless. Mulch over top of irrigation and around plants with straw, seaweed, landscape fabric, or plastic to maintain soil moisture and protect against soil-borne disease. If you don't have the ability to irrigate, make a small circular well around the base of the plant to hold extra water. Do not let tomatoes dry out between waterings. Inconsistent moisture leads to blossom end rot and cracking. I feed them using a gentle fish emulsion when they're young, but once flowers appear, I apply my homemade comfrey fertilizer to supply extra potassium to encourage flowers and fruiting. When tomatoes begin to ripen, cut back on watering to prevent cracking and splitting.

When your tomatoes begin to change color, you know harvest time is around the corner. Some have trouble knowing just when to pick their fruit, but I go by feel. Overall the tomato should be firm, with a bit of spring at the bottom. Use pruners or scissors to remove from the plant to avoid breakage during harvest. If an early frost is forecasted, pick all half-ripened tomatoes and set on a windowsill till they are ripe. Alternatively, store your tomatoes in a cool, dry drawer or wrap in brown paper bags to delay the ripening process and spread out your bounty until you're ready to use them. Avoid close quarters with bananas and apples, as they release an ethylene gas that hastens ripening.

Unfortunately tomatoes face a number of diseases, particularly those affecting leaves. Damping-off, verticillium wilt, and blight can all be an issue. When the hot, humid weather arrives in summer, be on the lookout for brown-black spots on your leaves, courtesy of blight. If infected, destroy immediately. The best defense against most disease problems in tomatoes is a three-year crop rotation, keeping the garden clear of debris, planting resistant varieties, and ensuring good air circulation. Space indeterminate tomatoes eighteen to twenty-four inches apart and bush varieties two feet apart to improve airflow and reduce the chance of disease.

Other common issues affecting tomatoes include phosphorus deficiency, characterized by purple leaf color, cracking, blossom end rot, and cat-facing. To lower your chance of splitting and cracking, mulch and reduce water two weeks before your tomatoes ripen. Discovering blossom end rot, which is caused by calcium deficiency and irregular watering, is discouraging.

Tomatoes are plagued by many pests, including aphids, whitefly, cutworms, and Japanese beetles, but chief among them is the tomato hornworm. A voracious predator, the tomato hornworm blends in along the foliage, with its large, fleshy, green body, white V-shaped marks, and black "horn" at its back. You will know you have one when whole tomatoes go missing and there is massive defoliation. Dark green droppings on top of your tomato leaves indicate the presence of the hornworm, and I can guarantee you'll find one hiding underneath some of the leaves upon closer inspection. Handpicking is the easiest way to manage those already munching, while parasitic wasps are an excellent biological control.

ROOT CROPS

Sun and loose, rich well-drained soil are the key to successful root crops, which are typically sown directly in the garden. Grown for what's under the soil rather than above, these vegetables are prized for their sweet, crunchy, and sometimes nutty roots. I usually incorporate organic matter such as straw, cover crops, and compost into the garden the previous fall. Root crops are not nitrogen enthusiasts, and if they're supplied with an over-

abundance, you will get lush top growth and small roots. For this reason, avoid fresh manure and nitrogen fertilizers. Slow and steady feeds like bonemeal, or superphosphate, are ideal. High in phosphorus (with a bit of nitrogen), they promote root development and strong growth, which are perfect for root crops. Rake in a handful for every four to six square feet of your prepared beds before planting. Roots like regular moisture so don't forget to mulch and ensure they get at least one inch of water a week in dry spells. And while their foliage is tasty for salads and stir-fries, don't remove too much top growth, or root development will slow or stunt. Root maggot is the primary pest that can wreak havoc with root crops in the garden, worming its way in and tunneling through your root vegetables. Prevent their flies from laying eggs on your vegetables with rotation, resistant varieties, and using insect barriers or row covers immediately after planting.

Beet (*Beta vulgaris*)

Family: Chenopodiaceae
Plant Type: Biennial, grown as an annual, zone 5–10
Light: Full sun
Soil: Well-drained, free of rock and debris
Height x Width: 6–12″ x 4–8″
pH: 6.5–7.5
Sow: ¼–½″ deep, 3″ apart
Succession: Every 2–3 weeks until midsummer
Days to germination: 4–10
Days to maturity: 49–91
Water: Regular, evenly moist
Feed: Moderate, low nitrogen
Friends: Bush bean, brassicas, corn, leek, lettuce, onion, and radish
Foes: Mustard and pole bean

A few years ago a friend had a bumper crop of beets and didn't know what to do with this wealth of produce, so she started making beet everything ... beet bread, beet salad, and even beet cake! Well, she made me a be(et)liever, and now my garden always has a row of beets growing. Although beets are a member of the chard family, I plant mine with other root crops that break up the soil for next year's crop. Beets make an ideal intercrop or catch crop as they are rapid growers, maturing in forty-five days.

Moreover, as a chard member its leaves are tasty and nutritious. Hence you can enjoy both the baby greens as well as the roots!

Amend your beds with well-rotted compost in a sunny spot. Do not use manure. The nitrogen will induce the roots to fork. As a root crop, beets dislike being transplanted. If you do start early, you will often only get leaves with rough, twisted roots rather than rich, round beets. Sow directly in the garden two to four inches apart, two to three weeks before your last frost, earlier if protected in a cold frame or hoop house. You may notice that after sowing what you think is a single seed will germinate as three or more seeds. This happens because what you think of as a beet seed is actually a fruit with several seeds enclosed. Simply thin to three inches apart once the seedlings are two to four inches tall. Avoid pulling, as any root disturbance can affect your growing beets. Instead use snips or sharp scissors to cut off the foliage at soil level. And waste not, want not—throw thinned leaves in your salad later that evening and those leftover roots will feed good bacteria in the soil as they decompose.

Sow your beets thick, so you can eat the baby leaves in salads when you thin out the bed.

Once growing, beets need little beyond water and harvesting. They appreciate and taste best when watered regularly. If watered intermittently, their quality dwindles significantly. Beets grow well in containers at least twelve inches deep, but you must ensure they get adequate water. I mulch with seaweed, which helps to retain moisture and is full of micronutrients that beets like. Unlike most other crops in the garden, beets don't require fertilizer. If you do feel the need to feed—avoid any high nitrogen fertilizers. Select only those with phosphorus and potassium, as too much nitrogen promotes sumptuous leafy growth but poor root development. The tops get woody if their shoulders are exposed to sun, so mulching or covering with soil protects the texture. Weeding is just as important as watering. Beets do not like to compete for their space, water, or nutrients. Warm weather produces full-colored and inferior-flavored vegetables, so once the temperatures start to rise in summer I sow my beets under other trellised crops. The shade provided by my cucumbers and peas keeps them a bit cooler.

Young beets taste better than older beets. Start harvesting alternating roots when they are at their peak of tenderness, typically about one inch in diameter, or three-quarters of matured size. This every-other pattern of harvest allows the remaining beets to grow a bit larger to harvest the following week when they are still

Beets should be harvested when young (about one inch across) for the sweetest, most tender crop.

tender at less than two inches across. As they grow bigger, their flavor diminishes, and they become squishy and develop an unappealing texture. I usually clip away all but one inch of the top growth to avoid bleeding when harvesting and storing my beets.

Alternatively you can leave beets in the ground protected by a thick twelve-inch layer of straw mulch, secured with a row cover or in a cold frame for harvest throughout the winter. Row covers can be used earlier in the season at planting to warm the soil bed and exclude pests like maggot flies and leaf miner, although they are rarely an issue. Scab and leaf spot are deterred by providing plenty of space and watering from the bottom. Higher pH, at or above 7, will also lessen the chance of beets getting scab.

MINIMIZE BEET BLEED

Hold each end of the beet in one hand (root in one and foliage in the other) and twist. This should significantly reduce the bleeding, making it less messy and improving its storage quality. Store in the refrigerator or in a root cellar.

Carrots (*Daucus carota*)

Family: Apiaceae

Plant Type: Hardy biennial, grown as annual, zone 3–12

Light: Full sun

Soil: Deep, loose, free of clods and rocks

Height x Width: 12–18″ x 12″

pH: 5.5–6.8

Sow: ¼–½″ deep 2–4 weeks after last frost, thinning to 2″ apart

Succession: Every 3 weeks until 3 months till first fall frost

Days to germination: 6

Days to maturity: 50–80

Water: Moderate

Feed: Light

Friends: Beans, celery, chives, leek, lettuce, onion, pea, peppers, radish, rosemary, and tomato

Foes: Dill, fennel, parsnip, and radish

Sweet, crunchy, and colorful carrots are so easy they should be in everyone's garden. Once growing they're a leave-'em-and-forget-about-'em crop making, them a favorite for even the most neglectful gardeners. I grow mine in full sun in raised beds enriched annually with compost. Carrots flourish in deep, well-drained beds free of rocks and clumpy soil, producing larger roots with better shape, flavor, and yields.

There is a carrot for everyone, from the gorgeous colored heirlooms to the traditional bright orange. The primary types of carrots include Chantenay, Danvers, Imperator, Nantes, and baby or miniature carrots. Chantenay are my

Gourmet cooks and kids love 'Parisian Market' carrots; they're the perfect size for little fingers.

favorites because they are sweet and crisp with great storage potential. From France, these wonderful all-purpose, five- to six-inch, slightly tapered carrots will tolerate shallow or heavier soils, making them an ideal choice for container gardeners and those with clay. Originating in Danvers, Massachusetts, Danvers carrots are a good all-around choice for cool climates. Their distinctive cone shape makes them similar to imperator carrots, but they are slightly shorter at six to eight inches. This makes them a good pot-grown and heavy soil selection. Aside from being crack and split resistant, their thicker skins elongate their storage life significantly. Just be careful, as they can get woody if left too long in the soil like Chantenay. Imperator is your typical skinny grocery store carrot with narrow shoulders and slight taper. Because they are so long at eight to ten inches, they perform best in deep— at least one foot deep—loose, sandy soil. The most popular carrot is the Nantes, because it is usually the easiest to grow. Like the Chantenay it is also of French origin, but it has a blunt tip and cylindrical shape. Growing five to seven inches, they are sweet and crisp with a limited storage life. Then there are baby carrots. These are the best choice for containers since they have shallow root systems and don't take up too much room. Also, many of the small, round varieties like 'Parisian Market' look like gourmet vegetables on a plate!

Sow directly a few weeks before your last frost in the garden, or ten to twelve weeks early in a cold frame. Soil temperatures of 60–75°F are optimal for germination, which is

Rainbow imperator carrots grow straight and long in deep, loose soil.

very slow. Do not sow early, as carrots really detest transplanting. This means just say no to buying carrot seedlings! You can broadcast or sow in rows six to eight inches apart. It can be challenging to space evenly, because carrot seed is exceedingly tiny. Often it's easier to mix one part seed with two parts coarse builders sand—not beach sand—to space more uniformly. This way when you sow your seeds there'll be less thinning. Alternatively you can mix carrot seed with radish seed. Radishes will germinate faster, and grow and be harvested in less than a month, long before carrots need the space. Additionally, these interplanted radishes break up the soil, stopping crusting that can make it difficult for weak seedlings to break through. Some gardeners will simply cover the seeds with fine sand or vermiculite, while others purchase pelleted seed. Pelleted seed is covered with an inert material that dissolves in water, making it slightly larger and easier to sow. Regardless, the key to good germination is consistent moisture and good contact between the seed and soil. Lightly cover newly sown seeds by scratching-in or raking smooth to increase the connection between the moist soil and newly sown seed. I water my bed twice a day, once in the morning and again in the evening until the carrots are an inch or so tall, when I reduce to once a day.

If you broadcast your seed, you will definitely need to thin. When planted too closely, carrots can become misshapen or stunted. Use snips or small scissors to cut the tops off at soil level to maintain spacing of one to two inches, and later three to four inches. Pulling can disrupt the growing crops. They also dislike weed competition. Carrots can be eaten fresh almost all year long. Leave room in the garden for successive sowing every two to three weeks. Sow fresh seed until eight weeks before your first anticipated fall frost. And if you don't have enough space, no worries—carrots grow just as well in large containers, a minimum of twelve inches deep.

Carrots are a cool-season crop. To keep their roots cool, mulch once the weather climbs into the mid to upper 70°F. Warmer temperatures encourage small, bland-tasting carrots, so shading the roots will keep them happier. Mulching will also protect the carrot shoulders from sun exposure, which turns them green and bitter.

LIGHT FROSTS IMPROVE ROOT CROP FLAVOR.

Forked carrots are the result of too much nitrogen (N), attempting transplanting, or the presence of rocks, weeds, clumps, or debris in the soil. Aside from the initial compost application, I rarely add any additional manure, and if I do I make sure it's well aged. Fish emulsion is the only feed I use to keep the carrots happy without overloading them with nitrogen.

A few light frosts will improve the flavor, so I leave mine in the ground well into fall. As the temperatures dip, the starches convert to sugars in the roots making them sweeter. In loose soils you can harvest simply by pulling on the green tops, but if you find them breaking off, ease them up with a garden fork first. To store I cut back the tops to one inch from the shoulder, pack them into containers filled with straw, moist sand, or sawdust, and leave them in my basement. A root cellar would be better, but I don't have one of those, so just make sure you find a spot with high humidity that hovers about 32°F. Otherwise they will store a month in the fridge. If you have the capability, mulch your carrots heavily. I mulch with six to twelve inches of straw and secure with burlap or row covers to keep everything in place. Later in the season you can trudge outside, pull back the cover, and mulch and dig fresh carrots as you need them. Remember to replace the insulated bedding once you're finished. One lesson that I learned the hard way: mark your carrot bed. Once the snow arrives it's like a truffle hunt, and you are the pig rooting about trying to find your treasure.

The only pest of note is the carrot root fly. Attracted to the sweet root smell, the flies lay their eggs on the shoulders and their larvae hatch and tunnel down into the root. While this does not make the carrots inedible, it does curtail their attractiveness. If possible, avoid thinning on warm days when the scents are easily carried. Instead thin on wet days, as water suppresses the sweet aroma. Row covers are also good preventative measures. Deer and rabbits like to munch on carrots and their tops, so fencing goes a long way to keeping them out.

Celery and Celeriac (*Apium graveolens*)

Family: Apiaceae
Plant Type: Biennial grown as annual, zones 5–10
Light: Full sun, tolerates light shade
Soil: Rich, well-drained
Height x Width: 16" x 8–12"
pH: 5.8–5.8
Sow: ⅛" deep, started indoors 10 weeks before last frost
Succession: n/a
Days to germination: 10
Days to maturity: 120–180 from seed to harvest
Water: Consistent and abundant
Feed: High NPK
Friends: Brassicas, leek, lettuce, onion, spinach, and tomato
Foes: Carrot, cucumber, parsnip, potato, pumpkin, and squash

Different varieties of the same plant, celery (*A. graveolens* var. *dulce*) and celeriac (*A. graveolens* var. *rapaceum*) are both members of the parsley family, are slow growing, and have the same cultivation needs. The distinction comes in the part eaten: celery is grown for its crisp, fresh stems and leaves, while celeriac, or celery root, for its knobby root. Celery stalks have a more fibrous, string-like texture, while celeriac is smoother and usually finely grated into salads and soups. Also, celeriac is not as discriminating as celery when it comes to soil fertility and water.

Rich, loose soil, amply amended with compost, full sun, and consistent, copious amounts of water are all celery and celeriac need to thrive. In the past these veggies got a bad rap as being difficult due to their growing requirements and blanching. Most of today's cultivars like 'Tango' are self-blanching, making growing these tasty treats even easier.

Because celery is a decidedly long-season crop, you need to start your seeds ten to twelve weeks early under lights. Years ago someone recommended that I soak my seed overnight to aid in germination. It seems to help, so I've done it every year since. Press seeds into the soil for good contact between the seed and the moist soil, and barely cover with fine sand or vermiculite. They need light to germinate. Then cover with a clear plastic dome, plastic bag, or plastic wrap to maintain humidity until emergence. Germination can be erratic, so the secret to successful germination is moisture and warmth. The seeds germinate better at warmer temperatures (70°F) and grow on at slightly cooler temperatures of 60–65°F, so use bottom heat to get your seeds started, removing the mat and plastic cover once they are sprouted. If using flats or propagation trays, you will need to transplant to larger pots when seedlings are one-half inch tall, but if you start your seeds in soil blocks, you won't have to transplant until they're ready to go into the garden. Thin to a single seedling per cell and keep moist. As a cool-season crop, your celery or celeriac needs to be hardened off for seven to ten days by restricting its water—not lowering temperatures.

Raised beds are ideal, since you can control your soil composition entirely and they warm a bit sooner than the ground. Plant celery and celeriac out in the garden six to eight inches apart when night temperatures

For best quality, water celery well the day before harvesting.

stay above 55°F. If they're exposed to ten or more days of cold night temperatures (55°F), they will bolt prematurely. Since celery and celeriac are biennial, the cold weather signals winter and they start to set seed. If you're concerned about frosts sneaking up on you, use a mulch and/or a row cover for protection or warm the soil with black plastic before planting. (A simple row cover will keep them warm and frost-free in early spring.) Be careful not to plant celeriac too deep, otherwise it will not develop its knobby bulb. Typically these crops are not successively sown. If you regularly harvest from the outside in, your plants will continue to produce stalks into the fall, but production will slow down and quality will decline. To ensure a high-quality crop, start a second wave of seeds when planting the first. Late summer and into the fall you will be rewarded with new, crunchy stalks. Water-in newly planted seedlings and gently fertilize with seaweed and

For a larger, smoother bulb remove celeriac's outer leaves mid-season.

fish emulsion at planting to give your seedlings a good start. Your second crop will be developing in the heat of the summer, so you may find you need to water and fertilize more than the first to keep them succulent.

The trick to growing celery and celeriac successfully is to provide food and moisture throughout to encourage crops to grow quickly. They can taste bitter if not given enough water. Mulching deeply once plants are four to five inches tall will help conserve moisture, keep the roots cool, and suppress weeds. Aside from the initial compost application, side dress with compost mid-season to keep the soil fertile and rich in organic matter. Celery and celery root are greedy feeders, so fertilize them every two to three weeks with fish emulsion and seaweed. Keep weeded—their shallow root systems don't like to share their water or nutrients. Since celery and celeriac are such slow crops, I sow leaf lettuce between. Interplanting with quick salad greens stops the bare soil from becoming weed city until the celery or celeriac develops more and makes the most of this valuable real estate in the garden.

Harvest is when you begin to see some differences between celery and celeriac. Celery can be harvested once it's large enough and has been in the garden for about five to six weeks. Since celery is one of my faves, I'll harvest the outer stalks throughout the season, leaving the heart to keep growing and producing into the fall. As you head into the winter, you can either harvest each plant by cutting the base at or below the soil line with a knife or mulching heavily to harvest later. For the highest-quality harvest, water the day before and store at 32°F or freeze.

Celeriac should not be harvested before one hundred days, or the bulb may not reach a satisfactory size. To promote larger, healthier roots and bulb development, remove and compost all outer leaves that have begun to flop over mid-season. Cutting away these stems and leaves results in a smoother bulb. This is a good time to hill with a side dressing of compost and mulch to keep plants tender and blanched. When you're ready to fully harvest celery root, dig and trim the foliage down to one inch. Rinse, carefully dry, and store at 32°F like regular celery.

Flavors of both celery and celeriac improve with a couple light frosts; however a hard frost can kill unprotected plants. Celery mulched with a foot or more of hay and held in place with row covers or netting can survive down to 20°F with little loss for late fall and winter harvests. Celeriac

BLANCHING

There are still some varieties that need blanching. In this case simply mound up the soil at the base to "bleach" the stem. Blanching induces tender stalks and a milder flavor.

Celery seedlings just getting started. Water well and you can begin harvesting outer stalks when they reach six inches tall.

on the other hand will keep exceedingly well at 32°F in high humidity from harvest until the next spring.

As members of the parsley family, celery and celeriac are most often plagued by aphids, carrot rust flies, leafhoppers, parsley or celery worms, and slugs. Handpicking is effective, and row covers offer good protection against these troublemakers. Cracked stems and distorted leaves are signs of a boron deficiency, easily remedied with a regular application of seaweed feed. Common diseases such as blight and celery mosaic, a virus transmitted via aphids, are best managed with good rotation plans.

Garlic (*Allium sativum*)

Family: Alliaceae
Plant Type: Perennial grown as an annual, zones 5–10
Light: Full sun
Soil: Fertile, well-drained
Height x Width: 12–24" x 6–8"
pH: 4.5–8.3
Sow: Plant cloves 2–4" deep, spaced 4–8" apart
Succession: n/a
Days to germination: 7–14, but not recommended
Days to maturity: 8 months from fall planting
Water: Low
Feed: Moderate
Friends: Beets, brassicas, celery, lettuce, tomatoes, strawberries, and fruit trees
Foes: All legumes

The flavor of homegrown garlic is incomparable to grocery store garlic—there is no contest. Whenever I see fresh garlic, I scoop it up for the kitchen and my tummy. I can never have enough. One of the best things about growing garlic is how easy and self-sufficient it is to grow. Almost no maintenance is required beyond the initial planting, and after about eight months you're blessed with a delicious harvest.

There are two subspecies of garlic: softneck (*A. sativum sativum*) and hardneck (*A. sativum ophioscorodon*). Most of the garlic you see in the supermarket is softneck because it's easy to plant and harvest mechanically. They have more cloves per head (twelve to sixteen), but are smaller. Adaptable to most climates, softnecks grow especially well in the South and on the West Coast, where the summer is warmer and winters temperate. If you see braided strands of garlic, you are looking at softnecks, as they have no central stem.

They keep well and have a shelf life of up to a year! They are further divided into silverskin and artichoke varieties. Silverskin has a stronger flavor and stores extremely well, whereas artichoke is milder with fewer, slightly larger cloves.

Requiring a dormant period of frigid temperatures to flower and bulb-up, hardneck garlic is ideal for northern and midwestern climates with cold winters and cool, wet springs. Offering a myriad of intriguing, delicious flavors ranging from subtle to fuller and more robust, hardneck garlic is characterized by a central stem that develops into a scape, or immature flower bud. Once the scape turns and loops on itself in early summer, cut it off right above the top leaf to encourage vigorous bulb development. Tasting of mild garlic,

Scapes taste amazing in salads or when blended into a garlic pesto!

Curing garlic.

the scape is great tossed in salads or as a pesto. Generally there are fewer cloves (four to ten), but they are substantially larger and easier to peel. Besides the extra work of harvesting scapes in mid to late June, the only disadvantage is they don't store as long as softnecks, only about six to eight months. Hardneck garlic is classified into three main varieties—Rocambole, Purple Stripe (including Marbled Purple Stripe and Glazed Purple Stripe), and Porcelain. Full-flavored and sweet, Rocambole flourishes after tough winters but dislikes overwatering. With beautiful, brightly covered skins, Purple Stripes taste incredible cooked. Porcelains, noted for strong, spicy flavor, are the classic white-skinned garlic with few cloves and perform well in cold climates. Creole, Asiatic, and Turban are known as weakly bolting hardneck varieties that don't always develop scapes, and if they do, they're less woody. Pretty and packing quite a punch, Creole tastes warm. Asiatics are large, firm, and quick growing, while Turbans are the most productive. All have a very short shelf life.

Elephant garlic is easy to mistake for Porcelain, but is in fact more closely related to leeks than garlic. These enormous heads contain several big, mild cloves and are less hardy.

Garlic enjoys rich, well-drained soil in a sunny spot, so incorporate plenty of organic matter and compost. Softnecks can be planted first thing in spring for a late summer harvest or in the fall for harvest next season in warmer climates. As a northern gardener I can only plant hardnecks, which go into the ground about one month before the ground freezes. Garlic needs a chance to root before it goes dormant in winter. Purchase your garlic bulbs through a catalog, garden center, or local farmers market—not the

REPLANT WITH THE BIGGEST BULBS NEXT SEASON.

supermarket. Many times grocery store garlic is irradiated or treated with sprout inhibitors. Break the heads apart to separate the cloves. Either trench or use a bulb planter to set your cloves two inches deep pointy end up, five to six inches apart in mounded or raised beds. Immediately mulch deeply (four to six inches) to insulate and protect against winter's soil heaves. Then forget about your garlic till the next growing season. Indian summers may bring about early emergence, but don't worry, your garlic will keep till the spring. Garlic can be started from the bulbils, immature bulbs in the scape, but they take a minimum of three years before they'll be able to produce any heads.

Overall I haven't found a need to fertilize my garlic, but you can hit the bed with fish emulsion first thing in the spring once their green shoots peek through the mulch, and again one month later. Mulch will help keep your garlic bed well weeded, and your heads will be larger if they do not need to compete against weeds for space and resources. Unlike with most vegetables, I let Mother Nature handle the watering unless it's been dry for over a week. Hardnecks need little care aside from the midsummer scape harvest to prevent the coiling scapes from stealing energy from the developing bulbs, and softnecks need even less. If you are supplementing one inch of water per week, lay off once bulbs start developing, stopping completely a month before harvest time. You want to give them plenty of time to dry and develop a protective papery skin.

Harvest when you see the bottom three leaves turn brown. Sometimes you can simply pull the garlic out, but to avoid any damage, use a fork to lift mature garlic. Gently brush off clinging soil—do not wash—and cure in a dry spot for two to three weeks out of direct sunlight with good air circulation. Cure your garlic on mesh, wire tables, or benches covered in newspaper in the your basement or garage. Softnecks can be braided together and hung to dry in bunches. Trim the roots and cut the stem down to one-half to one inch and store in a cool, dry site once they are finished curing. I keep mine tossed in wicker baskets in the basement at 55°F but mesh or paper bags work just as well.

While most gardeners experience few pest and disease issues, leaf miner, nemotodes, mites, and thrips are potential problems for garlic. Beneficial lacewings and predatory mites are good controls for these goons. Part of the allium family, garlic is most commonly affected by white rot. Leaf yellowing and dieback are signs your plants are infected. Although you might not see it, while the tops are wilting your roots are rotting. Crop rotation, fresh cloves, and good garden cleanup are key to preventing this fungal disease and many pests, but immediately pull any plants that appear infected.

WHEN IS MY GARLIC READY?

Check the leaves of your plants regularly. Once you see the bottom three have turned brown and died back, your garlic is ready to be harvested. Loosen with a fork and pull. Save yourself some money and save the biggest bulbs to replant for next season's harvest. Starting with larger cloves yields more sizable heads. In a few years you'll have plenty of your own seed garlic.

Leek (*Allium porrum*)

Family: Alliaceae

Plant Type: Biennial grown as annual, zones 3–10

Light: Full sun, tolerates part shade

Soil: Fertile, well-drained

Height x Width: 18–24″ x 6–10″

pH: 6.0–6.8

Sow: ¼″ deep, 8–10 weeks before last frost

Succession: n/a

Days to germination: 8–16

Days to maturity: 120–170

Water: Regular

Feed: Heavy

Friends: Beets, carrots, celeriac, celery, garlic, onions, parsley, and tomatoes

Foes: Legumes

Well-blanched leeks. Be sure to wash carefully before using—there is always a little dirt between the leaves.

Remarkably hardy, leeks are cold-weather vegetables that appreciate sun, regular moisture, and loose, nitrogen-rich soil. Leeks are great for those who enjoy onions but don't want to be overpowered by the flavor. Their bundled stems are edible, and between summer and winter harvest—also referred to as short and long season—you should have plenty to keep your kitchen stocked most of the year. Unfortunately, as tasty as leeks are, they don't do very well in containers. Both summer and winter leeks are planted at the same time, just after your last frost, but mature at different times. Quick-growing summer leeks are typically more sensitive to the cold, taller, thinner, and ready to harvest in just under three months. Winter leeks, on the other hand, take longer to bulk up and can be harvested all winter long providing they are adequately protected.

Like most in the allium family, leeks are slow growers, so start them eight to ten weeks early, or more, under lights. The bigger they are when planted out, the more sizable they

Plant your leeks low in a raised bed, and as they grow, add more soil to blanch the lower stems.

will be at harvest. Keep seedlings trimmed to three to four inches tall until ready to harden off, and transplant in the spring after your first frost. Raised beds are perfect for growing leeks when they're deep filled with loose, high-quality loam and compost. Plant out six to eight inches deep, six inches apart in the garden. Although it's possible, I've found direct seeding in spring a waste of time in Maine's cooler climate. Leeks are one of those vegetables that need to be blanched. Periodically throughout the season mound the soil around the base of the stems to block out the light to keep the leaves white and sweet. I like to plant mine deep such that only about an inch is above the soil line to reduce the amount of hilling. You can also plant in furrows or trenches, mounding up as they grow.

Leeks are greedy and enjoy plenty of water and nitrogen. Keep them uniform and mild with a good drink twice a week. Fish emulsion is my go-to feed, which I alternate with a side dressing of compost when blanching to keep these crops booming. You don't need to mulch until it begins to get colder, but I am a compulsive mulcher. A couple inches of straw or seaweed mulch throughout the season help retain soil moisture in the heat of the summer and keep the roots cool, and make a good defense against weeds. Leeks don't like weeds, so if you don't plan to mulch until later in the season, interplant with some quick greens like arugula or baby spinach.

You can start harvesting anytime your leeks are firm and substantial. I begin enjoying a few leeks every week in late summer through fall, leaving my winter leeks to overwinter in the ground. Before digging, loosen with a fork. Leeks are best used within a few weeks, even if refrigerated, so I dig my leeks on an as-needed basis. Wash right before use, because as leeks grow, dirt gets between the leaf sheaths. Like carrots, mulch your crop heavily (twelve inches), and secure with a row cover to hold the protection in place. The ground underneath won't freeze solid, allowing you to harvest fresh leeks throughout the winter.

Amazingly leeks suffer very little from pests. There are no disease issues, and thrips and root maggots only pose minor problems. A simple stream of water knocks off thrips, and a basic crop rotation strategy should keep root maggots away.

Onions and Shallots (*Allium cepa* & *A. cepa* 'Aggregatum')

Family: Alliaceae
Plant Type: Biennial, grown as annual, zone 3–11
Light: Full sun
Soil: Well-drained, rich
Height x Width: 24–36" x 6–8"
pH: 6.0–6.8
Sow: Seed ¼–½" deep, sets 1" deep
Succession: Staggered maturity
Days to germination: 4–12
Days to maturity: 80–120 from seed, 30–40 from sets
Water: Regular and consistent
Feed: Moderate
Friends: Beets, brassicas, carrots, lettuce, parsnips, peppers, spinach, strawberries, and tomatoes
Foes: Asparagus and legumes

These onions do not need any extra fertilizer. Feed only if you see yellowing of the leaves.

You wouldn't expect it, but I love growing onions. They are a small investment for such a big yield. They take almost no effort to grow and store well through the winter. Sweet onions are best enjoyed fresh, while the more pungent-tasting varieties store better and are savory in cooked dishes. The hardest part is deciding what type and how you want to grow them: seeds versus sets. Seeds need to be started super early for onions to bulb-up in time, but sets (immature bulbs) are simply popped in the ground and start growing. Tinier bulbs, one-half inch in diameter or smaller, produce healthier plants than larger bulbs and are less likely to bolt. While sets are easier to grow, there just aren't as many varieties available as with seeds. Onions started from seed not only store better, they are less likely to be infected with a disease. Buying transplants is a good workaround if you want the benefits of seed-grown onions without the time investment.

Day-length is the determining factor for which onions you can grow in your region. Onions are sensitive to the amount of light they are exposed to, and when they hit a specific threshold, it triggers the plant to stop putting out new foliage, sending all their energy into bulb formation. Short-day onions require ten to twelve hours of sunlight before they begin to bulb-up. They are good for southern gardeners who don't see much variation in light through the fall and winter seasons. If I were to grow these onions up in Maine, they would start bulbing too early in the season. Consequently, long-day onions are not prompted to bulb-up until they experience fourteen or more hours of daylight common in northern regions. If long-day onions were grown in the South, there would be lots of lush, green foliage, but when you pulled your onions at the end of the season, there would be very small bulbs since there were never long enough days to spark bulb development. Intermediate bulbs, also called day-neutral onions, will grow in most gardens and need twelve to fourteen hours of sunlight.

Milder tasting, green onions don't fall into either of those categories. Also referred to as scallions or bunching onions, they are explicitly bred to harvest while still immature. You can eat the young, undeveloped white bulb, as well as the green top-growth. Unlike regular onions

Onions are ready to be harvested when the tops bend and fall over.

they can be grown in all gardens regardless of day length.

Multiplier onions are just what you think they are—onions with more than one bulb per plant (similar looking to garlic). An old-fashioned plant with milder taste, they are also called potato onions. Give them a little more space, but other than that, they are grown the same as all other bulbs.

While waiting to plant out, strengthen seedlings with half-strength fish emulsion applications and trim the tops back to one inch whenever they reach four to five inches tall. Onions need a fair amount of potassium or their neck won't thicken, reducing their storage life. Prep the bed with compost before planting sets or seedlings. Sets should be planted one and one-half to two inches deep, pointy end up, and seedlings transplanted four to six inches apart in spring as soon as the soil can be worked in April (or two to three weeks before last frost). I water-in with weakened fish emulsion, repeating every two to three weeks. Onions don't like soggy conditions, which dilute their pungent flavors. Moisture fluctuations or an overabundance of nitrogen results in too many leaves and smaller bulbs. Mulch can help your onions maintain even soil moisture and suppress weeds that compete for resources, but avoid overdoing the water and fertilizer. An additional side dressing of compost is helpful as the plants bulb-up.

Onions are wonderful container crops. Give them a deep enough pot (ten to twelve inches) and treat them just as you would those in the garden, maybe just paying a little more attention to water and fertilizer.

Ease up on the water a few weeks before you're ready to harvest to improve the flavor and storage quality. When the green tops fall over, you know that your onions are ready to be harvested. Either pull your onions as they mature or wait until one-third to one-half the foliage has toppled and harvest the entire bed. Personally I find onion harvesting very fulfilling, gently tugging the onion out of the ground and brushing the dirt away. Then they need to cure for two to four weeks in a breezy, warm spot, otherwise they won't store well. Some gardeners will cheat by bending the tops, halting leaf development, which

SHALLOTS

Shallots are used similarly to onions, follow garlic in growth patterns, and are daylight sensitive to long days. Hardy and more tolerant of average conditions, these alliums have a subtle, or delicate, mild onion flavor. They are available in sets or seed—sets grow significantly faster. Separate the cloves just as you would garlic, and plant six inches apart such that the point is visible above the soil line. In temperate regions with mild winters, you plant from fall through winter, and in cold climates plant two to four weeks before your anticipated frost date and mulch. Like multiplier onions they produce multiple shallots per bulb, and similar to garlic they are ready to harvest when the lower leaves turn brown and die back.

encourages onions to bulb-up faster. This technique, called "lodging," forces the bulb to mature within a couple weeks once the foliage is creased. Once cured, trim the roots and cut off the leaves to one inch to store. Thick-necked onions have a reduced shelf life and should be eaten first. Onion bags, wooden crates, and wicker baskets are great storage options. Refrain from storing onions near apples or tomatoes. They release an ethylene gas that induces onions to sprout, which you don't want.

The onion's pungent scent repels most pests, but a few to keep an eye out for are onion maggots, small worms that tunnel into your onion bulbs, and thrips. Crop rotation, row covers, and resistant varieties are helpful in avoiding these insects as well as any disease. Soggy soil and lack of drainage are responsible for most disease problems, so make sure to include plenty of compost, organic matter, and sand if needed.

Parsnip (*Pastinaca sativa*)

Family: Apiaceae
Plant Type: Biennial, grown as an annual, zones 3–10
Light: Full sun to part shade
Soil: Loose, slightly sandy
Height x Width: 12–18" x 10–15"
pH: 6.0–6.8
Sow: ¼–½" deep
Succession: n/a
Days to germination: 5–28
Days to maturity: 95–120
Water: Moderate
Feed: Moderate
Friends: Beets, carrots, garlic, legumes, onions, peppers, potatoes, radishes, and other root vegetables
Foes: Brassicas and tomatoes

It would be easy to overlook parsnips, which can easily be mistaken for white carrots. But these hardy roots are oh-so-sweet and easy to grow. I don't know why they're not a staple in every garden. Frosts enhance their flavor, so be lazy and leave them in the ground well into the fall for super sweet, nutty parsnips. In recipes calling for carrots, turnips, or even sweet potatoes, substitute parsnips. You won't be sorry!

Sow two to three weeks before your last frost and again before your first fall frost if growing in a tunnel or cold frame. As with most deep-rooted vegetables, parsnips don't like

Parsnips taste better after their first frost. Here's a freshly harvested batch with some pelargoniums as garnish.

to be transplanted and instead should be planted directly in the ground one inch apart. Thin to three to four inches apart with snips (to avoid root disturbance) when four to six inches tall and mulch. Moist soil is the key to good germination. You can speed it up even more by soaking seeds overnight. Parsnips grow better in deep soil, free of rocks and clumps.

Usually I avoid stirring my dirt too much because I don't want to destroy my soil structure, but loosening with a fork one to two feet deep creates ideal growing conditions. Raised beds are a good option, allowing you to completely control the soil in the box and harvest nice, straight roots. You can also grow parsnips in deep containers on your deck or patio if you don't have an overabundance of space.

INTERPLANT PARSNIPS WITH LETTUCE AND RADISH SEED.

Mix parsnip with lettuce or radish seed and interplant. Baby greens are a good living mulch, but radishes help prevent soil crusting. Related to carrots, parsnips share many of the same qualities, including that their seedlings are weak and thus have trouble breaking through the surface. Radishes emerge long before your parsnips have even germinated, breaking up and loosening the soil, creating a more hospitable environment for parsnips to grow once harvested.

Consider parsnips a winter treat. Try to wait until you've had a few frosts before you harvest. You'll be rewarded with sweet and tender parsnips! You can harvest the entire lot and store in your root cellar (if you have one) or your fridge, but its easier—and tastier—to leave these roots in the ground until you need them. As with carrots, mulch heavily with twelve inches of straw before the ground freezes and secure with a length of chicken wire or row covers, and you will be able to go out and dig parsnips whenever you need them. You'll notice I used the word "dig," not "pull." That was intentional. Parsnips have a tendency to break when pulled (which you will quickly learn if you attempt it), so loosen with a shovel and fork to harvest. You should be able to enjoy the nutty sweetness of parsnips throughout the entire winter season.

While harvesting, you may notice some "fancy," forked and hairy parsnips. This is due to too much nitrogen, clumpy soil, or rocks, so be careful when amending in the spring. I use a light layer of compost in spring and avoid all nitrogen-rich manure. Carrot rust flies can be a problem, tunneling into the roots. Insect barriers or a lightweight row cover used at time of planting will exclude these pests from laying eggs. If you notice any black growths on your crop, it might be parsnip canker, a fungal disease. Remove and destroy immediately. Don't forget to disinfect any tools as well—you don't want to transfer the infection to other plants in the garden.

Radish (*Raphanus sativus*)

Family: Brassicaceae

Plant Type: Biennial, grown as annual, all zones

Light: Full sun, tolerates part shade

Soil: Well-drained, average moisture-retentive

Height x Width: 6–8" x 6"

pH: 5.5–6.5

Sow: ½" deep

Succession: Every 14–21 days

Days to germination: 4–10

Days to maturity: 21–35 (for spring, and 50–60 for winter)

Water: Moderate and even

Feed: Moderate

Friends: Beets, carrots, cucumbers, legumes, lettuce, peppers, and spinach

Foes: Fennel

Radishes are the ideal catch or intercrop. They break up the soil and are sown and harvested within one month!

The quintessential catch and intercrop, radishes are rapid growers that can adapt to most garden spaces. Perfect for young and amateur gardeners, this easy, cool-season spring crop is sown, grown, and harvested in a month. From its peppery root flavor to zesty greens, the entire thing is edible! I sow these "early types" all season long, planting in containers and under trellised beans, peas, and cucumbers to shade from high summer temperatures. Spring radishes are best enjoyed small, at one inch in diameter. There are also winter radishes, known as daikons, that need a bit more time to mature, usually two to three months. Larger than spring types, they can be overwintered in the garden with protection. Both spring and winter radishes are available in a wide array of colors, sizes, and shapes, with flavor ranging from mild to blazing hot!

Radishes are best sown in situ—do not start early under lights. Begin planting as soon as the soil can be worked, typically about six to eight weeks under protection and three to six weeks before your last frost in the open garden. You can use a row cover to warm the soil and speed germination in early spring. Sow in a sunny spot with average soil and water-

SPRING RADISHES ARE BEST ENJOYED SMALL.

Sow radishes in a row or broadcast.

in with a fish emulsion and seaweed feed for a good head start. They will germinate in just a couple days. Keep moist and thin spring and summer seedlings to two inches apart, and winter to five inches apart. I can almost guarantee that you will need to thin. Proper space is mandatory for optimal growth. An alternative to thinning is to mix your seed with slower-growing carrot or parsnip and sow together. This mix will sow more evenly, but I find there is still a small amount of thinning to be done. Because radishes are so easy and quick, sow every two to three weeks for a constant supply, or more frequently if you run out.

You can amend your beds with some compost, but don't overdo it. Too much nitrogen results in lots of top growth and hampers what's growing underground. Avoid manure completely. Most times I don't do anything special for my radishes, just popping them in wherever I have open space. Radishes like to be kept evenly moist, mulch helps. Too much water and they'll taste mild and crack, too little and they'll bolt, tasting hot and pungent.

In the heat of the summer radishes quickly go to seed, tasting hot and developing hollow or unappetizing woody centers. Combat this by selecting heat-resistant varieties like 'D'Avignon' or 'French Breakfast', or plant under the shade of other vining crops to keep cool.

Daikons, or winter radishes, can be planted in the spring or late summer for summer and fall harvests respectively. I usually sow late summer, six to ten weeks before my first anticipated frost. Like carrots, parsnips, and many other root crops, daikons can be left in the ground and sweeten when exposed to cold temperatures and frosts. Grow in a cold frame or protect the bed under a blanket of heavy mulch (twelve inches) and row cover. Harvest on an as-needed basis throughout the winter. And while I tend to stay away from any fertilization for spring radishes, unless in an interplanting situation, winter radishes benefit from a compost application and liquid feed during the season.

Spring radishes are tender and have a crispy, peppery taste when harvested young. Ideally they should be one to two inches wide when pulled from the garden. Enjoy this root vegetable right away, as they generally don't store well. Topping, or cutting off the top growth, can increase storage time to three or four weeks. Winter radishes, on the other hand, store very well, but as I mentioned earlier—storing them in the ground until you need them is the best way to keep them fresh.

Aphids, flea beetles, and root maggots are complications for radishes. Insecticidal soap and row covers are good controls, but often radishes are in and out before infestations or potential disease upset the plants. More problematic is stress, which causes stunted root development, cracking, or hot flavors. High summer temperatures, too much or too little water, lazy thinning, or weed competition result in the plant feeling pressure and acting out by producing unappetizing radishes.

Turnip and Rutabaga (*Brassica rapa* 'Rapa' & *B. napus* var. *napobrassica*)

Family: Brassicaceae

Plant Type: Biennial, grown as an annual, all zones

Light: Full sun, tolerates part shade

Soil: Well-drained, loam

Height x Width: 10–15" x 6–8"

pH: 5.5–6.8

Sow: ½" deep

Succession: Every 2 weeks

Days to germination: 3–10

Days to maturity: 30–50

Water: Regular

Feed: Low

Friends: Legumes, cucumbers, peppers, tomatoes, and squash

Foes: Potato

Like most cool-season crops, rutabagas taste better after a light frost.

I used to get confused by all the root vegetables until I started growing—and tasting—them in the garden. Nutty tasting and sort of like a raw radish and potato when cooked, turnips are one of the unsung cool-season veggies. Smaller is better when growing and looking for tender turnips at market. Enormous turnips may look succulent, but don't be fooled, they will be woody and tough. Once you eat one fresh like an apple or try them mashed up as you would a potato, you will be sold on why you must save space for this crop in your kitchen garden.

Turnips are often mistaken for rutabagas, even called yellow turnips in the store or at market. Both from the same family, they look and taste similar. Although rutabagas, a cross between a turnip and cabbage, are sweeter and their fleshy roots larger than turnips, they are often confused.

Avoid transplanting like most root vegetables and sow directly into fertile, well-drained soil. A relatively quick crop, maturing in thirty to fifty days, it can be planted every two weeks starting as soon as the soil can be worked for a steady supply of these roots. Space one to two inches apart, thinning turnips to two to four inches and rutabagas six to eight inches for root growth, tossing the baby greens into tonight's salad. Keep the bed consistently moist to grow a high-quality crop quickly. Let the rain take care of the watering unless you've had a stretch of five or more dry days, then give them about an inch of water. Don't worry about fertilizing, they rarely need any supplemental nutrients as long as they have decent soil. Turnips and rutabagas grow well in containers. If growing just for leaves you can choose a shallower pot, otherwise you will need a deeper pot to accommodate the roots.

Warm weather turns turnips and rutabagas woody, so plant successions in the shade of larger or trellised vegetables. Cooler temperatures and light frosts will sweeten these crops. Hard frosts can damage plants, so make sure to apply a heavy layer of straw mulch and protect under a row cover to handle severe weather.

Like most roots, turnips and rutabagas taste best young—whether harvesting greens or roots. Harvest turnips when no larger than a tennis ball—if they get too large they become unpalatable. Remove the soil from their shoulders to check if they're ready to be pulled, about thirty to forty days. Store in the refrigerator for seven to ten days or harvest as needed from a protected bed throughout the winter. Greens are enjoyed best young. Be careful not to gather too many, otherwise root growth will slow or stop. Rutabagas take 90 to 120 days to mature and taste better after a frost. It's easiest to leave them in the ground mulched and protected, digging roots when needed.

Cabbage root maggots, aphids, and flea beetles attack, but row covers, crop rotation, and cultural controls should manage them effectively. Diseases are seldom an issue, as most cultivars are resistant. Sometimes black heart, soft and watery centers, can be trouble. Only a soil test will show if you have a boron deficiency. It's easy to over-apply boron, so get a soil test, read the directions carefully, and apply only what is needed. Preferring to prevent it in the first place, I regularly employ a liquid kelp fertilizer or mulch with seaweed. Both contain a fair amount of boron.

TURNIPS ARE SMALLER THAN RUTABAGAS.

'Purple top white globe' turnips are purple above and white below the soil line with a zesty, mustard-like taste.

Sweet Potato (*Ipomea batatas*)

Family: Convolvulaceae

Plant Type: Perennial, grown as an annual, zones 6–12

Light: Full sun

Soil: Fertile, well-drained

Height x Width: 10–12″ x 4–8′

pH: 5.0–6.5

Sow: 2–3″ deep

Succession: n/a

Days to germination: n/a

Days to maturity: 150–175

Water: Low

Feed: Low

Friends: Marigolds

Foes: All root crops

Hot, hot, hot, and I'm not talking about taste. No joke, sweet potatoes like it hot! Not related to potatoes or yams, they are members of the morning glory family, which makes sense when you see their heart-shaped leaves. A perk when growing these tubers is that their foliage looks like a sumptuous ground cover. Traditionally a southern long-season, heat-loving crop, they are a little trickier to grow in cooler climates. Short-season cultivars are better choices for northern or midwestern gardeners.

Grow from certified, disease-free slips. Slips are small, rooted shoots, and the key to success is four long months of warmth and sun. Once planted the tubers require little work. Sweet potatoes do not like heavy soil. When dug up, they will appear

Remember to harvest sweet potatoes before it gets too cold. As a warm-weather crop they will only withstand one light frost.

spindly and distorted. Amend your bed with compost. Pick the hottest spot in the garden and wait until the soil has warmed to 65–70°F for two weeks before planting. Raised beds are good for cold-weather gardeners, heating up well before the ground does. Clear solar mulch, formerly termed IRT, suppresses weeds, but is used primarily for maximizing soil warming. If using the solar mulch, use a sharp tool to cut an X and plant directly through the plastic. Black plastic is useful too, but the clear is better. Plant your slip vines twelve inches apart, eighteen inches if you want larger sweet potatoes. You can also "ridge"

Sweet potatoes belong to the morning glory family—not the nightshades—which you can see by their characteristic heart-shaped leaves.

your slips. Planting in long raised hills is helpful for tuber formation and harvest. Floating row covers can be used after planting, they maintain a nice warm temperature throughout the day, and protect these tender tubers at night. Nitrogen fertilizers should be avoided, or you will have an abundance of gorgeous, heart-shaped leaves and small potatoes. Instead incorporate a small handful of a complete 10-10-10 fertilizer before you plant. Later in the season you can apply wood ash for some additional potassium, but avoid all other feeds.

Water-in slips well, and once they are established, let Mother Nature do the rest. The tubers are fairly drought tolerant, so let them dry out between watering. Irrigate in extreme cases only.

Sweet potatoes don't like weed competition, but as the vines begin running, they'll suppress any weeds that aren't already subdued by using mulch. Stop all watering several weeks before harvest for skins to toughen up and prevent rot.

Let your tubers stay in the ground as long as possible. The longer they grow, the sweeter they become. You can investigate your sweet potatoes after three months to see whether they are at a useable size. They will stop growing once the weather cools, and leaf yellowing is an indication that they are ready for harvest. Cold-climate gardeners will have their season curtailed with the arrival of the first frost. Sweet potatoes are frost sensitive and damaged by cold weather. Once your first frost blackens the runners, you need to harvest—the tubers will not withstand more freezing or cold soils. A good rule of thumb is to harvest once the temperature dips below 50°F. It's better to dig before frost if possible. Cut back the foliage, loosening the soil with a fork or shovel, being careful not to spear any valuable tubers, and dig up.

Don't try eating your sweet potatoes immediately unless you want to be disappointed—their flavor deepens as they cure. Prevent mildew by curing in the sun for a day, then brush off any remaining dirt and let them sit in a warm, humid spot for another ten to fourteen days before storing. Sweet potatoes need this time to convert the starches into sugars. I wrap mine in newspaper and store in a wooden box covered with burlap to maintain humidity, to be eaten throughout the winter (six months).

Rotating crops every three to four years will reduce your chance of disease and nematode, weevil, or wireworm problems. Resistant varieties and poor drainage usually account for any other disease issues—another reason some gardeners plant their sweet potatoes in ridges. Deer are by far the biggest thieves in the garden. They will come in and defoliate your leaves and shoots to a point where they can no longer photosynthesize and your tubers stop growing. Fence them out. As a bonus, it keeps all other snacking critters out as well.

Most salad greens have shallow root systems, making them ideal candidates for raised beds and containers.

LEAF CROPS

"Lettuce" get real here—you cannot compare the flavor of homegrown crisp, succulent greens to what's available in the supermarket. Whenever I find a barren spot in the garden I don't know what to do with yet, I toss a handful of leaf lettuce seed. They are the ideal catch or intercrop. Filling out open spaces, they keep weeds away and are harvested for your dinnertime salads before the spot is needed for another crop to grow or mature. Most greens are quick and thrive in cooler weather. Before the summer heat arrives, I sow my next crop underneath the shade of tall or vining vegetables. Lettuces like to be protected from the heat under the pole bean teepee or cucumbers crawling over the A-frame trellis where they are less likely to bolt. Start these nitrogen-loving plants indoors for an early spring crop and direct sow later successions for luscious greens all season long.

Arugula (*Eruca sativa*)

Family: Brassicaceae

Plant Type: Annual, zone 3–6

Light: Full sun, part shade in summer heat

Soil: Rich and moist

Height x Width: 12–24″ x 6–12″

pH: 6.0–7.0

Sow: ¼″ deep, thinning to 6″ apart

Succession: 2–3 weeks

Days to germination: 5–7

Days to maturity: 40–50

Water: Regular

Feed: Low

Friends: Just about everything

Foes: Pole beans and parsley

Wild rocket has deeply divided leaves.

Arugula is known as "rocket," or rucola, to many gardeners, because it rockets from seed to piquant, leafy greens in a month. Highly sought after by chefs for its distinctive leaves and peppery flavor, it is most tender and flavorful in cold weather. Arugula can be grown in a tunnel or cold frame for foliage all winter long and out in the garden from spring to fall. I still find it prolific during the hottest part of the summer if grown under the shade of some trellised crop.

Two types of arugula are available: the common arugula we're most familiar with, and wild, or Italian, arugula (*Diplotaxis tenuifolia*). Slower growing, wild rocket has a desirable nutty, spicier flavor and deeply divided foliage. Their yellow flowers taste good too. I actually prefer the more pungent wild arugula, it is perennial, more drought tolerant, and less likely to bolt. Both are excellent in containers with compost and loam, with the added perk of being mobile. You can move your pot to a shady spot when the weather warms up.

Start your first crop in late winter, again a month before your first frost, and then every two to three weeks until your first fall frost. Frost tolerant, your first and last crop should be grown under the protection of a polytunnel or cold frame. If concerned about freezing temperatures, add a floating row cover as a little extra insurance against the cold.

Direct sow in the garden as soon as the soil is workable and warmed to 40°F. Always amend with at least an inch of compost or well-rotted manure before planting.

Highly sought after by chefs for its distinctive leaves and peppery flavor, arugula is most tender and flavorful in cold weather.

Arugula germinates within a couple days in cooler temps and a bit slower in warmer ones. And although you can sow your seed three to four inches apart, I find it easier to broadcast and scratch-in with a fork or rake. Keep your seedbed moist. Fertilize young seedlings with fish emulsion to give them a little push. Once the seedlings reach three inches, thin to six inches apart. Eat your thinnings as a bonus salad crop.

Aside from the initial organic matter incorporation, don't overfertilize. Only dose your plants with fish emulsion if you find yellowing of the leaves. Keep weeded and water arugula regularly for succulent leaves. Don't follow your instinct to overwater. A surplus of water results in reduced sharpness of flavor. In the extreme heat of summer protect these greens with shade to prevent arugula from going to seed or the leaves from turning chewy. Overcrowding and water-stress will also produce less than delectable foliage. The only pests that seem to bother with arugula are flea beetles. You will know you have them if the leaves are filled with small pinholes. The best protection is a simple row cover.

Enjoy your arugula anytime from two- to three-inch thinnings, or as soon as it has produced an ample supply of leaves. Always harvest foliage as needed from the outside. Arugula grows inside out, from a rosette in which the young, inner leavers are mild and the outer more peppery. Although still edible once the warm weather hits, it bolts. After the heat arrives, the leaves grow tiny hairs and the plant sends up a flower shoot. If you're insistent on eating these tough greens, I suggest cooking them first. Flowers and seeds are a benefit of bolting arugula. Harvest some of the blooms to add a colorful, sharp bite to your salad and let the rest be (they are actually quite pretty for the kitchen garden). Collect the seed once it turns brown and dries, and you will have seed for your next crop.

Chicory and Endive (*Cichorium intybus* 'Foliosum' & *C. endivia*)

Family: Asteraceae

Plant Type: Perennial or biennial, grown as an annual, zones 4–10

Light: Full sun, light shade in summer heat

Soil: Fertile, well-drained

Height x Width: 24–48" x 6" and 8–12" x 3–4"

pH: 6.0–6.8

Sow: ¼" deep

Succession: 3–4 weeks

Days to germination: 10–14

Days to maturity: 115–120 and 90–95 days from seed

Water: Regular

Feed: Moderate

Friends: Leaf vegetables

Foes: Pumpkins and squash

Bitter leafed vegetables that are considered gourmet greens are often confused with each other. There are chicory, endive, Belgian endive, and radicchio to sort out. All part of the Asteraceae family, chicories includes the Belgian endive and radicchio. Belgian endives are tightly bound chicons with a blanched heart, whereas radicchio is an Italian, red-leafed, white-veined, lettuce-like head. Endives (different than the Belgian endive) are short, loose-leafed rosettes and further classified as frisée or escarole. Frisée has narrow, curled, frilly leaves, whereas escarole has wide, smooth leaves that taste milder. All are cold-weather crops that perform better in the spring, fall, and under protection in the winter.

Blanched endives are more tender, but non-blanched frisée endives can be treated as a cut-and-come-again salad green as long as the weather stays cool.

Before planting add a few inches of composted or aged manure to enrich the soil. Either start six to eight weeks early under lights or direct seed two to four inches before your last frost. Use row covers to shelter from frost and extreme cold. For mesclun mixes or baby crops, thin four to six inches or eight to ten inches for a full head.

Shade plants when temperatures rise above 85°F to prevent them from going to seed, as this results in an overly bitter taste and tough texture. Overcrowding and water-stress can also promote bolting. Water regularly for rich, plump leaves, mulch to keep the roots cool and soil moist, and position plants under A-frames and teepee-covered trellises to help shield from the heat. Feed every three to four weeks with fish emulsion and keep weed-free for happy chicories and endives. All do well when planted in containers, but the best-quality endives are grown quickly under cool, moist conditions.

Belgian endive (a chicory) seeds are sown in spring, and the heads left to mature until late fall, when they are cut back within an inch of the soil, leaving a stump. Dig up the entire root and replant tightly together and cover with soil. Alternatively if your winter season is too severe or you have clay soil, dig up and plant roots such that the shoulders are exposed in a pot, then cover with an inverted pot to block out the light. Keep moist and maintain a temperature of 50–64°F. In three to four weeks your roots will develop into chicons that can be harvested by cutting at soil level. Feed with fish emulsion, and in time your will see the tight bud of mild, waxy leaves and prominent veins develop above the soil. This process is called forcing, or outdoor blanching.

Forced chicons growing in a clay pot.

Radicchio does not rejuvenate after an initial cutting. Treat similar to lettuce—sow six to eight weeks early, plant in garden, and harvest in seventy-five to one hundred days. I prefer growing radicchio in early spring and in late summer for cool-weather harvests. The chilly temperatures enhance its purple and red variegation and mild flavor.

Endives grow from a rosette in the center, so collect outer leaves as needed once three to four inches.

Blanching the center rosettes creates the most tender and least bitter leaves. Just like cauliflower, tie or rubber band the outer leaves when it reaches twelve inches across. Or if you have enough space between endive plants, cover with a terracotta pot. The lack of sun and three to five days of cover turn the center growth to yellow-white. You can either harvest the entire head at ground level and succession sow every three to four weeks or treat endives as a cut-and-come-again crop. Cut back to one inch above the ground and feed with a fish emulsion and seaweed mix. In a couple weeks you should see the new endive resprout, unless blanched. Blanched plants are often exhausted and may not regrow. There are self-blanching varieties, but I've found they still benefit from some sun exclusion.

As with most cool-season crops, a light frost improves the flavor and texture of all chicories and endives. They store for about two weeks in the refrigerator.

Aphids, flea beetles, leafhoppers, slugs, and snails tend to be a problem for chicories and endives. Insecticidal soap or a strong stream of water handles the aphids, row covers bar beetles and leafhoppers access, and beer traps take care of slugs. Mildews and rots can be avoided with good air circulation and holding off on blanching if wet.

Lettuce (*Lactuca sativa*)

Family: Asteraceae
Plant Type: Annual, all zones
Light: Full sun, part shade in the summer heat
Soil: Fertile, well-drained
Height x Width: 4–12" x 6–12"
pH: 6.0–6.8
Sow: ¼–½" deep
Succession: 2–3 weeks
Days to germination: 2–10
Days to maturity: 40–55 for leaf lettuce, 75–90 for heading lettuce
Water: Regular
Feed: High
Friends: All vegetables
Foes: None

Grow a combination of lettuce colors and types (leaf, butterhead, and romaine) to ensure you have the perfect mix for homegrown salads.

Plant it everywhere and anywhere! Lettuce is the best friend of the garden. She can hang out with everyone, doesn't drain the soil, and doesn't overstay her welcome. Because it's a cool-season crop, I try to plant bolt-resistant varieties if I can, and lucky for me and the entire garden world, there are a seemingly endless choice of varieties, shapes, colors, and flavors.

Grow a collection of various types of lettuce, including butterhead (bibb), crisphead, leaf, and romaine. A favorite of most cold-climate gardeners, butter lettuce is known for its excellent cold tolerance, sweet, buttery taste, and tender leaves. Between their delicate flavor and soft foliage, they can't be beat. Crispheads include the grocery store staple iceberg lettuce and some of the Batavian types. Looseleaf is the perfect intercrop, filling in holes in the garden until needed. One of the easiest lettuce crops, leaf lettuce forms a loose rosette in just over a month. It also makes a vivid border and edgings along paths. Romaine looks more upright than round, with its conical head and crispy texture. Available in red, green, and speckled, it makes a striking addition to your salad. Occasionally you may see romaine lettuce described as Cos, because this type comes from the Mediterranean island of Cos. Mesclun mixes are a blend of different greens that are meant to be harvested young, usually a combination of brassicas, herbs, and spicy foliage.

All lettuces produce well in containers if provided with adequate moisture and nutrients. Baby greens grow just right in window boxes, and larger pots allow you to grow mature heads. Leaf lettuce makes a nice edge along large containers. Get creative—I personally love the look of lettuce grown with carrots in wooden wine crates. And as a bonus, they're portable. Once the weather heats up, pick them up and move them to a shadier location.

Given fertile soil, enriched with compost or aged manure, and regular moisture, your lettuce will thrive all season long! Amend your bed generously with compost to improve

Lettuce grows nicely in containers. Just make sure you drill a hole in the bottom for drainage.

your soil fertility and moisture retention. Whether transplanting seedlings or sowing in situ, ensure the soil is moist. When you rake or scratch-in seeds, there is good seed-to-wet-soil contact resulting in a higher germination rate. The key to sweet lettuce is rapid growth. The healthiest, tastiest, and prettiest heads are grown quickly. The healthier it is, the faster it matures and the yummier it tastes. You can sow under protective tunnels or in a cold frame six to eight weeks before your last frost or direct sow in the garden two to four

Extend your lettuce season by growing lettuce underneath a lean-to trellis. Once the heat of the summer hits, the squash will grow and cover the trellis, shading the lettuce underneath, keeping it cool (less likely to bolt).

weeks before your last frost. To have fresh lettuce all season and avoid it going to seed, sow successively every two to three weeks until fall. It's better to grow in smaller, more frequent batches. Continue sowing cold-tolerant varieties like 'Black Seeded Simpson' under cover into the winter.

Relatively undemanding, lettuce needs ample water to thrive. Mulch with seaweed and dose your leafy crops with fish emulsion every three weeks to keep them lush. Alternatively you can use compost tea, but I'm a particular fan of fish fertilizer. It has plenty of readily available nitrogen and contains many trace nutrients like calcium, sulfur, and magnesium. Keep weed-free. Weeds seem to have a sixth sense when it comes to sourcing nutrients, and you don't want them robbing your crop of any of the good stuff. As you do with other members of the Asteraceae family, protect from summer heat by planting those waves under another crop like squash, beans, or cukes. Daily watering and mulch also help keep lettuces cool and less likely to bolt.

I tend to broadcast seed thickly, knowing I plan to eat my thinnings as baby lettuce early in the season. When sowing a mesclun mix, shake the packet to mingle the seeds well. Initially thin to six inches apart, and later to twelve inches for full head development regardless of which type of lettuce you're growing. You can harvest lettuce one of three ways: as needed, whole head, or cut-and-come-again. If gathering leaves regularly for dinner, collect the outer leaves first. Leave the inner to continue growing. Whole head harvesting is pretty self-explanatory—cut at soil level and compost the roots. Comparatively, cutting-and-coming-again seems like a no-brainer to me. Instead of composting the roots after a whole head harvest, cut about an inch above the soil, leaving a stump. Then fertilize with fish emulsion and water regularly, and you should have a second, possibly even a third, harvest. I usually don't bank on the third since my successive crops are usually ready and fresher.

THE KEY TO SWEET LETTUCE IS RAPID GROWTH.

The biggest problems my lettuce has ever faced are slugs and snails. But I have heard from my fellow gardeners that aphids, cutworms, earwigs, flea beetles,

'Deer Tongue' is one of my favorite heirloom lettuces with its sweet, tender, tongue-shaped leaves.

and leafhoppers can be a problem. Insecticidal soap will kill the aphids, and row covers are a good defense against the rest. Earwigs can be tricky. As you would with slugs, set traps. In the evening, place wet, rolled up newspaper nearby and dispose of them in the morning.

Lettuce seedlings are prone to damping-off, so avoid overwatering. Overall I've rarely had issues with lettuce, but ensure proper drainage, keep up with your garden cleanup practices, and move your crops about the garden to prevent mildew, molds, wilts, and any other disease.

Birds will swoop in and eat your germinating seeds, so row covers are useful in protecting them. They keep your soil and seedlings warm at the start of the season, as well as pests and critters out. Deer and rabbits are apt to find lettuce very tasty—protection with fences or row covers can be crucial.

Mâche (*Valerianella locusta*)

Family: Valerianaceae
Plant Type: Annual, all zones
Light: Full sun, partial shade in summer heat
Soil: Fertile, well-drained
Height x Width: 2–8″ rosettes
pH: 6.5–7.0
Sow: ¼″ deep, thin to 6″ apart
Succession: 2–3 weeks
Days to germination: 10–14
Days to maturity: 50
Water: Regular
Feed: Moderate
Friends: All vegetables
Foes: None

Mâche is a plant designed for cold-climate gardening. It doesn't just "tolerate" chilly weather, it flourishes in extremely cold temperatures. You may have heard this cute, mildly nutty leafy green called lamb's lettuce or corn salad. It forms small (two- to four-inch) or large (four- to eight-inch) rosettes that are easily harvested whole. Because it is such a cold-weather enthusiast, plant in early spring and mid-fall for late spring and fall through winter harvests. The first time I grew mâche I didn't grow it under cover, and while it survived the snowfall, it was difficult to locate and harvest. Planting in a cold frame or a polytunnel makes it much easier to collect.

There are large- and small-seeded varieties of mâche. Small-seeded varieties are more flavorful and best sown in cooler temperatures, while the large-seeded are larger and more bolt resistant. Southern gardeners will have more success with the highly productive large-seeded mâche.

Mâche is more prolific in soil amended with compost or aged manure, fed with fish emulsion every couple weeks, and watered regularly. It's best sown in situ as soon as the soil can be worked. Scratch and water-in seeds well. Germination can take up to two weeks, but the secret to quick germination is cool soil. Warm weather will slow emergence even more, so plant in shade if you insist on growing them in the heat. And know that unless it's adequately shaded it will bolt as soon as it can. In zones 6–9 it's better just to hold off on mâche entirely until the summer heat abates. You can sow in rows or broadcast. Let's be honest—broadcasting is easier, and then you get to eat the thinnings! Once their spoon-shaped leaves are an inch or so in diameter, start thinning. Toss the baby greens in your salads for some tasty tenderness. Thin every other one each week, such that eventually they are spaced six inches apart.

Mâche rosettes are small and their root systems shallow, so they do extraordinarily well in containers and raised beds. Although hardy enough to survive to -20°F, it is the freezing rain, wind, and snow that take a toll on mâche. Fall and winter crops are most successful when grown under mulch, in the protection of a cold frame or tunnel if your winters are wet.

Mâche's flavor peaks in late winter, but you can begin harvesting once they're a couple inches wide. The small-seeded varieties are more tender and tastier. While it's possible to collect individual leaves, it is tedious. It's much better to simply harvest the entire plant by cutting it off at the base. While you can treat mâche as a cut-and-come-again crop, (cutting the plant an inch above the soil, leaving the stump to fertilize and regenerate), it is a waste of time. Rather, harvest whole and reseed. Also, whole rosettes make a very pretty salad dish—just plate them! Leave the roots and any uneaten greens in the ground, and at the end of the season, turn them under as a green manure—they're an excellent soil conditioner.

As a cold-season green, mâche is rarely affected by pests or disease—it's too cold for them!

Spinach (*Spinacia oleracea*)

Family: Amaranthaceae
Plant Type: Annual, zones 5–10
Light: Full sun, partial sun in summer heat
Soil: Fertile, rich in organic matter
Height x Width: 4–12″ x 6–8″
pH: 6.0–6.8

Sow: ¼" deep, thin to 12" apart
Succession: 2–3 weeks
Days to germination: 6–14
Days to maturity: 40–50
Water: Low, but even
Feed: Moderate
Friends: All brassicas, celery, legumes, lettuce, onions, radishes, and strawberries
Foes: Corn, pole beans, and potatoes

Anticipate lots of successive spinach sowings. It grows relatively fast, but bolts quickly as well. This makes it an excellent catch crop. A cool-season green, spinach performs best between 45 and 75°F. Therefore, unless you plan to shield your plants from the summer heat, it's best to sow every two weeks until midsummer, picking up again at the end. In addition to planning succession, you need to determine which type of spinach is for you, savoyed or smooth leaf. More common in cooler temperatures, savoyed (or semi-savoyed) spinaches have dark green, crinkled leaves. Smooth leaf is just what it sounds like—it's smooth and better in the spring and summer. This is what is traditionally used for baby spinach.

As you thin spring spinach, gather the young leaves in a bowl and bring them in for an evening salad.

Direct sow first thing in spring when the soil is workable, or get a head start indoors. I sow my first crop eight to ten weeks before the last frost and transplant out a month later. Start successive sowing immediately and keep on it until summer. Spinach germinates quicker in cool, moist soil. Once temperatures reach 85°F, spinach will not germinate (I told you it doesn't like the heat!). Grow smooth leaf types in the warmer weather. Spinach likes even moisture and regular nutrition. It can tolerate a wide array of less-than-ideal soils, but thrives with additional nitrogen-rich organic matter like compost or well-rotted manure like other greens. Incorporate either alfalfa or blood meal, or feed your plants monthly with fish emulsion if you haven't already enriched your soil. Too much nitrogen causes spinach to

'Bloomsdale, is a new favorite of mine. It's an excellent-tasting, rapid-growing, heavily savoyed spinach that thrives in both cool and cold seasons.

taste bitter. Lay off the fertilization on your next crop and you'll taste the difference. Spinach needs to be thinned twice—once to two to four inches and again to four to six inches apart.

A couple of spinach plants will fill out six-inch-deep pots nicely. I like to keep one next to my back door because it's shaded, and thus the plant will last longer before bolting. It also provides easy access! Bolting is a problem with spinach. It is both heat and light sensitive. Too much of either, and it goes to seed. That is why I highly recommend successive sowing. Regular watering, plant stacking, and growing bolt-resistant varieties are good ways to delay bolting.

Spinach is very frost tolerant, so start your cold-season crops in late summer. Sow about six to eight weeks before your first autumn frost. Since your seeds will be germinating in warmer weather, sow thickly. Germination will be slow and erratic. Sow later successions under cover. Spinach needs over a month of growth before being hit with a hard frost for a good winter crop. Mulching in cold frames or polytunnels helps spinach overwinter in extreme temperatures. If you feel the need for more protection, you can add a row cover, but keep in mind the cold weather also enhances spinach's flavor!

Once your final thinning (four to six inches) is complete, do not pull the entire plant from the garden. Instead, harvest single leaves from the outside of the plant when they are three inches long. Make sure to leave at least six central leaves for continued photosynthesis and growth. Don't leave the greens on the plant too long, otherwise they become gritty, bitter, and more likely to bolt. Force a second harvest when the spinach sends up a flower shoot and starts going to seed. As you do with lettuce and some of the brassicas, cut back within a few inches of the soil. Water well and fertilize with the famed fish emulsion, and in a month you should see the plant leaf out a second time—if it's not too warm of course.

The leaf miner is one of the few bothersome pests for spinach. Aphids, flea beetles, slugs, and snails are controlled the usual ways: hosing off, insecticidal soap, insect barriers, and baits. Improved air circulation through thinning keeps most diseases and rot at bay. Resistant varieties and good drainage also play a role in healthy, disease-free spinach.

Swiss Chard
(*Beta vulgaris* var. *vulgaris*)

Family: Chenopodiaceae

Plant Type: Biennial, grown as annual, zones 2–10

Light: Full sun

Soil: Well-drained

Height x Width: 12–16" x 6"

pH: 6.0–6.8

Sow: ½–¾" deep, thin to 8–12"

Succession: 2–3 weeks

Days to germination: 7

Days to maturity: 45–55

Water: Regular

Feed: Low nitrogen, moderate phosphorus, and potassium

Friends: Cabbage, chicory, garlic, leek, legumes, mustard, and onions

Foes: Beets and spinach

Swiss chard makes a beautiful, edible border plant, especially the 'Bright Lights' variety with its rainbow-colored stems and savoyed leaves.

Delightfully colorful, productive, and versatile, swiss chard is one of the more popular vegetables because it tolerates the warm weather better than any other salad green and doesn't bolt. Although you can grow chard from the spring, straight through the summer, and past the first frosts of autumn, it tastes best in cooler temperatures. Grown for its leaves and stalks, swiss chard is equally edible and ornamental. Its foliage is available in red, green, and bronze hues, and its stems in a myriad of colors ranging from white, pink, and green to orange and gold. Swiss chard makes an attractive border and intercrop, filling in open spots in the garden.

As with other leafy greens, enrich your bed with compost or well-rotted manure before seeding or transplanting. Direct sow or start early, three to five weeks before your last frost, setting seedlings out in the garden a few weeks later. You can plant a couple weeks earlier if planning to grow under season extension devices such as tunnels or cold frames. Space seeds and seedlings two inches apart, thinning to six inches once a few inches tall, and later twelve apart. And set rows twelve inches apart for mature chard plants.

You may notice more than one seedling once germinated. Chard is related to beets, and as such the seeds are actually dried fruit. If that is the case, thin to the strongest seedling once emerged. Successive plantings are crucial to having a consistent supply of tender baby greens and tasty, mature stalks. Despite handling the warm weather better than its leafy relatives, the leaves are not as tender as they age or the plant goes to seed, and they will benefit from a quick cook before eating. Postpone bolting by cutting back the flower stalk. If you garden in warmer climates, check your seed catalogs for more heat-tolerant varieties for better, less bitter flavor during your growing season.

Swiss chard is just as happy in a pot as in the garden, provided the container is at least eight inches deep and you give it plenty of water when it is establishing. Chard is more drought tolerant once settled, but don't let it wilt. Mulch to keep the soil evenly moist and weed-free. And to enhance flavor and speed growth, fertilize with fish emulsion or compost tea when six inches tall, and again midsummer. A mid-season side dressing of compost is also appreciated.

Hardy enough to sustain cooler temperatures, the touch of light frost improves chard's flavor. Sow your fall crop the same time as you do spinach, in late summer, about six to eight weeks before your first fall frost. When planting in tunnels, you can start your winter crop a little later. To protect from unexpected or hard frosts, mulch with straw and use row covers.

SWISS CHARD IS EDIBLE AND PRETTY.

Between succession plantings of young, salad greens and more mature stalks you should have enough swiss chard to make it through the year. Beyond baby greens, you can begin harvesting regularly anytime. Pick the outer stalks and leaves first. Let the heart continue developing for an endless harvest, or rather, treat chard as a cut-and-come-again crop. Cut the entire plant so all that is left is a stump and rejuvenate with fish fertilizer and water. Within a few weeks your second harvest will be growing and on its way.

Related to both spinach and beets, swiss chard is most often nibbled on by deer, rabbits, mice, and slugs. Fence the deer and small critters out. Handpick or bait beer traps for the slugs. Destroy and treat any aphid-infested stems. Other gardeners have had issues with leaf miners. If it's a problem in your garden, forbid them access with row covers. Although swiss chard is infrequently plagued with disease, downy mildew and leaf spot can be problematic if your soil doesn't drain well or you don't practice crop rotation.

OTHER CROPS

These vegetable crops generally take up a lot of room, and can fill in wherever you find space in your crop rotation. As you grow more and more crops, you'll find that the number of your beds grows too. Once you have six or more beds, you can start rotating by plant family. Many plants in this section are cucurbits, or belong in the gourd family. Familial groupings are helpful because those veggies have similar needs and wants. And as a bonus when it comes to planning, many of the plants described below can grow with other types of crops without impacting their nutrient demands. The only consideration is space—these guys need a lot of it!

Corn interplanted with a mustard cover crop.

Corn (*Zea mays*)

Family: Poaceae
Plant Type: Annual, zones 3–11
Light: Full sun
Soil: Fertile, loam
Height x Width: 4–12′ x 18–48″
pH: 6.0–7.0
Sow: 1″ deep outdoors
Succession: 2 weeks, or stagger maturity rates
Days to germination: 4–10
Days to maturity: 60–100 days
Water: Regular until flowering, heavy afterwards
Feed: Heavy
Friends: Beets, cabbage, cucumbers, legumes, melons, potatoes, pumpkins, and squash
Foes: Cane berries and tomatoes

It doesn't get any more all-American than sweet corn in the summer. The yellow, gold, white, and bicolor kernels will brighten up any picnic table. Store-bought corn just doesn't compare. For corn to be tasty, tender, and productive it needs heat, nutrients, and water. Growing corn is a little different than most crops—it is wind pollinated. Farmers growing on a large scale can plant in long rows because there are so many plants. But for the home gardener planting in thick masses ensures the best pollination. Four or more short rows guarantee that as the wind blows, the pollen has a higher chance of being distributed, rather than if the corn is planted in a single long and narrow row.

When perusing your catalogs for seeds, you will discover there are three designations, or types, of corn: normal sugary (su), sugary enhanced (se), and supersweet (sh2) corn. Sugary corn grows best in cold soils and has the classic sweet taste. But unfortunately its sugars quickly turn to starch, and it should be eaten immediately. This makes sugary corn less than ideal if you're a farmer shipping your corn across the country, but it's typically not an issue when growing it in your backyard. Sugary enhanced tastes sweeter and creamier, with supersweet earning its name. Germinating better in warm, moist soil, supersweet corn's sugar content is maximized. Its starches are slow to turn into sugar, increasing its longevity and making it ideal for commercial production and transport. Although considered to be the sweetest of them all, it's a bit tougher and less tender. Normal sugary

Corn should be harvested when the ear feels solid, the kernels full and the silks green at the top of the husk, turning brown at the ends.

and those varieties described as "open pollinated" or "standard" are not affected by cross-pollination. But hybrids and other varieties need to be grown at least twenty-five feet away from other corn. Alternatively, sow them two weeks apart to stop cross-pollination. Also, if you see "treated seed" in the blurb, it means the seeds were treated with a fungicide. Stay away from these if gardening organically.

Warm-weather gardeners can sow fresh blocks of corn every two weeks for continued harvests. But since corn takes a minimum of sixty frost-free days to grow, succession planting in the traditional way doesn't make sense for those in cold climates. Instead, elongate your harvest by planting early-, mid-, and late-season varieties of each type. They are all planted at the same time, but mature at different rates.

Wait until the danger of frost has passed before sowing your corn. It needs warm soil to germinate—your seeds will not sprout unless it stays moist at a consistent 60°F. Corn is a heavy feeder—it requires a lot of nitrogen especially—so add a few inches of compost or rotted manure in the fall and mulch. Autumn-planted nitrogen-fixing crops like hairy vetch or red clover will also improve your fertility. Let the winter kill and turn under in the spring. I

HARVEST CORN IN THE MORNING WHEN IT'S AT ITS SWEETEST.

find it helpful to warm the soil before planting. Apply solar or black plastic mulch to the garden two weeks before you expect to plant to get to that "sweet spot" of 60°F. Keep in mind where you are planting your corn. It starts out small, but by the end of the season it will reach six feet. Plant it on the north end of the garden surrounded by salad greens and cool-weather crops, like brassicas, that will benefit from the summertime shade.

Interplant corn with other plants to save space in the garden. Brassicas and leaf lettuces benefit from the late-season shade. One of the most common companion plant groupings is the Three Sisters. This method originated with the Native Americans, who grew corn with beans and squash. The beans provide lots of nutritious nitrogen, corn acts as a trellis for the beans to climb, and squash or pumpkins act as a living mulch and discourage predators from snacking with their spiny stems and leaves.

Corn does not transplant well. It should be planted in "hills." This does not mean you mound your soil. Because germination is erratic, plant three to four seeds together one inch deep, eight inches apart, and later thin to the strongest seedling. Improve germination by keeping the soil warm and moist and protecting seeds from unexpected frosts. Row covers do all three nicely, but once night temperatures stay above 60°F, remove them. As I mentioned before, corn likes to eat, so feed with fish emulsion, blood meal, or your favorite organic fertilizer several times a season. Fertilize after a month, or when twelve to fifteen inches tall, bimonthly, and again when tassels appear. Weed regularly. Corn has a shallow root system, so any competition for nutrients or water will negatively impact your crop. Soaker hoses or drip irrigation can facilitate consistent moisture. Mulching helps control weeds and maintain moisture. Water regularly, but really kick it up a notch once your corn tassels. This signifies that pollination—and kernel formation—are going to start, and it likes lots of water at that point. Pollen is typically transferred by wind from the top tassel (male flower) to the silks (female flowers) below. Shaking the stalks can help wind and gravity get pollen to the silks, but this is the primary reason I recommend planting in short blocks. Interior plants usually develop more ears than those at the edge. If planting in a container, you will need at least three to four plants for pollination. An eight-inch-deep pot should accommodate the corn's shallow root system, but make sure to keep the pot weighted down or moist, because once the corn grows tall it may topple over.

The first time you harvest corn is nerve-wracking. Is it ready or not? There are a few easy ways to tell. First, look at the silks. They should be green near the husk and starting to shrivel, dry, and turn brown at the ends. The ear should feel firm and the kernels plump. Once you think it's ripe, check its milk stage. Pull back the husk a bit and prick a kernel with your fingernail. If it squirts out a milky liquid, it's ready for harvest. Wait until morning to harvest if you can, because that is when sugar content is at its highest, and store in the fridge until dinner. Low temperatures slow the sugar to starch conversion.

The yellow-headed earworm is corn's biggest nemesis. Control it with a few drops of mineral oil dropped into the tip of the ear several days after the silks appear. The regular assortment of pests, aphids, cutworms, flea, and Japanese beetles can be problematic. European corn borers also burrow into ears. Crop rotation and sanitation are the best ways of preventing these pests and diseases like wilt and corn smut from becoming an issue. Netting and fences will keep birds and deer from grazing or stealing seeds.

Cucumber (*Cucumis sativus*)

Family: Cucurbitaceae
Plant Type: Annual, zones 4–12
Light: Full sun
Soil: Fertile, well-drained
Height x Width: 3–10′ vine x 12–15″
pH: 6.5–7.5
Sow: 1″ deep
Succession: 2 weeks until midsummer
Days to germination: 5–7
Days to maturity: 55–65
Water: Regular until flowering, heavy afterwards
Feed: Heavy
Friends: Brassica, corn, dill, eggplant, kale, legumes, lettuce, melon, nasturtium, radish, pumpkins, squash, sunflowers, and tomatoes
Foes: Potatoes and herbs

Cucumbers like to climb. Let them grow over a homemade A-frame trellis made of lattice or chicken wire.

If cucumbers are kept off the ground, they grow more uniformly, without the yellow/white spot on the bottom.

The mighty cucumber, when provided with a steady supply of water and nutrients, will be tremendously productive. There are bush and vining types. Bush cucumbers are wonderful for small-scale or urban gardeners who may only have a tiny space or room for a pot on the patio. Though less productive than their vining counterparts, they still produce fruits and do well in containers at least eight inches deep. A short trellis will also increase their productivity. Vining plants are obviously larger, rambling across the garden and up the trellis. They like to climb and will produce much better off the ground. A trellis system is critical. Your fruits will grow straighter and more uniformly and won't be marred by a whitish-yellow spot, the result of sitting on the ground. An A-frame, fence, or even a tomato cage will work as a support system.

The first year I grew my cucumbers from seed I was dumbfounded at the selection. Slicing and pickling I was familiar with. Slicers are the traditional dark green six- to eight-inch cuke. Picklers are smaller with spines. Growing rapidly, they need to be picked daily to maintain high yields. Enjoy fresh or as pickles—they are crisper with great flavor. Harvest at three to five inches for best quality. These are my favorites for their versatility. Specialty cucumbers include a wider assortment than I ever imagined. Persian cucumbers, also called Middle Eastern or Beit Alpha cukes, are milder but tasty. Small (four to six inches) and almost seedless, they can be used just like traditional slicing cucumbers, but these you don't have to peel. Their skin is so thin, it doesn't have to be removed—what's not to like? Milder than Middle Eastern, Asian cucumbers can be used fresh or pickled. Sweet and long, they reach up to fifteen inches in length. Then there are lemon cucumbers (one-and-half to two-and-a-half inch round balls), which—you guessed it—taste (and look) just like lemons. Save some space in your garden to try some of these sweet novelties. Plan to grow varieties with different maturity rates for a longer harvest or sow successive crops every two weeks from the last frost till midsummer.

Position your cukes in a sunny patch, amended with a few inches of compost. While most references suggest you direct seed when the soil warms to 70°F, we northern gardeners can't wait. There isn't enough warm weather in the season to grow if sown in situ. Start your seeds four to six weeks before your last frost. Plant two to three seeds per block, or pot, and keep moist. Carefully transplant (avoid root disturbance) in the garden once frost has passed and the soil warms. Out in the garden plant in hills—as you would corn. Cucumber seed will not germinate in cold soil, so use plastic mulch (black or solar) two weeks before planting to warm the soil. Sow two to three seeds one-half inch deep, two to four inches apart. Once your seedlings have their first set of true leaves, snip the weaker sprouts out. Thin trellised plants to eight inches apart and those on the ground to sixteen inches apart. Frost tender, cloches, row covers, and tunnels help keep seeds and plants toasty until the summer heat kicks in—just remember to vent on warm days. Remove all your season extenders once the temperature has stabilized around 65°F.

As plants grow, help them latch onto the trellis. Once they're on, they should climb mostly on their own. Suppress weeds and keep the roots cool and moist with mulch. To encourage rapid growth, feed your cukes with fish emulsion bimonthly, starting when they're a few inches tall and grabbing for support. If you notice a yellowing of your leaves, boost with a nitrogen feed. Maintain steady moisture until flowering begins.

HARVEST CUKES EARLY AND OFTEN.

An inch of water a week is standard. Once your cucumbers set flower, amp up the water and fertilizer. This is the time to feed with comfrey tea to promote flower and fruit development.

I follow the motto of harvesting "early and often" once my cucumbers are large enough to eat. Small, immature cukes have the fewest seeds, taste good, and have the best crunch. Harvest daily—cucumbers left on the vine too long turn yellow and seedy and lose their flavor. It also slows fruit production. Yellowing of the blossom end signifies that the cukes are overly ripe and should be composted. Also, I recommend clipping, rather than pulling, your cucumbers from the plant to avoid damaging the growing vines.

Cucumber beetles. Such a non-threatening name for such a destructive bug. They carry and transmit a disease called bacterial wilt that will destroy your plant. You will know when your plant has succumbed to wilt—it will collapse—and it is not salvageable. A minimum three-year crop rotation is especially important in controlling these beetles. Protect early in the season with insect barriers or row covers, removing once buds appear to let pollinators do their job. Aphids, slugs, snails, squash bugs, and worms also present problems, but are easily managed with handpicking, hosing off, and bait trapping. Aside from wilt, powdery mildew and cucumber mosaic virus are particularly detrimental, among other diseases. Improved air circulation through trellising, planting resistant varieties, pest exclusion, and watering from the bottom in the morning (so the leaves are dry by evening) combined with a good rotation strategy are the best defenses against disease.

Melons (*Cucumis* spp. & *Citrullus lanatus*)

Family: Cucurbitaceae
Plant Type: Annual, zones 4+
Light: Full sun
Soil: Deep, well-drained loam
Height x Width: 24" x 3–4' vine
pH: 7.0–8.0
Sow: 2–3 seeds ½–1½" deep, thin to 24–36"
Succession: n/a
Days to germination: 4–10
Days to maturity: 70–140
Water: Regular until ripening
Feed: Low nitrogen, high phosphorus and potassium
Friends: Corn, pumpkins, and radishes
Foes: Cucumbers and winter squash

Position your melons in the sunniest spot you've got. They love light and heat. Any plant from the Cucurbitaceae family with fleshy, edible fruit is considered a melon. To the backyard gardener this includes cantaloupes, honeydews, crenshaws, charentais, and the almighty watermelon. The four former melons are considered muskmelons and can have smooth or rough skin. Grouped by maturation rates, cantaloupe and watermelons are summer melons; the rest are winter melons. While watermelon comes from a different botanical genus, it's grown the same way as all melons. Seedless varieties and hybrids are available, but don't be mistaken—seedless watermelons are not completely seed-free. Instead of the large, black seeds that you need to spit out as you eat, the seedless seeds are white, soft, tiny, and edible. In addition to being finicky to germinate (you need really warm soil and to separate the seed coat from the cotyledons), in order for pollination to occur you will need to plant one seeded variety for every three seedless plants. I like the 'Moon and Stars' watermelon because its distinctive markings make it easy to identify in the garden. But whenever you're growing watermelon or muskmelon, the secret to delicious, fleshy melons is ample sun, steady water, and rich soil.

Like all warm-weather crops, do not plant out until the danger of frost has passed. In warmer climates, direct sow once the soil is a consistent 70°F. Cold-weather gardeners have more success with short-season varieties and should start their seeds indoors three to five weeks before their last frost, harden off, and set out two weeks after. When transplanting, be careful not to disturb the roots too much. Season extenders like polytunnels will get you planting a few weeks earlier than that

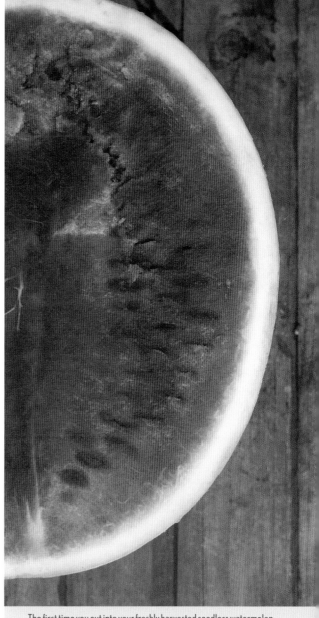

The first time you cut into your freshly harvested seedless watermelon you may notice small, white seeds. Don't worry, you didn't do anything wrong, seedless watermelons are not completely seed-free.

with some extra protection. Prep your bed with a generous helping of compost or well-rotted manure. Employ black or solar plastic mulch a couple weeks before your last frost to warm the soil, inhibit weeds, and maintain soil moisture. Regardless of when you plant, hill your seed. Plant two to three seeds per hole, soil block or pot one inch deep, and cover.

When transplanting, set out in two- to three-foot-tall mounds or ridges for better drainage. Muskmelons should be planted three feet apart and watermelons two to three feet apart for plenty of room for their vines to run. Thin to a single plant (with snips) once their true leaves develop. Insect barriers and row covers will protect against unwanted invaders. The covers also keep your soil warm and tender seedlings frost-free, but need to be removed once the plants bloom in order for pollination to occur.

High fertility and steady water are essential when growing melons. In addition to copious amounts of compost, feed monthly with fish emulsion or a balanced 10-10-10 organic fertilizer. You should plan these feedings around the time the vines start to run and again after the first harvest. As heavy feeders melons don't like to compete with weeds for anything. If you aren't using a plastic mulch, mulch with something else—it's important for weed control and moisture, particularly right after germination. Keeping the soil evenly wet is vital for large, sweet melons—an inch of water per week is typical. Melons do not tolerate drought. Install soaker hoses and drip lines under your mulch to ensure that plants get adequate moisture. Once blossoms appear, pinch out buds to allow only four flowers to develop into fruit, which funnels all the plant's energy into growing large, sweet melons.

If you're short on garden space (melons take up a lot), grow them vertically. Trellises, arbors, and A-frames are good ways to get small melons like cantaloupe or honeydews up off the ground. Just remember the growing fruits need support. A net or melon sling will help hold the weight of developing melons. For this very reason, melons are not great for small-scale gardens or containers.

Muskmelons are ready to be picked and eaten when they turn from green to their matured coloring. Melons can be harvested either when they naturally detach from the vine, called "full slip," or at "half slip," when a gentle tug frees the fruit. Each muskmelon plant should produce four to six fruits, and watermelon, two. Watermelon harvest is a little more difficult to discern. I was taught to "thump" the melon to determine whether it's ready to eat. A dull thud means you're good to go; if it sounds hollow let it keep growing. Other helpful clues your watermelon is ripe include the hardening of the rind, which should turn dull in color. When growing, the rind looks glossy and bright. Also, the curly stem that attaches the watermelon to the vine will turn brown or shrivel and die. Lastly, the green underbelly will turn a soft white (seeded) or yellow (seedless). Do not harvest early—melons only ripen on the vine. If picked too early, they won't continue to ripen.

Squash bugs and cucumber beetles are troublesome to growing melons. Keep squash bugs under control by handpicking in the morning, when they are more lethargic. Protect young crops from cucumber beetles with barriers or row covers. The beetles transmit bacteria wilt, which kills your vines. Wash aphids away or cut out infested stems to prevent the spread of mosaic virus or other viral disease. Other pests cause minor damage. Water from below to discourage powdery mildew, which affects leaf appearance and reduces flavor. If your melons develop a yellow patch on the rind, they are suffering from sunscald. Mostly cosmetic, this is sunburn for melons. Protect affected melons with an old sheet or overturned basket.

Pumpkins and Squash (*Cucurbita pepo, C. maxima & C. moschata*)

Family: Cucurbitaceae
Plant Type: Annual, zones 3+
Light: Full sun
Soil: Rich, well-drained
Height x Width: 12–15″ tall. Vine length depends on variety.
pH: 5.5–6.8
Sow: ½–1″ deep, thin to 24–36″. Space 3–5′ between rows
Succession: n/a
Days to germination: 7–10
Days to maturity: 50–65 for summer squash; 60–100 from seed (60–80 after transplant) for winter squash
Water: Heavy
Feed: Heavy
Friends: Celeriac, celery, corn, legumes, nasturtiums, melon, onion, and radish
Foes: Brassicas, potatoes, and pumpkins

You're more likely to overplant squash than underplant it. There are two types of squash: summer and winter, sometimes referred to as courgettes, they both belong to the gourd family. As warm-season crops, squash thrive in full sun, are frost sensitive, and come in a plethora of colors, shapes, and tastes. They differentiate themselves from one another in that summer squash is harvested immature, when the rind is soft and thin; whereas winter squash are picked much later after the rind is hardened.

Summer squash is a producing machine. It is a rare day when there aren't at least a few zucchini to harvest!

When harvesting, cut the stem—do not pull. If the stem breaks, the shelf life is reduced.

Harvested young for highest-quality fruits, summer squash is one of the most productive plants I've ever grown. I have to literally give the fruit away. Do not plant more than a couple plants of each variety, that is usually more than often enough. Most grow as a bush rather than running vines. There are a handful of different types of summer squash. Zucchini, the classic cylinder-like courgette, grows in shades ranging from soft to dark green, white, and yellow. These versatile fruits should be picked when they reach four to six inches. Pattypans, or scallop squash, look more like an alien spaceship than something you eat. Crunchier and denser than other types, they hold up longer in cooking. Their scalloped edges and wide array of colors make them pretty to look at—or stuff! Then there are straightnecks and crooknecks, which look just like they sound. Both have a bulbous bottom and tapered neck, but crookneck squash curves in between. Middle Eastern squash is usually a pale green, stout (four- to six-inch) tapered cylinder. Known for their mild taste and creamy texture, these prolific squash may be called Cousa, Kuta, Lebanese, or 'Magda' in catalog descriptions. And lastly there are 'Tatume' and globe courgettes. Both seedless,

'Tatume' is a small, Mexican variety, often oval shaped, while globes are round and taste similar to zucchini.

Winter squash are beasts in the garden. Grown the same way as summer squash, they just need more of everything (time, sun, space, fertility, and water). These vigorous vines are bigger than summer squash and more diverse. Choosing between acorn, buttercup, butternut, delicata, hubbard, and spaghetti squash can be overwhelming. Deeply ribbed acorn squash are excellent in cooler climates with shorter growing seasons. Resembling a flattened acorn, buttercups store well, which is good since they are prolific producers. Beige and bottle-shaped, butternut squash is grown for its rich flavor and smooth texture. But it's their resistance to squash vine borers that makes them stand out. Delicata squash is very sweet. I like them because they are easy and rapid growers for northern gardeners. These ivory and green striped cylinders turn yellow as they age and last three to five months in storage. Hubbards, or kabocha, are quite large. They have a variety of looks from smooth or bumpy, molted or not, and develop into a pretty bluish-gray, green tones, or orange. Sacrifice these and use them as a trap crop for squash vine borers—they love them! Spaghetti squash is average sized and oblong with stringy flesh. Feed them heavily for their sweet, mild nutty flavor.

'Buttercup' squash may be dark green on the outside, but are known for their sweet taste and rich, orange flesh.

'Sweet dumpling' is the perfect single-serving, stuffed delicata squash for the fall, brightening up the table with its cream and dark green coloring.

Kabocha squash, available in green, grey, and red, taste sweeter a few weeks after harvest.

Protect plants from squash bugs. Cover with row covers immediately after planting, leaving on until flowering begins. Squash need pollinators to fruit.

Grow your pumpkins and squash on landscape fabric to keep them disease and bug-free.

Pumpkins are just a large, orange, winter squash. Grown the same, harvested the same, and enjoyed a little bit more—not only can you eat these giant squash, you can carve them too! Toss your toasted seeds with salt for a savory autumn treat.

Bush varieties perform very well in pots at least ten inches deep—wine barrels look great and give plenty of room for growing squash. Plant two to three seeds in the center, eventually thinning to a single seedling. Protect against unexpected frosts with a sheet or row cover.

All squash need sun, warm, fertile soil, and room to sprawl. Courgettes make beautiful borders—I often plant mine at the edge of my garden. Apply a few inches of compost to your bed, the more the better. Once the soil reaches 70°F, direct sow in hills (three to four seeds planted in one spot, later thinning to a single plant). Squash seeds do not germinate in cold soil, so warm with solar or black plastic in cold climates and start four weeks early. Traditionally squash does not transplant well, so sow three to four seeds in larger, four-inch pots. Thin to the strongest seedling and harden off before setting out a couple weeks after your last frost. Space squash seedlings twenty-four to thirty-six inches apart, on the short end for smaller or bush types and three feet for larger. Small summer squash can be grown on tripod or teepee trellises.

Quality and quantity begin to wane after a month of producing. Summer squash enthusiasts should plant a second crop at the time the first is transplanted into the garden. The newer crop will produce past the first, into the fall until frost. Growing your second crop under row covers or in polytunnels enables you to extend your harvest even further. And as a bonus you can close it off to vine borers and other pests!

Steady moisture and nutrition are important. Drip or soaker hoses under a thick layer of mulch will keep your squash cool and sated. I feed monthly with fish emulsion to maintain strong plants and healthy leaves. But if your plants look sad or their leaves yellow, feed more often. Once the plants

"EARLY AND OFTEN" ALSO APPLIES TO SQUASH.

begin to flower, I fertilize every two weeks with my homemade comfrey tea to promote bud and fruit development. You may notice that the first couple blooms on your plant fade—this is all right. Sometimes pollination is delayed because the female flowers open before the males. This should correct itself quickly.

A smorgasbord of my favorite squash (clockwise from left): 'Butternut', 'Delicata', 'Carnival' sweet dumpling, green 'Kabocha', 'Blue Hubbard', 'Jet' (acorn), 'Buttercup' (Burgress strain), 'Magda' (Middle-Eastern summer squash), and spaghetti squash.

Cropping is when you really experience the difference between growing summer and winter squash. The "early and often" mantra is fundamental to harvesting summer squash. The more you pick, the more productive your plants will be. Additionally, young squash will have softer skin and taste best. Harvest straightnecks and crooknecks when four to six inches long, and small, rounded (including pattypans) squash when two to four inches wide. The flowers are edible. Gourmet home cooks should collect male flowers in the morning when still turgid to maximize their longevity. Male blossoms tend to bloom farther out from the center with a straight stalk, while female flowers are borne from the center and have a swollen base.

Wait to harvest winter squash until the rind hardens, before your first frost. As the summer winds down, newly pollinated flowers won't have time to develop and will be wasted. Instead, reduce your water and pinch out the remaining buds to refocus the rest of the plant's energy on ripening up its last fruits. Squash color will indicate when they are ripe, but double-check with the fingernail test. Push your nail into the skin—if it leaves an indent, let your plants keep growing; they're not ready. If there's no depression, it has adequately cured and you can harvest. But keep in mind that the longer squash are left on the vine, the longer they will store. To maximize winter courgettes' shelf life, let cure in the sun for an additional week or two, protected with a sheet or row cover in the event of a surprise frost. Then store at 55°F for three to nine months. Root cellars, pantries, or under the bed in your spare room all work well.

I advise wearing gloves when harvesting squash, because they have spiny stems and leaves. Don't treat the stem as a handle, it's better to cut, not tug, the fruit off the vine. Pulling can damage the still growing plant or break the stump off winter courgettes. The stems break easily, which decreases the squash's storage life.

Unfortunately squash bugs overwinter in the soil and are resistant to most organic pesticides. Handpicking is really the only way to manage these goons. Scrape their shiny, orange-colored eggs from leaves' underside early in the season, and handpick adults first thing in the morning when they are more sluggish. Then there are those sneaky squash vine borers. Midday wilting leaves are the first indication that you have a problem. Squash vine borers feed on stem tissue, making it impossible for plants to drink and feed, killing them. Insect barriers and row covers are the best defense against cucumber beetles and vine borers (remember to remove once buds form for pollination). To confirm you have borers, look for a sawdust-like frass at the base. To save the plant, slit the stem where the residue is coming from with a knife and remove the pest. Mound up soil beneath the wound and bury, just like you would when layering a plant, so it can reestablish itself. Mildews and viruses transmitted via beetles can also be problematic. Most of these pests can be avoided with insect barriers, crop rotation, disease-resistant varieties, or by sowing late and transplanting.

PERENNIAL CROPS

Artichokes, asparagus, and rhubarb are set apart from other vegetables. They are perennial, returning year after year. Whereas you can make last-minute decisions on most crop placements in the garden, you cannot with these. Where you plant them is where they're staying. Spend some time thinking about this. Rather large, these crops will need ample space once they get growing. And you have to keep in mind what plants might shade them, and how they may cast a shadow on others. Plan to side dress each spring and fall with compost or aged manure and mulch to keep your plants content. Once established, Mother Nature takes care of watering. And remember that production may decline at some point, and you will have to divide or replace plants. The silver lining with this group is once you have them growing, you're good for a long time!

Artichoke
(*Cynara scolymus*)

Family: Asteraceae
Plant Type: Perennial, sometimes grown as an annual, zones 7–10
Light: Full sun
Soil: Fertile, well-drained
Height x Width: 36–60" x 60–72"
pH: 6.0–6.8
Sow: ¼" deep
Succession: n/a
Days to germination: 10–14
Days to maturity: 85 for annual (harvest first or second year)
Water: Regular
Feed: High nitrogen
Friends: Brassicas, sunflowers, and other perennial vegetables
Foes: Vines

Grown for their buds and bracts—not their flower—artichokes add some interesting architecture and flavor to the kitchen garden. Although they are considered perennial in temperate (zone 7 or above) gardens, treat them as annuals in colder climates, as they won't survive the winter. A new variety called 'Imperial Star' is making the rounds in northern gardens. It's easy to grow and produces artichokes from seed in its first year. There's just one catch—their seedlings require at least ten days of 45–50°F in order to set buds. Other than that quick vernalization condition, grow them just like you would in warmer growing zones. Artichokes are easily confused with cardoons, which do not produce any flower buds, but rather are grown for their edible leaves.

Artichokes can be grown three ways: from seed, dormant roots, or softwood cuttings. Getting a jump on the season is crucial if growing from seed. Start your seeds six to eight weeks before your last frost, waiting until danger of frost has passed to plant out. Sow two to three seeds per soil block or four-inch pot. You can start them in tiny plug trays, but you're just going to have to transplant them later into something bigger. Why create more work, especially if you aren't planning to grow on a commercial scale? Because they germinate better in warm soil, use bottom heat to speed up the process. As soon as you have emergence, start feeding with half-strength fish emulsion and keep the soil moist to strengthen your seedlings. If gardening in a cooler climate, you will need to vernalize and harden off before transplanting out. When your seedlings are about six weeks old, expose them to colder temperatures (45–50°F) for at least ten days, tricking them into thinking they've experienced a mild winter. Protect from nighttime frosts with row covers, but remove them first thing in the morning. Plants need to be subjected consistently to the cooler weather to induce budding—any fluctuations will interrupt the process.

All artichokes should be planted out in the garden four inches apart once the danger of frost has passed, eventually thinning to two feet apart. Not all plants will grow true to seed, so it's better to grow more than you need and thin to the strongest seedlings. As mentioned earlier, they grow fastest and are most productive when given generous amounts of food and water. This is why fertile soil and drainage are so important. Start off the season amending your bed with lots of compost or well-rotted manure. Black (or solar) plastic mulch will help speed along growth as artichokes thrive in warmer weather and soil. And since artichokes are very thirsty plants, drip irrigation or soaker hoses situated under moisture-conserving mulch are worth the investment. Feed growing artichokes monthly with fish emulsion. They are just as hungry as they are thirsty, and they will reward you will large, flavorful buds. Unless you are growing one of the new annual varieties, your plant will not produce its edible buds until its second year. If ambushed with a late frost warning,

Artichokes and cardoons are bold, stately thistle-like plants with a similar flavor. But while artichokes are grown for their buds and bracts, cardoons are harvested for their leaf stems.

throw a sheet or row cover over your plants. Frosts will either toughen up or kill growing flower buds, but who really wants to take that chance?

Artichokes make excellent container plants—especially in cold-weather gardens. Since they are large and statuesque plants, select a large (minimum three-feet-deep) pot. These plants make a striking focal point in the garden. And the biggest benefit to growing in a pot is that they're mobile! If you don't like it where it is, simply move it.

Now, if you're one of those lucky people living in milder climates (zone 7 and above), you can grow artichokes from dormant crowns or rooted shoots from a fellow gardener's plant. Two weeks before your last frost, plant your dormant roots vertically, four to six inches apart with their buds at soil level. Rooted shoots, or suckers, need to be sliced from the parent plant when about ten inches tall. Use a sharp trowel or spade to cut the shoot away, while digging as much of the root system as possible. Then replant into a four-inch hole, such that the buds are above soil level.

Although they look quite pretty in bloom, do not let your artichokes flower if you're planning on eating them. You want to harvest the edible bud, which includes the heart and scale-like bracts. Once the thistle opens and starts to flower, its flavor diminishes. Green buds will develop at the end of the plant's terminal and lateral shoots. Cut your artichokes when the firm bud is still tightly closed. They will be tastiest if harvested in cool and moist conditions.

Artichokes should overwinter with almost no work in regions with temperate winters (zone 7 and up). Once the season is passed, chop your plant to the ground and cover with a layer of straw mulch. It should send up new shoots the following spring. Cooler zones (5-6) need a little more care. Cut back to twelve inches, mulching around and over the stem. Then cover with an upside down basket or large pot and top it off with a weatherproof tarp. Perennial artichokes will start producing buds in late summer for three to five years after the initial year of vegetative growth. Or, you can grow one of the annual hybrids.

Pests don't seem to bother artichokes much. Hose away or destroy aphid-infested branches, and slugs can be baited in wet conditions. Artichokes can be affected by disease, but generally it's not a problem. The bigger concern is drainage. Unimproved soil can become compacted, and if overly wet, it will lead to root rot. Also, covered, overwintered plants may rot over the winter in poorly drained soil.

Asparagus (*Asparagus officinalis*)

Family: Asparagaceae
Plant Type: Perennial
Light: Full sun
Soil: Loose, fertile, well-drained
Height x Width: 30–60" x 24–48"
pH: 6.5–7.5
Sow: Seeds ¼–½" deep. Crowns 6" deep, space 12–15" apart.
Succession: n/a
Days to germination: 14–18
Days to maturity: n/a (harvest in second or third year)
Water: Heavy
Feed: Heavy
Friends: None. Hates any competition
Foes: All root vegetables

Once established, asparagus can live for decades. There is a bit of work and waiting up front, but after they hit their stride in their third year, they are underground producing machines. Pick your spot carefully. Because they're perennial, they're staying where you've planted them for a long while. Asparagus enjoys full sun and weed-free soil. Surrounding weeds steal resources from the growing plant, producing substandard spears and reducing productivity and longevity. You'll start to see their pencil-thick shoots pop up in May. Harvest these tender stems for another six to eight weeks—then they'll go into storage mode—and begin prepping for the following year.

Asparagus is customarily started from crowns, which are one-year-old dormant root bundles with buds (called eyes). Crowns have the advantage of being easier to grow and quicker to harvest, allowing you to cut shoots in the second year. You can start asparagus from seed, but it will take an additional year before you can begin harvesting—and that

doesn't take into account the time and effort of propagation and transplanting. Dormant roots are more expensive, but also more productive than plants grown from seed. Most crowns available to purchase are male hybrids, which outperform females. The males produce significantly (three times) more shoots. When starting from seed, you will likely have more females than you would if you bought older crowns, thus reducing your yields.

Prepare your bed with copious amounts of compost and organic matter and ensure it is weed-free. If you're willing to part with one of your raised beds to make it a permanent home for asparagus, that's ideal. The deep beds warm more quickly, are weed-free, and improve drainage, which is particularly important for asparagus. Wait until the soil has warmed to 50°F before planting, typically a few weeks before your last frost. Traditionally asparagus is planted in a trench and gradually filled in with soil as the asparagus grows. However, years ago I read about a technique in which you plant

Harvest when buds are tight and the spear is the diameter of a pencil.

ASPARAGUS CROWNS PRODUCE IN THE SECOND YEAR.

Fern development is important for aspuragus. Without it they won't be as productive the following year.

the crowns at soil level and slowly mound up around them with extra compost, which I loved. This method positions the crowns a bit higher for improved drainage and makes planting easier. Asparagus roots look like shriveled octopus legs when they arrive and should be planted relatively quickly before the crowns dry out. Space twelve to eighteen inches apart on small, individual mounds of soil in a staggered formation. Sit the crowns such that the roots are draped over each mound, and cover with three inches of compost and loam. Then every couple weeks add a few more inches until your asparagus are growing in six- to eight-inch-tall mounds. Alternatively, you can dig a six- to eight-inch-deep trench, plant the crowns on mounds at the base, and backfill as they grow. Water freshly planted beds thoroughly.

Growing asparagus from seed is decidedly cheaper, with the added benefit of a wider selection. You need to sow your seed super early, twelve to fourteen weeks before your last expected frost. They are finicky germinators, taking two to eight weeks to pop. To speed up and improve germination, soak your seeds the night before and sow in four-inch pots. After your last frost, harden off for a week, then transplant your six- to eight-inch-tall seedlings in the garden just as you would crowns (in a six- to eight-inch trench or mound).

Keep the bed weed-free, mulch, and provide ample amounts of water while spears, or ferns, are growing. Asparagus has a big appetite and does not like to share its nutrients, space, or water with resource-sucking weeds—or even companion plants. Each spring I pile on three to five inches of compost, every other year incorporating a complete organic fertilizer (10-10-10) to maintain and encourage healthy, abundant shoots. Once the asparagus is harvested, I apply fish emulsion. This is the point in the asparagus life cycle in which they develop into ferns. Fern production is essential—they store energy in the roots for next season, and they need food to do that. In the fall, the ferns turn brown and naturally die back. If not, cut them back to one inch off the ground. Apply another generous layer of compost and mulch heavily (six inches). Mulch is multifunctional: it stifles weeds, conserves moisture, and insulates the soil against extreme temperatures. In the spring, pull back the mulch, weed, add a fresh layer of compost, and start all over again.

After two or three years, depending on whether you started with one- to two-year-old crowns or seed, you will start harvesting. The first time you harvest restrain yourself. Harvest lightly for a couple weeks, allowing some of the spears to develop into lush ferns. This helps build up the roots and makes for stronger plants in the long run. By the following year, your asparagus should be successfully established, with each plant yielding approximately one-half pound over six to eight weeks!

Harvest your spears when they are pencil-thick, six to eight inches tall, and have tight buds. Follow the old adage of picking early and often to keep your plants productive. Cut daily when warm, and every two to three days in cooler weather. There are two techniques for harvesting asparagus: the bend and snap method (which is exactly what is sounds like) and cutting at the base with a knife. When I'm lazy or forget my snips, I bend the stalk until it snaps, but more often I cut them just below the soil surface so my stalks include a bit of the white at the base. This extra length reduces water loss, thus increasing its shelf life.

COVER SPEARS FOR WHITE ASPARAGUS.

Asparagus does not store well—its flavor peaks immediately after it's been cut. Freshly harvested stalks should be kept upright in a shallow bowl or container in your fridge until ready to cook and serve. When the tops of your spears start to open and become feathery, asparagus is signaling its season is over.

Asparagus beetles, slugs, and rust are bothersome and inconvenient. Handpick slugs and adult beetles before they snack on your shoots. Also, when cutting back fern foliage, dispose of or hot compost them rather than letting them fall to the ground to stop asparagus beetles from overwintering. Getting rid of old, infected foliage will also help reduce your chances of asparagus rust. Resistant cultivars and positioning your bed such that it is not subjected to fog or mist will also prevent rust. But beyond pests and disease, asparagus' most devastating adversary is weeds.

Rhubarb (*Rheum rhabarbarum*)

Family: Polygonaceae
Plant Type: Perennial, zones 3–9
Light: Full sun to part shade
Soil: Fertile, well-drained
Height x Width: 24–36″ x 48″
pH: 6.0–6.8
Sow: Crown shoots should be planted at the soil surface.
Succession: n/a
Days to germination: n/a
Days to maturity: n/a (harvest in second and third year)
Water: Regular
Feed: Low
Friends: Brassicas and other perennials
Foes: Legume and root crops

What I love about rhubarb is how easy it is. Besides its initial planting and some root division every 5–6 years, there is almost no work involved! Rhubarb is a large plant, the anchor of the kitchen garden—every garden should have at least one. Grown for its juicy, tart stalks, it's treated more like a fruit than a vegetable. Make sure to place it in a spot where it gets full sun and the soil drains well. I positioned my rhubarb to be ornamental as well as edible. Its Jurassic-like foliage and stately flower stalk and seeds make quite the focal point in the garden, so I have several, one at each corner and one in the center.

Start with root divisions. Find a friend willing to share or purchase a small plant—rhubarb does not grow true to seed. Plant three to four feet apart (I told you it was big) as soon as the soil can be worked in spring or fall. Dig a large hole, and shovel in fresh compost. Then set the crown so its buds are slightly elevated, peeking out at the soil surface and continue backfilling with a compost and soil blend. Water well. The slight mounding will improve drainage. All the soil will not go back in the hole, so find a spot that could use a little extra.

Overall, rhubarb doesn't require much. Regular water and a hefty side dressing of compost or aged manure in early spring are all it needs. Many gardeners consider mulch unnecessary, but I add a decent layer to help maintain even soil moisture. Elongate stem harvest by snapping off flower stalks to delay blooming. Lack of water, high temperatures, and overcrowding can cause premature flowering. Crowded plants not only bloom early, but produce smaller, not-as-tasty stems.

Plant rhubarb so its crown is level with the soil surface.

Dividing rhubarb improves stalk productivity, yield (because you now have more plants), and general plant health. Rhubarb grows rapidly and in time becomes overcrowded. Stalk production ebbs after five or six years, but root division will rejuvenate weakened plants. The best time to divide is in the spring when it's cool and moist, before the buds pop, but fall will work in a pinch. First loosen the soil twelve inches out from around your plant, and, being careful not to damage the roots, dig up your rhubarb. Remember this is a larger plant, and it may take some muscle and time to get it out. A bunch of soil should come up as well. Then using a sharp knife, cut between the buds and down the roots. This can seem tedious for especially big root balls. You can use a sharp spade to cut apart the plant instead. Regardless of how you accomplish the division, each section should have at least three buds. Replant one section, incorporating fresh compost, and either share your divisions with friends or spread them around your yard. Rhubarb makes a lovely landscape plant even if you aren't eating its stems.

Newly planted—or divided—rhubarb should not be harvested for one year. So stagger your division schedule to ensure you will never be without their succulent stalks. As with asparagus, only harvest a few stems in the second year. Let the plant establish itself. By the third year, harvest all you want!

Rhubarb is a cool-season crop, it needs the winter chill to grow thick, succulent stems. They taste best in spring, with frost improving its flavor and texture. Once temperatures reach 80°F, you will find production begins to wane. Pink and red stems are traditional, but a few varieties like 'Victoria' are available as green stems with red tinges. The leaf stalk is edible, the leaves are not—in fact they are poisonous. Cut them off and compost them. To harvest, bend stalks back and twist. They should break off easily at the crown.

Forcing rhubarb was discovered by accident in Britain in the Chelsea Physic Garden. A few crowns were accidently covered with large pots and forgotten about. When they were spotted and lifted, the gardeners discovered fresh out-of-season rhubarb ready

Rhubarb is the anchor of the kitchen garden—large, ornamental, and edible.

for harvest. But while you can force rhubarb to produce, it completely depletes the plant of all its energy, rendering it useless in the future. Although forcing rhubarb may be an experiment, unless you need to force it for a specific rhubarb dish you plan to cook, it's best to grow and harvest according to its traditional schedule.

Generally free of pests and diseases, rhubarb may be bothered by aphids, beetles, or flea beetles, but they rarely cause any serious damage. Overcrowding can cause crown rot. As long as you cut the infected portion away and divide regularly, it should be a non-issue.

BERRY DELICIOUS

No kitchen garden is complete without a few sweet berries. Strawberries, raspberries, blueberries, or grapes are all excellent additions to your garden borders.

Strawberries benefit from a serious cutback late in the season. I prefer the bush-like everbearing raspberries since they produce in autumn from their first year on and only require an annual cutback. Blackberries and June-bearing raspberries perform better on a trellis to keep them upright. Blueberries are available in early, mid and late season types. Since blueberries fruit on newer wood, thin or prune periodically so you always have six to ten thick, bud-laden productive canes. Climbing grapes are great in small spaces and add some well-needed structure to any garden. American varieties are ideal choices for cold climates, and need light, heat, and selective pruning to set a productive crop. Always purchase on grafted rootstocks, which are resistant to two primary root pests: grape phylloxera and parasitic nematodes.

Most berry bushes should be pruned when dormant in the winter according to how they bear fruit (on new or old wood). The fruit should detach easily from the plant when it's ready to harvest. Birds are the biggest berry thieves, but other scavenging critters as well as aphids, Japanese beetles, and fungal diseases can become a problem. Nets and fences, regular monitoring, and good garden cleanup are the best and easiest ways to protect fruiting berries in your garden.

CHAPTER 5

HERBS AND FLOWERS

A kitchen garden would not be complete without being interwoven with herbs and flowers, and how you do it adds personality to your space. Vegetables will fill your table and pantry, but herbs add flavor and flowers beauty. I cannot fill a space without scattering a few nasturtiums or planting a dahlia—it just wouldn't be right. So I'm going to share with you the herbs and flowers I simply cannot do without in my garden.

HERBS

Basil (*Ocimum basilicum*)

Basil is synonymous with summer tomatoes in my mind. How can a gardener grow one and not the other? It is one of the most versatile herbs, complementing Italian, French, and Mexican foods. The best part about this annual is it's super easy to grow, and the more you pick, the more you get! Give this leafy green herb rich, well-drained soil, sun, and water, and it's almost impossible to screw up. It grows quickly from seed, but this is one of those plants that you'll find on your kitchen counter in a glass growing its own roots. Basil germinates

Pick basil early in the morning when still turgid to maximize its shelf life.

Start your basil early inside, and plant your seedlings after frost danger has passed.

better in warmth and requires a seven- to ten-day hardening off period. Monitor your seedlings as these little guys will fall victim to damping-off from overwatering. Downy mildew and gray mold are characterized by a grayish fuzzy growth on the underside and both sides of the leaves respectively, later turning brown. Use fresh clean seed, space 24 inches apart for improved air circulation, and water from the bottom to inhibit the humid, stagnant air that invites these spores to develop.

Most traditionalists go for the Genovese or sweet basil, but from Thai to cinnamon to lemon there is a variety for every discerning home chef. Some basils like Spicy Globe or Bush basil are more ornamental, forming tight balls of small leaves that can be grown as topiaries. 'Aromatto' and other purple basils are more attractive than edible, providing the perfect pop of color for homegrown bouquets. Personally I can't grow enough to satisfy my family and me, but if you're not an addict and just looking for a small taste, basil is a wonderful addition to your container garden. It's happy to grow in the garden or on your windowsill. Just be sure to give it plenty of light and pinch back regularly to keep it bushy and healthy.

Chives (*Allium schoenoprasum*)

One of the easiest herbs to grow, chives are fundamental in my kitchen garden. I like to use them as an edible, flowering border, letting them go to flower once or twice a season. This perennial can be started from broadcasting seed, inside or outside, or by division. One year I had too many divisions and threw a huge clump in the compost pile ... and early next spring what do you think was growing in my bin? Chives! These are incredibly hardy, and established plants enjoy being divided every three years in the spring.

The chive flower is also edible, making a striking addition to a salad and giving it a hint of subtle onion flavor.

Unless you plan to use chives as an ornamental plant, deadhead the flowers to promote leaf production. Rich, moist soil with good drainage, four to six hours of sun, an annual side dressing of compost, and a regular liquid feed will keep your chives happy and productive in the garden. As the season winds down, chives die back to the ground. If you want to keep your family in plenty of chives through the winter, sow or divide into a smaller pot and bring inside. They are excellent potted plants provided they get enough light.

Cilantro (*Coriandrum sativum*)

Although it can be polarizing, cilantro is one of my favorites. Summer salsa is not the same without it. Another herb that's easy to sow, this is actually a two-for-one deal. Leafy cilantro is the same plant as the spice coriander, differing in the part of the plant used and flavor. An annual growing in two phases, cilantro is the green, active growth, whereas coriander is the dried seed. Favoring cool weather, this herb will bolt, or run to seed, in the summer heat. I deal with this in two ways: selecting bolt-resistant varieties like 'Santo' or 'Slo-Bolt' and planting it under other warm-season trellis crops like cucumbers or peas. Keep in mind that cilantro is a thirsty plant, so plan to give it plenty of water.

Take advantage of this cool-season herb and get your cilantro off to an early start with transplants.

For those without lots of garden space, cilantro often gets leggy in pots, putting in an average show. But if you're desperate for those lacy, pungent leaves, use a larger pot than you would typically think of, give it plenty of TLC, and direct sow. Cilantro does not like to be transplanted, so whether in the garden or containers sowing in situ is best. Also, beware of overfertilizing as it can diminish the flavor.

I also enjoy it in bouquets. Let it go to flower and you will get these pretty white umbels that add a spiciness to arrangements. If left on the plant, they will mature into seed heads. Once the round seeds begin turning from green to brown, cover with a brown paper bag, rubber band, and cut. Hang and let dry in a dark, well-ventilated space for several weeks. Harvest the dried seed and store in opaque, airtight jars to elongate the shelf life. Also, you should wait to grind the seed until you need it for the freshest coriander flavor.

Leave space in your garden to successively sow dill every 2–3 weeks to maintain a consistent supply of both leaves and seeds.

Dill (*Anethum graveolens*)

Dill, another double-duty herb, is coveted for its feathery foliage and seed heads. The leaves enhance salads, marinades, and dressings, and their sharper-flavored heads are used in pickling. They are also a wonderful, long-lasting cut flower. Growing almost five feet tall, they need to be sheltered from wind. A sun-loving annual, dill greatly dislikes being transplanted. You'll have better success sowing out in the garden rather than in pots or soil blocks. Just toss a handful over the soil, scratch in, and keep moist until leaves develop.

If you are not diligent about harvesting the seed heads, dill will self-sow and you will see seedlings emerging on their own. But if you're like me and harvest periodically for leaf and seed, you will need to sow successively. In fact, I sow dill every three weeks from one month before the last frost until ten weeks before the last to guarantee that I'll be provided with enough seed and leaves for my wholesale customers and myself. And unless you enjoy inferiorly flavored dill, plant far, far away from fennel. Otherwise they will cross-pollinate and neither will taste very good.

Mint (*Mentha* spp.)

When I first began growing seedlings for sale, I thought no self-respecting gardener would want a thug like mint in the garden. Well, boy was I wrong! I had discounted all its diversified uses in teas, marinades, grills, vegetable dishes, salads, Italian, and other ethnic dishes. So I began offering the generic spearmint as well as other fun, savory flavors like 'Apple', 'Chocolate', 'Orange', and variegated 'Pineapple'—with the caveat of how to care for these invasive herbs. Mint is known to spread mercilessly, and you need to make sure you know how to contain the problem. Often I'll suggest sinking a large two- to three-gallon nursery pot with drainage holes into the garden to help control the sprawl. A single plant is often enough to supply you with plenty of leaves to use in the kitchen.

For maximum flavor plant in full sun in rich, well-drained soil and water well. Mint should not be sown from seed as it does not come true and tastes mediocre. Cuttings or purchased plants from nurseries that propagate with cuttings are the only way to get the true culinary-valued flavors. In summer, cut back hard. Don't worry: mint is tough and it will come back. Fertilize with fish emulsion, compost, or comfrey tea and divide every couple years to keep healthy. The only issue besides its rampant nature is rust. If you see any orange-brown spotting or discoloration on the leaves, destroy—don't compost—any infected plants. Mint is an excellent specimen for container plantings and as scented foliage in bouquets.

Mint is a promiscuous herb. Planting in large pots will help contain it and stop it from running amuck in your garden.

Oregano and Marjoram (*Origanum vulgare* & *O. majorana*)

Part of the same family, oregano and marjoram have slight differences in their leaves and flavor. Oregano is a perennial with stiffer, dark green leaves with a pungent, slightly minty flavor, whereas annual sweet marjoram has tiny, light green leaves and a floral fragrance. Like most herbs they taste better in sunny positions and develop better if pinched. Both are super easy to sow from seed and grow without a lot of fuss, needing just sun and well-drained dry soil. Flavors peak just before flowering, and a hard cutback midway through the season results in a flush of new leaves. I fertilize twice a season with liquid feed, once in the spring and again after the hard cutback. Both do well in pots, particularly terracotta or other clay pots that wick moisture away, in soil with a bit of extra grit. If you've collected plenty of leaves for the winter months, let a few plants go to flower as their purple and white blooms look airy and delicate on a vase on your kitchen table.

Marjoram distinguishes itself from oregano with its milder flavor, lighter leaves, and small, round seed heads.

Rosemary (*Rosmarinus officinalis*)

Just as happy in the ground as it is in a pot, rosemary is my favorite herb (do I say that often?). The compelling scent draws me in, its evergreen leaves and blue, pink, or white flowers make a statement in the garden, and it can be shaped! Rosemary has three main growing habits: upright, mounding, and trailing. The first two are ideal for the garden—their flavors are maximized for the kitchen. The trailing, or prostrate, type makes an interesting centerpiece as it can easily be trained into sphere, small tree, spiral, or any other wire-framed topiaries.

Rosemary is another plant whose seed is not true and needs to be propagated by cuttings. Softwood cuttings taken in early spring root more easily than those taken after flowering. As a Mediterranean plant it thrives in full sun and well-drained soil. The trick to success with rosemary is water. It does not like wet feet, and although a warm-weather herb, it is not a succulent. Make sure to cut back by approximately one-quarter after flowering to keep it healthy and flowering. To maximize leaf production, feed with liquid seaweed and replace your plant every five to six years. Remember, you don't need to purchase a new plant, just take a few cuttings off your current plant and overwinter them for the following year.

While rosemary may be able to grow as a hedge in the Mediterranean, it will never make it that large in cooler regions. For cold-climate gardeners, 'Arp' and 'Hill-Hardy' cultivars are hardy to zone 6, otherwise they are considered tender perennials. I have personally been able to overwinter these, as well as 'Gorizia' in my zone 5 garden with heavy mulching and frost blankets. Regardless of climate, rosemary is a very happy container plant. And as a bonus, it can be overwintered indoors if you can give it at least two hours of direct sunlight!

It's easy to make beautiful topiaries with rosemary.

Flat-Leaf Parsley (*Petroselinum crispum* var. *Neapolitanum*)

One of the most valuable plants in the garden is parsley. It is used in virtually everything. Since I use so much in the kitchen, it's more cost-effective to grow from seed than buy transplants. The biggest gripe I hear about growing parsley is germination. It's either spotty or non-existent. The secret is consistent soil temperature, moisture, and patience. Unless it's later in the season I always use heat mats until germination is complete, and it still may take two to three weeks for an entire tray of seedlings to successfully emerge, but they will.

Although a biennial, parsley is grown as an annual. First year plants taste better, particularly flat-leaf Italian varieties like 'Giant of Italy'. They grow well in full sun to part shade and like deep, fertile soil. If you notice the leaves yellowing, cut back and fertilize with fish emulsion. Parsley grows as happily in a pot as it does the garden, so it is perfect for gardens of any size.

Sage (*Salvia officinalis*)

Common gray-leafed sage with its narrow leaves is the best culinary sage available. 'Berggarten' has a broader leaf, but it can be overpowering and musty, and therefore needs to be used at half strength in cooking. Other varieties such as 'Holt's Mammoth', 'Pineapple', and 'Tricolor' are attractive in borders, and while they can be used in the kitchen, they are less flavorful. They all

Parsley is one of the main components of the French bundle of herbs known as bouquet garni used to flavor many French savory, slow-cooked meals.

Sage is known as a staple ingredient for stuffing, but it is just as tasty with fatty meats like beef, chicken, duck, or pork.

perform well in containers, but must be repotted annually or they can become rootbound and decline.

A sun-loving perennial, sage does best in well-drained but not overly fertile soil. The key to success is drainage and ensuring it is never waterlogged. Basic garden sage is easily grown from seed with the specialty varieties best propagated from cutting. Sage benefits greatly from an early spring pruning and again after flowering. And remember to pinch back any flowers to keep leaf production high. I've found that leaf flavor begins to decline after four or five years, so replace your plants to maintain good flavor.

French Tarragon (*Artemisia dracunculus*)

Tarragon is essential to all French cooking, and that is why the only variety you should be using is 'French' tarragon. If the plant does not have this distinction, you are getting the far inferior tasting "Russian tarragon." Additionally, don't be conned by seed packets claiming to be culinary tarragon—it is the unpalatable Russian variety. 'French' tarragon cannot be grown from seed. It needs to be propagated by layering or stem or root cuttings. As a perennial with a fibrous root system, it can be divided in the spring or fall, but you will be far more successful with cuttings.

All tarragon is not the same. Unless it is clearly noted as 'French' tarragon do not buy it, as it's most likely the distasteful Russian variety.

This herb hates wet feet and needs a sunny, dry spot in the garden with well-drained soil. French tarragon is a heavy feeder, and I give mine weekly applications of fish emulsion to keep it happy and producing. You need to prune it early in the summer to ensure a late summer flush. French tarragon is another herb that thrives in a container as well as the garden. Regardless, it will need to be divided every other year or replaced every three years to keep the flavor and leaf production up. For gardeners in warm climates where French tarragon doesn't get its required dormant period, the annual Mexican tarragon (*Tagetes lucida*)—which really isn't tarragon at all, it's a member of the marigold family—is a good flavor substitute.

French Thyme (*Thymus vulgaris* 'Narrow-leaf French')

I have one more herb I cannot do without ... thyme. Like many herbs, there is an over-abundance of varieties, but 'French' thyme far outshines the others in flavor. 'Lemon' and

'English' thyme taste good and can be substituted in a pinch, but professional chefs prefer the 'French'. Then there are the more decorative varieties that are variegated, creeping, or mounding, which become wonderful ground covers, shine in borders, and usually taste awful. So make sure you buy edible thyme when purchasing.

You can start thyme from seed, but it is better grown from softwood cuttings. It's quicker and guarantees the plant is true to its flavor intensity. A perennial, thyme is a super easy-to-care-for plant. It enjoys full sun and sandy, well-drained soil, and does great in containers. It is s a dry-land native herb, so do not overwater or over-fertilize. Thyme thrives on neglect. The only thing you must remember is to prune after flowering. I cut back hard at the end of June, resulting in a bushy, second flush later in the summer.

FLOWERS

Bells of Ireland (*Moluccella laevis*)

Perfect in the garden and in bouquets as foliage or the star, bells of Ireland are a showstopper. The spikes of lime-green, bell-shaped blooms have all the height and drama you can ask for. The actual flower is tiny, sitting inside each of the chartreuse shell calyxes. I love them particularly because they are easy to grow from seed, smell delightful, and have a long vase life. Bells grow best in place and take just under a month to germinate once the soil warms

There are many different varieties of thyme, all with their own characteristics and uses. Some have a creeping habit that works well as a ground cover, while others, like the dark-leafed 'French' thyme pictured here, are prized for their flavor in cooking.

Bells of Ireland are striking in borders.

to 55°F. If you want earlier flowers, start them in large pots for transplanting eight to ten weeks before planting out twelve inches apart in full to partial shade once the danger of frost has passed. Barely cover the seeds—they need light to germinate—and water in well.

Add a touch of airy whimsy to your kitchen garden with some old-fashioned cosmos.

These top-heavy spires topple easily, so I plant mine where they're protected from wind. Since these plants don't rebloom, I succession sow every couple weeks to ensure I have plenty of bells of Ireland throughout the summer.

Cosmos (*Cosmos bipinnatus*)

Super fast growing and productive, cosmos should be a staple in every gardener's plot in my opinion. Arriving in just over two months from seed, they are available in a multitude of colors and single- and double-flowered type. Brighten your arrangements with frilly leaves and delicate blooms rising on stems three to four feet tall. Don't worry about exhausting your supply, as the more you cut, the more flowers you get. Start from seed, space one foot apart, and plant in full sun. Pinch back when they reach twelve inches tall for bushier, stronger plants. They don't need heavily amended soil and do well in dry, hot conditions, making them a marvel-ous choice for the busy gardener. And if you let them, cosmos will self-sow!

Dahlias (*Dahlia* spp.)

Oh where to begin ... the dahlia, one of my absolute favorites and an iconic flower. They grow from one to five feet (even a bit taller in a hoop house) tall, are available in over ten different flower head types (anemone, ball, cactus, collarette, formal decorative, informal decorative, orchid, peony, pompon, semi-cactus, and single), and are classified by size. My white and blush dinnerplate 'Fleur' and 'Café au Lait' dahlias are the backbone of my garden, with more planted each year. Since they are tender, you need to wait until the soil warms up above 55°F, typically about two weeks before the last projected frost. Plant the tuber with the "eye" (small nub or tube-like growing point) facing up four to five inches deep in soil

If you were too busy getting your vegetables off to a good start in the spring, no worries, you can plant your dahlias as late as mid-June and still get a good show by summer's end.

amended with compost. I toss a small handful of bonemeal in the hole before planting to promote good root and bud development. Space twelve to eighteen inches apart, backfill, and mulch well. Because dahlias need lots of water throughout their growing season, I use multiple lines of drip tape underneath the mulch. Once the plants reach twelve to eighteen inches tall, pinch back the growing tip several inches to the next leaf joint to encourage better branching and stronger plants. And stake your plants. This is easier to do when they're small rather than later when they've grown and are laden with giant blooms. Unlike most flowers, you harvest dahlias when they are fully open. They will not finish opening up if picked when they're only partially open.

Love-in-a-Mist (*Nigella papillosa*)

An old-fashioned annual, Nigella evokes the sentiment its common name implies, with lovely star-shaped flowers sitting on a blanket of fringed, green mist. Lacy, finely divided bracts surround blue, white, or pink flowers, followed by their balloon-like seedpods, making this an elegant flower choice for arrangements no matter the stage. 'Delft Blue' and 'Miss Jekyll Alba'

Nigella is the perfect flowering annual, it's easily grown from seed and its flowers and seedpods look just as lovely fresh as they do dried.

are two of my favorite cultivars in deep blue and semi-double white flowers respectively. Broadcast love-in-a-mist seed in situ in the spring or previous fall, as it is not a fan of transplanting. It compensates for that by readily self-sowing. With sun and well-drained soil, it should take approximately three months till the flowers bloom. Nigella isn't high maintenance—regular watering and feeding improve production. And although it is a relatively short flowering plant, you should succession sow every three weeks for continuous color all summer long.

I use nasturtiums throughout the garden. They are perfect for softening and camouflaging unsightly borders with their sprawling habit.

Nasturtium (*Tropaeolum majus*)

Nasturtiums can fill up a container and smooth out the edges of beds and borders like nobody's business. Dwarf varieties are well suited to borders and pots, but I still prefer the cascading profusion of the vining types to topple out and over. And not only do they make a beautiful ground cover or stun climbing up a fence or trellis, but you can cut them for your arrangements or even eat them! The flowers and leaves are edible, adding a yummy peppery tang to salads and cakes. Nasturtiums are vigorous growers with bright blooms available in colors ranging from yellows and oranges to pinks and reds. Whether you are growing trailing or compact types, nasturtiums need full sun and dry, well-drained soil to thrive. If you find your plants leggy, they are getting too little sun. Sow seeds shallowly—they need light to germinate—in open ground or in propagation trays to get a jump on the season. Nasturtiums shouldn't be fed, otherwise you won't get many flowers, and their rambling blooms are one of the main reasons to grow these guys.

Pot Marigold (*Calendula officinalis*)

Give the garden some pop with pot marigolds in shades of orange and yellow. I love these edible annuals because they taste yummy in a salad, brighten up the beds and borders, and make a nice cut flower. As a bonus, its colored petals are used in natural dyes. In warmer climates calendula can be considered a perennial, but for those of us in the north it is an annual. It grows well in full sun to part shade in well-drained soil. Pinching back regularly maintains a good shape, keeping plants from becoming leggy. Calendula doesn't like too much fuss, and in fact does better with less frequent waterings and average soil. Deadhead regularly to encourage its flowering period to extend from spring through fall. Another self-seeder, it is easy to collect their curved seeds once the flowers fade and save them for the following spring.

Sunflowers (*Helianthus* spp.)

Summer is not complete without the sunflower, which reminds me of growing up at the shore. Whether you prefer a traditional or unique shaggy, burgundy variety, they are one of the great all-American flowers. Arriving in summer, sunflowers are the hero of any bouquet. Plant them in a spot with plenty of sun, pinch back for stronger plants when a foot-and-a-half tall, and water regularly. Sunflowers can be direct seeded or started a couple weeks early in blocks. Cut the stems as soon as the first few petals being to open for the longest vase display, stripping the lower three-quarters leaves.

If you are looking to harvest sunflower seeds, you'll have to show some restraint and wait until the petals fade and fall. If you collect too soon, there will be little meat in the seed, and if you are too late, they'll be too dry—if the critters haven't beaten you to them first! You'll know its time when the petals fall, the seeds appear plump, and the green base of the seed turns brown. If you're worried about scavenging birds, use a fine netting to protect

Single-stem sunflowers need to be succession planted to keep your kitchen in cut stems all season long, otherwise you'll be inundated with blooms all at one time.

the plants. While many gardeners will harvest directly from the garden, I prefer to use the paper bag method. When two-thirds to three-quarters of the seeds are mature, cut the stem four to five inches from the head, insert into a paper bag, and tie. Hang upside down in a dry, dark, well-ventilated space for two to four weeks. Then all you have to do is shake the head in the bag or run your hands along the head to separate the seeds from the flower.

Blue and light-colored sweet peas from the Spencer series are grown for their incredibly scented, large, frilly flowers with long stems (pictured variety is 'Nimbus').

Sweet Peas (*Lathyrus* spp.)

Fragrant and utterly graceful, sweet peas should be a staple in every kitchen or cottage garden. Available in many colors, the Spencer series is known to have the strongest scents. They may look like peas, but germination is a bit trickier for these beauties. Regions with mild winters can germinate in the fall and overwinter till spring, but for everyone else, you'll need to start them in early spring. I usually start mine in February or March under lights, but first you need to break dormancy. Due to its tough seed coat, I soak the seed in a jar of water overnight. Do not leave in the water for more than twenty-four hours, or you run the risk of drowning the seed. By morning the seeds should look swollen. If not, I use a sharp knife to nick the seed coat and soak for another six hours. Then I plant the seeds one-half inch deep in three- or four-inch pots. Sweet peas have large root systems and need deep pots, particularly if started months early. Use clear

SWEET PEAS SHOULD BE A STAPLE IN EVERY KITCHEN GARDEN.

plastic domes or plastic wrap to cover the pots to maintain the humidity and even moisture required for germination. Promote branching by pinching back the main growing stem just above a set of branching leaves when four to six feet tall. Once danger of frost has passed, plant out in full sun into well-amended soil. I prep the bed with a hefty dose of compost or decomposed manure and bonemeal and feed regularly with a fish emulsion and seaweed mix. You will need to keep your sweet peas well watered if you want them to perform well, and give them some sort of trellis to scramble and climb up. I help the plants initially by tying them to my makeshift trellis until they are about a foot tall when they can grow and grab on their own. Harvest regularly, water well, feed weekly, and deadhead any spent flowers, and you will be rewarded with an endless supply of sweet pea blooms throughout the season.

Verbena (*Verbena bonariensis*)

Verbena is outstanding as an airy filler in bouquets or in the garden. I use it liberally throughout all my plantings knowing what a lovely, architectural effect it will have once it reaches its full height of three to six feet. This tall plant doesn't need staking and bears

Even though these billowy stems tower over the garden, growing up to six feet tall in optimal conditions, they look perfect with their purple flowers seemingly floating among your vegetables or in ornamental borders.

A high-yielding, large (four- to six-inch) double bloom, 'Benary's Giant Salmon Rose' is a workhorse in the garden with a long vase life.

bunches of floating purple flowers evoking an ethereal aura in the garden. A perennial in warmer climates, it is a quick-growing annual in colder. You can direct sow or start two to three months early. Since they can be slow to establish, give them a head start in deep pots, then transplant after frost. Lazy gardeners love these plants because they require little beside full sun and moist, well-drained soil. Verbena has a long bloom period that can be extended by deadheading and regular harvesting. Butterflies, hummingbirds, bees, and other pollinators are drawn to this heat-tolerant plant, and I've found if you let some of the plants go to seed, it will self-sow for next spring!

Zinnia (*Zinnia elegans*)

If you are looking for a beautiful, long-lasting, bright flower for the garden that will produce like mad, plant some zinnias. It wasn't love at first sight for me, but once I began growing some of the more showier 'Zinderella' and 'Benary's Giant' varieties, I never stopped. Coming in a variety of stunning colors and shapes, zinnias are the perfect complement in the garden and on the kitchen table, lasting over a week (up to 10 days)!

Although zinnias can be sown in situ, I start mine early in soil blocks when I have little over a month before our last frost to give them a jump on the season. Zinnias enjoy full sun and moist soil. I use drip irrigation so I don't get the

ZINNIAS ARE THE PERFECT COMPLEMENT IN THE GARDEN.

leaves wet and space them ten to twelve inches apart for good air circulation; otherwise powdery mildew can be a problem. Pinch out the center growing tip when your seedlings are a foot tall for better, stronger branching. You will know it's time to harvest when you grab the stem and it is unbending and sturdy. Don't be afraid to go too far; hard cutbacks result in longer, firmer stems. Zinnias benefit from regular harvesting for bouquets and deadheading, leaving you with a bushier, more productive plant in the garden.

CHAPTER 6

THE GARDEN CALENDAR

I know many gardeners can't wait to dig their hands into the soil come January, but I almost enjoy the self-imposed exile from the garden. Nature is resting and I am hibernating. There is a time and place for everything in the garden: chores to take care of, seeds to sow, seedlings to plant, and gardens to grow and harvest. So let nature be your guide and harmonize with the environment.

When I first began gardening, I had almost no direction. All the books talked as if I already knew when to sow my seeds or transplant them out. So as I share with you my garden calendar, it is important to keep in mind what part of the country you live in. Whether you live in chilly USDA hardiness zone 5B like me, the more temperate climates of zones 6, 7, and 8, or the warm, almost tropical 9+, you'll need some direction. So as you look over the monthly chores below, remember you might need to consider your garden region and adjust when you plant out your tomatoes or harvest your cabbage.

MIDWINTER

There's nothing like starting out the year with a bundle of your favorite new and old seed catalogs. This is the moment when the eyes are bigger than the garden and you've got to rein it in. Also, if you've already been growing for a few years (or more) and have kept a garden journal, break it out! Look over what worked and what didn't. Did you test out a new variety of lettuce that you just loved or wish you had given a bit more room to your brussels sprouts? Now is the time to make note of it and factor all those things into this year's garden.

Planning is best done when you're *not* at the nursery and *not* in the spring garden. Think about what you really want to grow and what you ate or enjoyed. Maybe you need more herbs—and if so, you need a new bed to grow them in. Where do you plan to build it?

If you're feeling blue and had the foresight to pot-up bulbs last fall, it is time to starting bringing out the color! Many small bulbs like muscari, snowdrops, and crocus need only eight weeks of a cold treatment before you will see their green leaves emerging from the soil. Once brought out into a cool room and exposed to indirect light, they will bloom and fill your tables with fresh flowers. Other bulbs like daffodils, alliums, and tulips require longer exposure to cold temperatures to bloom. So when your imagination is not running rampant with seed and bulb ideas, check to ensure your stored autumn harvest isn't spoiled and inspect your dahlia tubers and other bulbs for rot, discarding any that show signs of drying out.

JANUARY GARDEN CHECKLIST

- Harvest kale, brussels sprouts, and other winter vegetable crops.
- Order seeds.
- Compare/review notes from last year and plan the garden.
- Begin to bring out any of your forced bulbs.
- Check on your stored crops and overwintering bulbs, corms, and tubers, discarding any unsavory or rotting pieces.

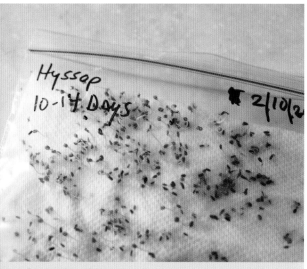

Testing viability of old hyssop seeds.

LATE WINTER

This is the hardest month for me. It's easy to get overzealous and start sowing everything at your disposal, but restrain yourself and only sow slow-growing veggies like onions, leeks, celeriac, celery, and sweet peas. Test whether your leftover seeds are still viable. Lay out a few seeds from each pack (labeled of course) on a damp paper towel and expose to light. If you see germination you are good to go! Chuck whatever seeds don't show any signs of life. This is also a good time to set up your growing system. It doesn't have to be fancy—a few shop lights from your local hardware store with grow bulbs suspended a few inches above your seedlings are all you need. Bottom heat can also be useful in getting your plants off to a good start, so stock up on any heat mats on sale.

In my world garden plans are fluid and ever changing, but it is important to finalize your ideas for the upcoming season so you know you'll have a place for all the seeds you've ordered. Most flowering branches can be cut and forced starting at the end of January through mid-March, making this a primo time to force witch hazel, dogwood, forsythia, and cherry blossoms to name a few.

EARLY SPRING

March is one of those wait-and-see months. You can begin to start seeds inside, sowing beans and brassicas as soon as the ground can be worked, but make sure it isn't wet and soggy. Wait until mud season is over—especially if you live in northern climates—and your soil has warmed to at least 45°F. Otherwise you will be trampling all over the ground, damaging your soil structure and running the risk of damping-off in muddy conditions. Use an online seed starting calculator (johnnyseeds.com has a good one) to help you determine the best time to start your seeds and begin prepping the ground. Now is the time to weed, turn any green manures you grew last autumn, and use plastic mulch to heat the soil. Plant bare-root plants, prune your fruit trees and late flowering shrubs while still dormant, and divide any perennials that you didn't get to last fall. It's also an ideal time to sharpen and clean your tools and sterilize any pots and trays you plan to reuse. Vegetables and herbs like rhubarb, artichokes, lovage, and French tarragon enjoy being divided every few years. And lastly don't forget to protect any tender seeds and seedlings from killing frosts and hungry critters.

FEBRUARY GARDEN CHECKLIST

- Order seeds, if you haven't already.
- Prune fruit trees, grapes, and other dormant, late-flowering plants.
- Continue to retrieve your pots of forced bulbs as they meet their vernalization requirements.
- Test viability of old seed.
- Set up your indoor seed starting system.
- Sow slow-growing seeds.
- Finalize your garden layout.
- Force branches.
- Check on your stored crops and overwintering bulbs, corms, and tubers, discarding any unsavory or rotting pieces.
- Prune off winter damaged trees and shrubs.

MARCH GARDEN CHECKLIST

- Soil test if your soil has thawed.
- Sharpen, clean, and organize your tools.
- Continue forcing branches.
- Start sowing seeds.
- Sterilize recycled pots, trays, and tools.
- Prep garden with compost and other amendments, weed, and warm the soil.
- Turn any living mulches.
- Lift and divide perennials.
- Plant new bare-root plants (fruit trees, shrubs, trees).
- Prune fruit trees and woody shrubs that flower after June.
- Vent cold frames and tunnels on warm days (40–45ºF).
- Protect young seedlings in the garden from frost.

MID-SPRING

If you have not yet done so, it's not too late to soil test! Go out, get a sample, and send it off. You still have time to amend your soil for the upcoming season. Continue cutting back and dividing perennials, finish pruning your fruit trees, and perform general garden cleanup. Tomatoes, cucumbers, and other tender crops are sown in the greenhouse, cold frames, or indoors under lights. They don't get planted until the danger of frost has passed.

Plant your asparagus crowns when they arrive and sow in situ crops like lettuces, peas, beans, and onion sets. Trellises and plant supports are most easily installed now before plants get too large. I like to plant quick-growing radish or spinach crops alongside slower-growing ones such as carrots, parsnips, and celery. Then round out the month by transplanting cool-weather brassicas. Remember to monitor nighttime temperatures so you know if—and when—you have to protect your seedlings.

APRIL GARDEN CHECKLIST

- Soil test and amend.
- Finish pruning dormant plants before plant buds swell.
- Cut back and divide overgrown perennials.
- Turn your compost pile.
- Plant early crops and transplant cool-weather plants in the garden.
- Clean up border and plant bed edges.
- Mulch plants.
- Sow tomatoes and other warm-weather crops under protection.
- Vent cold frames and tunnels on warm days (40–45ºF).
- Begin to pull back mulch and frost blankets from winter-protected plants.
- Soak bare-root plants before planting.
- Protect young seedlings in the garden from frost.
- Build new garden beds.

LATE SPRING

Continue sowing seeds for late-season crops and succession plantings. Harden off your seedlings for at least a week or so before you transplant into the garden, water-in, and mulch garden beds. Once you hit your frost-free date, plant away! Tomatoes, potatoes, herbs, and flowers can go in the ground now (double-check your frost date, especially if you're a cool-season gardener). Once squash are planted, cover to protect against pests and cold. It is usually about now that I have confirmation that I have more plants than space, so a few new beds are installed and planted. Stay on top of those weeds—they're much easier to manage when small. Mulching, whether plastic, landscape fabric, seaweed, or wood chips will go a long way to suppress weeds and retain water. And lastly begin pruning early flowering shrubs once they finish flowering. If you fail to prune and deadhead, next year's blooms won't be as plentiful.

EARLY SUMMER

The garden should be planted, and as the weather warms up, the garden will start to take off. Asparagus should be in full swing and other early crops such as lettuce and

Lettuce and onions interplanted under a cucumber A-frame trellis.

MAY GARDEN CHECKLIST

- Continue sowing seeds and direct seeding.
- Harden off and transplant seedlings.
- Weed, water, and mulch.
- Deadhead bulbs and spent flowers.
- Take softwood cuttings.
- Start harvesting your rhubarb.
- Protect crops from surprise frosts and nibbling pests.
- Plant annual containers.
- Prune spring-flowering woody shrubs after they flower.

peas should be harvested regularly to maintain high production yields. Water regularly, and other than a steady sowing of succession crops, fertilizing and staying on top of those weeds, there isn't much to be done. I alternate feeding the garden between a fish emulsion and seaweed mix and comfrey tea every few weeks. To reduce time spent watering, consider installing a drip line irrigation system. Like plastic mulch or landscaping fabric, the time invested is well worth the time saved over the season.

The lavender starts blooming at the end of June, running into July. Cut just as the first bud begins to maximize essential oil content and scent.

JUNE GARDEN CHECKLIST

- Harvest early crops regularly (particularly asparagus).
- Thin seedlings.
- Succession sow.
- Direct seed warm-season crops like squash, melon, and cucumbers.
- Water and weed.
- Pinch back seedlings for bushier growth.
- Feed with a fish emulsion and seaweed blend or a high potash fertilizer like comfrey tea.

- Stake and trellis tall plants or vines.
- Wet down and turn compost.
- Continue taking softwood cuttings.
- Prune early-flowering shrubs once they finish blooming and deadhead flowers.
- Monitor and protect plants from pests—especially those pesky Japanese beetles.

MIDSUMMER

This is my favorite time of year in the garden—the growing season is at its peak! Your main concern midsummer is staying on top of the harvest, weeding, fertilizing, and watering. If you have an irrigation system set up, watering should be easier, and mulch should take care of much of the weeding. Stake and trellis any vining crops, pruning tomato side shoots and suckers to increase production and later ripening. Continual deadheading of flowers will keep the garden clean and full of blooms. At this point I walk through the garden every night harvesting vegetables, herbs, and flowers and weeding whatever I see. It only takes about fifteen minutes each evening, and you leave with so many goodies it almost doesn't feel like work. Slugs, aphids, Japanese beetles, and other pests can be an issue at this point, so while walking though the garden, keep an eye out for insects and potential disease, cutting away and destroying any damaged or infected plant parts. It is also time to open any insect barriers or row covers for plants like pumpkin, squash, and tomatoes, which need pollinators to develop and bear fruit.

JULY GARDEN CHECKLIST

- Harvest regularly.
- Pinch back herbs.
- Continue succession sowing.
- Watch out for blight on tomatoes.
- Water, weed, fertilize, and mulch.
- Support plants when necessary.
- Deadhead spent blooms.
- Protect crops from pests and blight.
- Wet down and turn compost.
- Sow/plant kale and other cold-weather crops.

LATE SUMMER

Enjoy your garden as the end of summer draws near. The garden should still be jammed full of deliciousness to harvest, meaning you should be out regularly to collect as many tomatoes, beans, potatoes, and cucumbers as you can to keep production high. If you find you have a surplus, share with friends, donate to Harvest for the Hungry, or preserve it! There are so many options between canning, freezing, and drying that you should be able to enjoy your fruits and vegetables well into the fall and winter. Make sure to process and store each to maximize its flavor. Garlic and onions

The harvest is peaking and the kitchen is overflowing.

should be dried and cured, and I prefer my peas and tomatoes frozen, my cucumbers pickled, and my herbs preserved.

As you harvest, bare patches in the garden will open up. If you have succession or winter crops to transplant, get them in. If not, consider planting a green manure. Cover crops return nutrients to the soil, protect against weeds, and improve soil structure. Continue pruning, deadheading, and weeding to keep the garden looking good. It's easy to neglect it a bit with the heat of summer.

Sow kale three months before your first frost, for late fall and winter harvest.

AUGUST GARDEN CHECKLIST

- Harvest regularly.
- Complete your last succession sowing and plantings.
- Water, feed, and weed.
- Prune summer fruit bushes after fruiting.
- Plant green manures in bare beds.
- Wet down and turn compost.
- Plant kale and other cold-weather crops.
- Divide spring perennials.
- Watch out for powdery mildew.
- Monitor for pests and disease.
- Order bulbs.
- Preserve and store your harvest.

EARLY FALL

September is the month in which you will see your garden breathe and take a rest. Nighttime temperatures begin to drop and growth rates slow down, but there is still a lot of produce to come out of the garden. Plant out the last of your successions, fall cabbage, or winter lettuce. Reduce your watering as the plants won't be needing the extra cool down, and prune away yellowed, damaged, or diseased leaves and branches from plants. Gather, preserve, and store mature celery, ripened tomatoes, squash, and other veggies. Cut down perennials, compost barren plants, and then plant winter cover crops to keep open soil weed-free.

If you live in colder climates, this is the time to erect or begin using some of your season extension tools like cold frames, low tunnels, and row covers to elongate your season.

Dahlias are a great kitchen garden flower, because while most plants bloom in spring and summer, the dahlias are just getting started in late summer and produce heavily through your first frost.

Winter squash and cool-weather crops are in abundance this time of year.

SEPTEMBER GARDEN CHECKLIST

- Harvest, preserve, and store.
- Prune, weed, and mulch.
- Employ cover crops.
- Cut back and divide perennials as they die back.
- Begin garden cleanup and compost non-diseased plant debris.
- Employ season extenders.

MID-FALL

Autumn has arrived, and with it cooler temperatures and surprise frosts. Vegetables like kale, carrots, and brussels sprouts enjoy, and in fact taste better with, the kiss of Jack Frost, so continue harvesting your cool-season crops and those under the protection of cold frames, hoop houses, and row covers. If you didn't get an opportunity this year, now is the ideal time for a soil test. The ground is easy to dig, and you can't beat the pricing and wait time of the off-season. You may get your results quickly enough that you can apply slow-acting amendments in the fall so your beds are ready by spring. This is also a great time to build new raised beds or prepare lasagna beds using the sheet mulching technique.

Plant cover crops and garlic, and protect winter-sensitive plants. Herbs like lavender and rosemary can be overwintered in cold climates by heavily mulching with straw and using heavy-duty row covers to protect from high winds. As much as it hurts to consider, if you haven't already done so, it is time to put the garden to bed—with the exception of cold-weather crops or those using season extension tools. This includes digging up and storing tender bulbs and corms like dahlias and ranunculus. On the upside you can plant your spring bulbs and pot-up bulbs to force to beat the winter blues!

OCTOBER GARDEN CHECKLIST

- Harvest vegetables and store.
- Soil test.
- Plant winter cover crops.
- Plant garlic.
- Mulch winter-sensitive plants and cover.
- Divide perennials.
- Build and prep new beds for next year.
- Protect tender and cool-season crops.
- Clean up garden and compost.
- Employ season extenders.
- Dig up tender bulbs.
- Move cold-sensitive plants indoors before frost.
- Plant fall bulbs.
- Pot-up bulbs to force.

LATE FALL

As it gets colder, it is time to get out of the garden. Finish up any last-minute garden chores and clean your tools, seeding equipment, and pots. Continue harvesting till the plants are no longer producing, and get those bulbs in the ground for goodness' sake (if they haven't already been planted)! Then just relax. Order some new seed catalogs and enjoy the start of the holiday season.

NOVEMBER GARDEN CHECKLIST

- Make final harvest.
- Carry out season extension harvest.
- Provide support for tall winter crops (brussels sprouts or kale).
- Plant bulbs.
- Pot-up forced bulbs.
- Finish putting garden to bed.
- Clean and store garden tools and equipment.
- Order seed catalogs.

Make sure you do a good job cleaning up plant debris in the fall. Pests and diseases can overwinter and attack next year's crop if you don't.

EARLY WINTER

December always breezes by quickly between the holidays and end-of-the-year roundup. You don't need to think about the garden too much at this time. Simply enjoy whatever is left for you to harvest, appreciate the bounty you preserved, and think about what you liked and didn't in the garden. A garden journal comes in handy here! You can look back and see when you planted what, when it matured, and how much it yielded. Maybe you want to move your tomatoes to a brighter location, plant your cucumbers a little later, or start your leeks earlier. You'll have a record of what varieties you grew, and where you grew them. So when it comes time to plan your garden rotation for next spring, you will know right where to plant everything. Or you can wait until the new year and hibernate with a warm blanket and a glass of wine and let your imagination run wild with planning!

DECEMBER GARDEN CHECKLIST

- Carry out season extension harvest.
- Assess your garden.
- Inspect stored crops, and discard what's spoiled.

FURTHER READING

Albert, Stephen. *The Kitchen Garden Grower's Guide.* 2008.

Bradley, Fern Marshall, Ellis Barbara W. and Martin, Deborah L. *The Organic Gardener's Handbook of Natural Pest and Disease Control: A Complete Guide to Maintaining a Healthy Garden and Yard the Earth-Friendly Way.* Rodale Organic Gardening Books, 2010.

Coleman, Eliot. *Four-Season Harvest* (revised edition). Chelsea Green Publishing, 1999.

Coleman, Eliot. *The Winter Harvest Handbook.* Chelsea Green Publishing, 2009.

Cunningham, Sally Jean. *Great Garden Companions: A Companion-Planting System for a Beautiful, Chemical-Free Vegetable Garden.* Rodale, 1998.

Fowler, Alys. *The Edible Garden.* Viva Editions, 2013.

Greer, Allison. *Companion Planting for the Kitchen Gardener.* Skyhorse Publishing, 2014.

Hemenway, Toby. *Gaia's Garden: A Guide to Home-Scale Permaculture* (second edition). Chelsea Green Publishing, 2009.

Jabbour, Niki. *The Year-Round Vegetable Gardener.* Storey Publishing, 2011.

Nardozzi, Charlie. *Northeast Fruit and Vegetable Gardening.* Cool Springs Press, 2012.

Roberts, Juliet. *Organic Kitchen Garden.* Conran Octopus Limited, 2005.

Smith, Edward C. *The Vegetable Gardener's Bible* (second edition). Storey Publishing, 2009.

Stuckey, Maggie and McGee, Rose Marie Nichols. *McGee & Stuckey's Bountiful Container: Create Container Gardens of Vegetables, Herbs, Fruits and Edible Flowers.* Workman Publishing Company, 2002.

RESOURCES

Baker Creek Heirloom Seeds
471-924-8917
RareSeeds.com

The Cook's Garden
800-457-9703
CooksGarden.com

Fedco Seeds
207-873-7333
FedcoSeeds.com

John Sheepers Kitchen Garden Seeds
860-567-6086
KitchenGardenSeeds.com

Johnny's Selected Seeds
877-564-6697
JohnnySeeds.com

Select Seeds
800-684-0395
SelectSeeds.com

Pinetree Garden Seeds
207-926-3400
SuperSeeds.com

Stokes Seed Company
800-396-9238
StokeSeeds.com

Renee's Garden Seeds
888-880-7228
Renee'sGarden.com

Tomato Grower's Supply Company
888-478-7333
TomatoGrowers.com

Richter's Herbs
800-668-4372
Richters.com

Veseys Seeds
800-363-733
Veseys.com

Seeds from Italy
785-748-0609
GrowItalian.com

W. Atlee Burpee & Co.
800-333-5808
Burpee.com

WEBSITES

Cornell University, Department of Horticulture
Gardening.Cornell.edu
gardening.cornell.edu/homegardening

Master Gardeners Associations
American Horticultural Society Interactive Map
ahs.org/gardening-resources/master-gardeners

Organic Farming Research Foundation
ofrf.org

Rutgers University
njaes.rutgers.edu/garden/

USDA National Institute of Food and Agriculture
Local Cooperative Extension Offices
nifa.usda.gov/extension

INDEX